Advanced Sciences and Technologies for Security Applications

Indexed by SCOPUS

The series Advanced Sciences and Technologies for Security Applications comprises interdisciplinary research covering the theory, foundations and domain-specific topics pertaining to security. Publications within the series are peer-reviewed monographs and edited works in the areas of:

- biological and chemical threat recognition and detection (e.g., biosensors, aerosols, forensics)
- crisis and disaster management
- terrorism
- cyber security and secure information systems (e.g., encryption, optical and photonic systems)
- traditional and non-traditional security
- energy, food and resource security
- economic security and securitization (including associated infrastructures)
- transnational crime
- human security and health security
- social, political and psychological aspects of security
- recognition and identification (e.g., optical imaging, biometrics, authentication and verification)
- smart surveillance systems
- applications of theoretical frameworks and methodologies (e.g., grounded theory, complexity, network sciences, modelling and simulation)

Together, the high-quality contributions to this series provide a cross-disciplinary overview of forefront research endeavours aiming to make the world a safer place.

The editors encourage prospective authors to correspond with them in advance of submitting a manuscript. Submission of manuscripts should be made to the Editor-in-Chief or one of the Editors.

Robinson Tombari Sibe · Christian Kaunert

Cybercrime, Digital Forensic Readiness, and Financial Crime Investigation in Nigeria

Springer

Robinson Tombari Sibe
Faculty of Life Sciences and Education
International Centre for Policing
and Security
University of South Wales
Pontypridd, UK

Christian Kaunert
Faculty of Life Sciences and Education
International Centre for Policing
and Security
University of South Wales
Pontypridd, UK

School of Law and Government
Dublin City University
Dublin, Ireland

ISSN 1613-5113 ISSN 2363-9466 (electronic)
Advanced Sciences and Technologies for Security Applications
ISBN 978-3-031-54088-2 ISBN 978-3-031-54089-9 (eBook)
https://doi.org/10.1007/978-3-031-54089-9

This Springer imprint is published by the registered company Springer Nature Switzerland AG
The registered company address is: Gewerbestrasse 11, 6330 Cham, Switzerland

Paper in this product is recyclable.

This book is dedicated to the loving memory of my late parents—Mr. Godwin Sibe and Mrs. Charity Sibe, and to all the Law Enforcement Agents in Nigeria, working round the clock to keep us safe.

Dr. Robinson Tombari Sibe

To my daughter Elisabeth and my son Raphael. You are my eternal pride until my last breath. To my wife Sarah—I will always love you. To my parents—many thanks for all your support and love.

Prof. Christian Kaunert

Preface

Nigeria is one of the hotbeds of cybercrime. Over the last decade, the cybercrime caseloads have been on a steady rise, and increasingly overwhelming the financial crimes institutions in Nigeria. Several reasons have been attributed to be behind the surge in cybercrime incidents. One of these is the apparent lack of digital forensic resources by the cybercrime investigating institutions. While a few studies have highlighted the lack of forensic resources among financial crimes institutions in Nigeria, no study had investigated in detail, the specifics of this lack, and the impact on financial crimes in Nigeria. This book, for the first time, attempted to investigate this from a law enforcement point of view. In this book, Dr. Robinson Tombari Sibe and Prof. Christian Kaunert investigated the digital forensic readiness of the two leading institutions, responsible for investigating and prosecuting financial crime in Nigeria—the Economic and Financial Crimes Commission (EFCC) and the Nigeria Police Force. Good knowledge of the scale and scope of the lack of digital forensic resources is an essential first step to developing a digital forensic readiness model or digital forensic capability maturity model, and this book attempted to provide this foundational knowledge. Also, Nigeria is often listed as one of the nations behind the global surge in cybercrime activities. While there are some organized studies supporting this assertion, a lot of these discussions are anecdotal in nature, with no empirical basis. This book also attempted to investigate the specifics of the caseloads and conviction records, looking out for trends and patterns supporting or refuting this. The book investigated the other cybercrime complexities in Nigeria, such as common cybercrime taxonomies, prosecution, and conviction dynamics, juxtaposing it with select case studies in other jurisdictions. Drawing on extensive research, this book offers crucial insights for policymakers, researchers, and the public interested in new trends in cybercrime, digital forensic readiness, Nigerian financial crimes institutions, and cybercrime investigations.

Pontypridd, UK — Robinson Tombari Sibe
Pontypridd, UK/Dublin, Ireland — Christian Kaunert

Acknowledgements

Dr. Robinson Tombari Sibe is grateful to his lovely wife, Dr. Marie-James Sibe, and their children, Nakadi, Fole, and Giodi for their immeasurable love, sacrifice, and support, always. He is also grateful to his siblings—Ledum, Barinem, and Barida for their love and prayers. Prof. Christian Kaunert is very grateful to his amazing wife, Prof. Sarah Leonard, and their children Elisabeth and Raphael. They are his eternal pride. He is also very grateful to his parents for all the support and love. We are grateful to a great number of people—family members, friends, and colleagues—who have helped us through the various stages of the writing of this book. Without these very special people, the writing of this book would have been impossible.

This book is a qualitative case study, involving semi-structured interviews with cybercrime investigators, prosecutors, and digital forensic examiners from the Economic and Financial Crimes Commission (EFCC) and the Nigeria Police Force. We are grateful to the leadership of both institutions for graciously permitting their staff to participate freely in this research. We are also particularly grateful to the EFCC for providing supporting information and statistics that enriched our research. Special thanks to our interviewees for their invaluable insights, knowledge, and contribution to this research.

This book was inspired by Dr. Robinson Tombari Sibe's Ph.D. research at the University of the Cumberlands, Kentucky, USA. For this, he is grateful to his dissertation mentors who read and critiqued the original research, which provided the foundation for this book. Thank you, Dr. Bernard Sharum, Dr. Shaughnn Raschid Muller, and Dr. Amelia Phillips.

The findings presented in this book are based on research supported by various institutions, including Dublin City University, the University of South Wales, and the Institut Barcelona d'Estudis Internacionals (IBEI). Prof. Christian Kaunert also wishes to thank the European Union for funding his Marie Curie Doctoral Training Network EU-GLOCTER (coordinated by Dublin City University). This book has also been written with the support of the Erasmus+ programme of the European Union (Jean Monnet Actions), notably Prof. Christian Kaunert's Jean Monnet Chair EUCTIRL in EU Counter-Terrorism, as well the Jean Monnet Centre of Excellence VIRTUE, the Jean Monnet Module EUHYBRID, and, finally, the Jean Monnet

Network in EU Counter-Terrorism EUCTER. While writing this book, we also benefited enormously from the comments and insights of numerous experts in the field. We thank them for their time and support.

We are grateful to the entire team at Springer Nature, for their support, encouragement, and understanding throughout the publication process. We are deeply grateful for the editorial support and expertise put in to get this book to the readers.

We reserve a final mention for those individuals who have offered tremendous support throughout this book adventure. First and foremost, we sincerely thank our respective parents and families, who have always been a source of inspiration. We also express our appreciation to our friends, who have provided encouragement at just the right moment.

Contents

About the Authors

Dr. Robinson Tombari Sibe is a Visiting Fellow of the University of South Wales (International Centre for Policing and Security), Lecturer at the Computer Engineering Department of the Rivers State University, Nigeria, and the Founder/Lead Forensic Examiner of Digital Footprints Nig. Limited.

Prof. Christian Kaunert is Professor of International Security at Dublin City University, Ireland, Director of the International Centre for Policing and Security, Jean Monnet Director (Chair, Centre, and Network) on EU Counter-terrorism, and Professor of Policing and Security at the University of South Wales.

Abbreviations

ARPANET	Advanced Research Projects Agency Network
AU	African Union
BEC	Business Email Compromise
BYOD	Bring Your Own Device
CAC	Cybersecurity Advisory Council
CBN	Central Bank of Nigeria
DDoS	Distributed Denial of Service
DFRWS	Digital Forensics Research Workshop
EFCC	Economic and Financial Crimes Commission
EU	European Union
FATF	Financial Action Task Force
FBI	Federal Bureau of Investigation
GAFI	Grouped'actionfinancière
GSM	Global System for Mobile Communication
ICPC	Independent Corrupt Practices Commission
ICT	Information and Communication Technologies
NCC	Nigeria Communications Commission
NCCC	National Cybersecurity Coordination Centre
NDFL	National Digital Forensic Laboratory
NDIC	Nigeria Deposit Insurance Corporation
NIBBS	Nigeria Inter-Bank Settlement System
NIP	NIBSS Instant Payment
NITDA	National Information Technology Development Commission
NITEL	Nigerian Telecommunications
OBT	Obtaining By Tricks
ONSA	Office of the National Security Adviser
RAT	Routine Activity Theory
TAM	Technology Acceptance Model
TOE	Technology-Organization-Environment
TRA	Theory of Reasoned Action
UAE	United Arab Emirates

UK	United Kingdom
US	United States
UTAUT	Unified Theory of Acceptance and Use of Technology

List of Figures

List of Tables

Chapter 1
Background and Introduction

Abstract This chapter presents the background, contexts, and overview of the cybercrime challenge in Nigeria. The chapter presents foundational information of the rising caseloads of cybercrime in Nigeria. Specific challenges as well as the various reforms by government to tackle this, are also presented in this chapter. This chapter also presented the various institutional reforms, including the Economic and Financial Crimes Commission (EFCC), the Independent Corrupt Practices Commission (ICPC), and others with the mandate to tackle cybercrime in Nigeria. This chapter presents the two theoretical framework that shapes this study—Cohen and Felson's (Am Sociol Rev 588–608, 1979 [20]) Routine Activity Theory (RAT) and Technology Organisation and Environment framework developed by Tornatzky et al. (Processes of technological innovation. Lexington Books, 1990 [86]). This chapter also presented the conceptual framework for this study, the digital forensic readiness model, first introduced by Tan (Forensic readiness. @ Stake, Cambridge, MA, pp. 1–23, 2001 [84]). Using this conceptual model, the chapter presents a major challenge faced in the fight against cybercrime, which is the lack of forensic resources at the financial crimes agencies in Nigeria. The chapter ends by summarizing this challenge and the need to study the specifics of the lack of forensic readiness of the cybercrime agencies.

Keywords Cybercrime · Internet fraud · Financial crimes · Digital forensic readiness · Economic and Financial Crimes Commission · Nigeria Police Force · Independent Corrupt Practices Commission · 419

1.1 Overview

Nigeria has increasingly become one of the hotbeds of cybercrime since the liberalization of the telecommunication industry commenced in 1996. The scale and magnitude have been quite disturbing, not just to Nigeria but also to the international community, given the limitless boundaries of cybercrime [25, 71]. The Nigeria Deposit Insurance Company [65] report shows Nigeria lost 15.15 billion Naira (approximately

R. T. Sibe and C. Kaunert, *Cybercrime, Digital Forensic Readiness, and Financial Crime Investigation in Nigeria*, Advanced Sciences and Technologies for Security Applications, https://doi.org/10.1007/978-3-031-54089-9_1

$43 million) to fraud in the banking sector alone in 2018. This amount represented an increase of 539% from the 2.37 billion Naira recorded in 2017. Cybercrime accounts for most of these. Recent figures show this trend has continued to increase exponentially. The Nigerian Communications Commission (NCC) puts total annual loss to cybercrime at $500 million. That is, cybercrime contributes to about 0.08% loss in GDP [40]. The victims cut across the financial sector to other institutions and even individuals across different jurisdictions.

Like any other type of fraud, Internet fraud is driven mainly by financial gains [21]. This fraudulent scheme originated from Advance Fee Fraud, and is said to have its history in West Africa [51]. Globally, this scheme is mainly associated with Nigeria, which has influenced its naming—"419"—with the "419" code being Nigeria's criminal code for fraud [7, 6]. Besides averaging the highest loss per victim, Nigerian "419" scams are the second most reported cybercrime [19]. Symantec Corporation and African Union [83] reported that out of a large pool of email addresses used by online scammers, 46% were Nigerian Internet Protocol (IP) addresses.

Like other cybercriminals elsewhere, Nigerian Internet fraudsters have increased in sophistication over the years. They have metamorphosed from the stage of sending bulk emails to unsuspecting victims to carrying out spear-phishing attacks and sophisticated Business Email Compromise (BEC) schemes that compromise their corporate email accounts. For instance, Nigerian cybercriminals reportedly caused a breach involving confidential health records of over 750,000 persons in Los Angeles [12, 13]. They now use sophisticated malware tools such as Zeus, Darknet, Predator pain, ISpySoftware, and other malware families [41]. This increased sophistication has become an incentive for more attacks and perhaps explains the numbers. Such a high prevalence is of significant concern to the country.

A major driving force behind the use of complex and sophisticated tools, specialist hacking tools and powerful malware is the increasing role of availability of these dangerous tools on the internet. These tools are readily available on the cyberspace for less expensive amounts. Thus, people with less sophisticated skills can now procure these tools and deploy same to vulnerable and unsuspecting people. This model is now increasingly sophisticated and evolved to Cybercrime-as-a-service or crimeware as a Service [56, 58]. The proliferation of cybercrime-as-a-service is a major driving force behind the increase in cybercrime, opening the cybercrime space to both the experienced and inexperienced. Today, a rookie cybercriminal can easily procure dangerous tools for as little as $20 dollars, with full instruction on how to deploy it, and in some cases money-back guarantee.

Nigeria has responded to these increasing caseloads by implementing reforms and setting up structures to combat cybercrime. The primary investigating agency for cybercrime is the Economic and Financial Crimes Commission (EFCC). Set up by the Economic and Financial Crimes Commission (EFCC) Act 2004, the commission's mandate extends beyond Internet fraud to other financial crimes [66, 88]. In 2022, the commission secured a total of 3785 convictions across all it's command, representing an improvement of 70.5% and a success rate of 98.93% in convictions (losing only 41 cases—representing 1.07%). Following the previous trends, the zones with the top three convictions are Lagos (765), Ibadan Command (573 convictions) and Port

Harcourt Command (567 convictions) [26]. Previous conviction statistics shows that majority of the convictions by EFCC are cybercrime related. For instance, in 2021, 80% of the convictions by EFCC were cybercrime related [39].

However, other agencies often play overlapping roles in this regard. For instance, the Nigeria Police Force has a dedicated cybercrime unit with a mandate to crack down on cybercrime [61]. This unit investigates and prosecutes Internet fraud [90]. In 2022, the Inspector General of Police announced a merger of all cybercrime related departments, under the newly formed Nigeria Police Force National Cybercrime Centre, currently under the Force Criminal Investigations Department, Force Headquarters, Abuja [76]. This was to give way for focused unit for better efficiency in investigating and prosecuting cybercrime.

Also, the Office of the National Security Adviser plays a central role in cybercrime investigation, as host to Nigeria's Computer Emergency Response Team [83]. They coordinate the nation's corporate response to cyber-attacks. Also, in exercise its responsibilities as contained in the Cybercrime (Prohibition, Prevention, etc.) Act 2015, the Office of the National Security Adviser coordinates stakeholder input and releases the National Cybersecurity Strategy and Policy, on behalf of the President of the Federal Republic of Nigeria. Two editions have since been released; one in 2014 and a review in 2021. The last edition which was released in 2021 also outlined structural measures in line with the extant provisions. For instance, the National Computer Emergency Response Team, also known as the Nigeria Computer Emergency Response Team (ngCERT), the focal point of the nation's cyber incident response management is now domiciled under the National Cybersecurity Coordination Centre (NCCC). Also to be domiciled under the NCCC is the National Digital Forensic Laboratory (NDFL), to provide the requisite tools and facilities for investigation and intelligence gathering of cyber related issues. Also, in reflection of the growing call for the amendment of the Cybercrime (Prohibition, Prevention, etc.) Act 2015, the Cybersecurity Advisory Council (CAC) is charged with the responsibility of driving the process for the amendment [67].

Beyond this, the Independent Corrupt Practices and Other Related Offences Commission (ICPC) also investigates cybercrime related offences. Although the establishment act predates the cybercrime act 2015, and did not specifically mention cybercrime, however, specific sections of the Establishment Act, such as sections 15 and 43 did make reference to investigating computer related crimes. Therefore, while the commission is focused on investigating corruption, they also investigate the intersection of computers and digital technology used for perpetrating crime—and this falls within the context of cybercrime. For instance, in 2022, the ICPC busted a cybercrime syndicate in connection to a N30.4 million fraud 44. To boost their investigative capacity, the commission had in 2012 set up a digital forensic laboratory [43].

Despite the various institutional and structural reforms embarked upon, this has not been sufficient to meet one of the highest cybercrime caseloads in the world. While there are many other reasons for this failure to stem the surging incidents of cybercrime in the country, one primary reason is the lack of technical capability and forensic resources [27]. The current system has a noticeable gap in digital forensic infrastructure and resources. Apart from the lack of forensic technology, there is also a shortage of investigators with forensic capabilities [69, 73]. For instance, the EFCC digital forensics unit at the agency's head office has an eight-man team. With caseloads averaging about two per day—each case with a possibility of multiple devices—it is challenging to cope with [68].

This book presents the findings of a study that investigated the extent of the lack of digital forensic resources in Nigeria's financial crime agencies. The study adds to the growing body of knowledge and clarifies the scope of the lack of digital forensic resources. Understanding the extent of the lack of forensic resources and the impact on the caseloads could be crucial to developing a roadmap towards building forensic capability and readiness for the agencies. This chapter is structured to introduce the study, statement of the problem, the purpose of research, and conceptual framework. This chapter also presented the research questions and significance of the study.

1.2 Background and Problem Statement

Information technology plays a central role in all facets of human endeavors [50, 78]. In Nigeria, a significant landmark event that catalyzed the rapid growth of information technology was the liberalization of the telecommunication sector [1]. Before this, the telecommunication sector was run centrally by the federal government's NITEL. With only about 500,000 landlines in 1991 [63], the sector's liberalization led to such exponential growth that by June 2023, the total number of mobile phone subscribers had risen to 220 million, translating to a teledensity of 115.30%. This rapid increase also triggered other associated development. For instance, the total number of active Internet subscribers increased to 194 million [64]. While this deepened access and connectivity, it also enabled a new kind of crime—Cybercrime.

Cybercrime has continued to be of growing concern over the years. The scale and dimension have increased exponentially in a short period. Studies have pointed to several reasons behind this surge. A significant reason behind this is the exponential growth in the use of computers in almost all spheres. Such widespread use of computers increased the attack surface and catalyzed the growing threat of cybercrime. This widening attack surface had become a significant attraction to criminals to take advantage of the increasing vulnerabilities in the cyber world [11]. Interpol [48] described cybercrime as the fastest growing transnational crime. It is now a primary concern of an international dimension.

There are several other factors behind the rapid rise in incidents of cybercrime. A significant driver behind the increase of cybercrime is the exponential increase in connectivity [89]. The International Telecommunication Union [47] put the total number of persons using the Internet at 4.1 billion. This number translates to 53.6% of the global population. In Nigeria, Internet connectivity had grown exponentially from just a few exclusive access in 1999 to 194 million Internet subscribers in June 2023 [64]. With a large pool of connected users, cybercriminals have a high probability of success. With such exponential growth in connectivity, there is also an increased propensity that more persons will turn to cybercrime with a possibility of more victims.

Another incentive is the virtual anonymity of cyberspace [78]. The very nature of cybercrime is such that the perpetrator seems to have a sense of anonymity. Thus, they derive additional comfort from their seemingly anonymous criminal activities online. Another motivation is the borderless cyberspace, not limited by geographic boundaries. The fact that criminals could potentially commit Internet fraud in one country from another country presents complex jurisdictional roadblocks to law enforcement agencies [48]. The complexities of cross-border investigation and prosecution, the bottlenecks of extradition, and other bureaucracies present a significant challenge. Thus, the speed of cybercrime is far more than the slow grind of cross-border prosecution [46]. Cybercriminals exploit this gap between the fast pace of cybercrime and the slow grind prosecution to escape without trial or conviction.

Furthermore, for the perpetrator, cybercrime is less risky than other crimes that involve dangerous field operations. Cybercrime operations are typically bloodless [24]. Hackers have committed serious online bank heists from the comfort of their homes, thousands of miles away. In contrast, the traditional bank robbery will have to go through dangerous drills and face potentially fatal shootouts to cart away their loot. This convenience, comfort, minimal risk, and primarily bloodless characterization are behind cybercrime's growing threat.

The increasing number, scope, and sophistication of expert hacking tools, powerful malware, and antiforensic techniques make tracking down a cybercrime complex and challenging. These tools are increasingly accessible and are even sold and leased in cyberspace. Therefore, people with less sophisticated skills can now procure these tools and deploy same to vulnerable and unsuspecting people. This model is now increasingly sophisticated and evolved to Cybercrime-as-a-service [56, 58]. The proliferation of cybercrime-as-a-service is a major driving force behind the increase in cybercrime, opening the cybercrime space to both the experienced and inexperienced.

Globally, law enforcement agencies have also increased their complexity in dealing with emerging cybercrime tools. In Nigeria, the EFCC and the Cybercrime units of other related investigating agencies have both acquired some measure of digital forensic capabilities. With the improved complexities in investigation and prosecution by law enforcement, the Nigerian Internet fraudsters also retooled and evolved to a more complex scale. The scheme has grown from flooding Cyberspace with spam emails to a spear-phishing and more sophisticated Business Email Compromise (BEC) [57]. They are more deliberate and precise in their current operations. In Business Email Compromise, also known as Email Account Compromise, the Internet fraudster targets businesses and individuals engaged in legitimate transfers. In 2022, an estimated $2.7 billion was lost by BEC victims, in a total of 21,832 cases reported to the Internet Crime Complaint Center [33]. This trend is also reflected in Africa. For instance, in 2022, there were reported high concentration of BEC actors in West Africa, and particularly Nigeria, launching attacks both within and beyond the continent [49].

There have been a few notable successes from Nigerian Law Enforcement Agencies in clamping down on BEC. For instance, joint operations such as "Operation Delilah" and "Killer Bee" operations, respectively, led to significant disruption of BEC activities in Nigeria. The joint operation included Interpol's Africa Cybercrime Operations Desk, private partners such as Group-IB, Palo Alto Networks, and Trend Micro, as well as the Nigeria Police Force [49]. Also, with impressive figures (prosecution success rate of 98.93% in 2021 and an improvement of 70.5% in total number of convictions) by the EFCC, clearly, progress is being made in this regard.

Despite these recorded successes, the Nigerian law enforcement agencies continue to struggle with the scale, pace, and magnitude of financial crimes. The gaps in digital forensics resources are such that they could be overwhelming to the law enforcement agencies [68, 69, 73]. The law enforcement agencies in Nigeria lack the requisite tools to tackle the growing sophistication of cybercrime. The agencies have not invested sufficient funds to ensure the forensic readiness of the organization. Most investigators lack the required level of forensic capability to combat the rising scourge of cybercrime in the country [15]. Therefore, it is essential to investigate, in greater detail, the extent of the lack of forensic resources as a necessary step towards developing a roadmap for building forensic readiness of the law enforcement agencies in Nigeria.

1.2.1 Statement of the Problem

Nigeria is one of the cybercrime hotbeds in the world. This increasing number of youths taking to cybercrime has escalated the caseloads, making things increasingly difficult for law enforcement [25]. A few studies have been conducted, highlighting the deficiencies in the law enforcement agencies as a significant impediment to the fight against cybercrime. For instance, Olayemi [69], Oraegbunam [73], and Bello and Griffiths [15] all pointed to this lack of forensic capabilities of the law enforcement agencies. However, previous studies did not drill into the specifics of this lack of technology, human resources, technical capabilities, and others. For the Nigerian law enforcement agencies to successfully confront the growing threat of financial crimes, it has to ascertain the capabilities of these agencies. The absence of such clear information on their capabilities makes it challenging to develop a roadmap for digital forensic readiness and capability maturity for the law enforcement agencies in Nigeria. This book addresses this, which is an important step in building the forensic readiness of Nigeria's cybercrime agencies. The book also establishes the specifics of the rising caseloads and other dynamics affecting Nigeria's fight against cybercrime.

1.3 Purpose of the Study

The purpose of this qualitative case study is to identify the extent of the lack of digital forensic resources amongst law enforcement agencies in Nigeria and how this affects the cybercrime caseloads and prosecution. Law enforcement agencies in Nigeria continue to struggle with the cybercrime caseloads [25]. Although this apparent lack of forensic resources is evident from the outside, this study identified the extent of the deficiency from the insider's perspective and available literature and documents. Good knowledge of the scale and scope of the lack of digital forensic resources will be an essential first step to developing a digital forensic readiness model or digital forensic capability maturity model.

Also, there is lot of information pointing to the high caseloads of cybercrime in Nigeria. Nigeria has also been accused of being behind the global surge in cybercrime activities. While there are some organised studies supporting this assertion, a lot of these conclusions are anecdotal in nature, with no empirical basis. The study presented in this book evaluated these conclusions and opinions in the public opinion, looking at empirical and scholarly sources. The book presents some of the cybercrime cases in Nigeria, looking out for trends and patterns. Also, the book presents some celebrated cybercrime cases by Nigerians, perpetrated outside of Nigeria. This is done to study the modus operandi and establish connections where necessary.

1.4 Nature of the Study

This research is a case study. The research population is the Nigerian financial crimes and Internet fraud investigative agencies—the Economic and Financial Crimes Commission (EFCC) and the Nigeria Police Force (NPF). Case studies are exploratory research into complex issues. Case studies allow the researchers to closely examine a case within a specific context [96]. Yin [95] defines case studies as an empirical inquiry that investigates a contemporary phenomenon in depth and within its real-life context, especially when the boundaries between phenomenon and context are not evident. They deepen understanding or gain insight into a specific case. Case studies are empirical investigations for a single unit or related units, using data collection tools such as interviews or surveys [30].

Specifically, the research adopted the case study approach, which is a type of qualitative paradigm. Yin [94] gave four scenarios when to use qualitative case studies. These include:

1. When answers to the "how" and "why" questions are critical to research;
2. When it is impossible to manipulate research participants;
3. When the contextual conditions are relevant to study; and
4. When there is an unclear boundary between the phenomenon of interest and the prevailing contexts.

This research fits the four conditions specified by Yin [94]. Therefore, this informed the choice of a qualitative case study. It is possible to analyze several data sources that will provide a multidimensional view of the phenomenon under review with case studies [14, 96]. Case studies explore details from the lenses of participants from multiple sources. It is essential to have a comprehensive perspective for an in-depth investigation, and this study provides that [85]. By structuring this as a case study, the lack of forensics resources amongst law enforcement agencies in Nigeria can be analyzed in-depth, from different sources, including interviews with serving officers, documents, publications, and other stakeholders, where necessary.

1.5 Significance of the Study

A few existing studies outline the myriad of challenges law enforcement agencies face in the combat of cybercrime. For instance, Mohammed et al. [59], Omotubora [72], and Ajayi [3] all pointed to the deficiencies in the significant legislation governing cybercrime—the Cybercrime (Prevention, Prohibition, etc.) Act 2015. Olayemi [69], Oraegbunam [73], and Ehimen and Bola [27] both pointed to the lack of forensic capabilities of the law enforcement agencies. Bello and Griffiths' [15] took this further to interrogate the technical capabilities of Nigerian law enforcement agencies to combat cybercrime. However, despite these studies, there are no studies that drill into the specifics of the lack of resources—technology, personnel, and capabilities—at the agency level. Bello and Griffiths' [15] effort took a more strategic and global overview, cutting across stakeholders. As a result, this study identified digital forensic resource deficiencies. The outcome of this study could be a good starting point to developing a roadmap for digital forensic readiness and capability maturity for the law enforcement agencies in Nigeria.

Also, this study also interrogates the cybercrime cases to establish things such as the caseloads, complexity of the crime, frequency, patterns, etc. This is quite important to understand the dynamics of cybercrime in Nigeria, beyond the newspaper headlines that often shape opinion on the subject.

1.6 Research Questions

The study has two primary research questions and nine research subquestions listed below:

Primary Research Question: What is the assessment of digital forensic resources and capabilities of law enforcement agencies in Nigeria?

Research Subquestion 1: What challenges prevent law enforcement agencies in Nigeria from having adequate forensic capabilities and being forensically ready?

Research Subquestion 2: What is the extent of digital forensic tools adoption by Nigerian law enforcement agents?
Research Subquestion 3: How has the lack of digital forensic resources affected the law enforcement agencies in Nigeria, and by extension, their efficiency in the fight to stop cybercrime?
Research Subquestion 4: What are the areas of digital forensic skills deficiency needing an upgrade?
Research Subquestion 5: What is the specific digital forensic training needed by law enforcement agents in Nigeria?
Research Subquestion 6: What specific digital forensic tools are in short supply or with expired licenses needing an upgrade?
Research Subquestion 7: What are the daily cybercrime caseload and available digital forensics resources?

Primary Research Question 2: What is composition and complexity of the cybercrime cases in Nigeria?

Research Subquestion 1: What are the frequent cybercrimes committed in Nigeria?
Research Subquestion 2: How many persons are convicted of cybercrime in Nigeria?

1.7 Theoretical Framework

Two theoretical frameworks guide this study: the Routine Activity Theory (RAT) and the Technology-Organization-Environment (TOE) framework. RAT is a famous theory in criminology developed by Cohen and Felson [20]. Essential aspects of the RAT—such as the concept of capable guardianship—shaped this study. The TOE framework is a technology adoption framework that is suitable for studying adoption at the firm level. This theory is related to this research which investigated the lack of digital forensics resources in the financial crimes agencies in Nigeria.

1.7.1 Routine Activity Theory (RAT)

Cybercrime has grown in popularity in the last two decades and is now an established research area in criminology [53]. Routine Activity Theory is a renowned situational theory of crime developed by Cohen and Felson [20]. The theory states that for crime to occur, three conditions must occur. The conditions are a motivated offender, a suitable target, and the absence of a capable guardian. This study is rooted in the third element: the absence of a capable guardian.

There have been debates as to the suitability of this theory in other areas beyond the terrestrial world. Specifically, there are varying perspectives and arguments regarding

RAT's suitability to analyze the causation of cybercrime and Internet fraud. For instance, Yar [93] thinks RAT cannot explain the causation of Internet crime reliably given the Spatio-temporal nature of cyberspace and the ecological nature of the RAT. Grabosky [37] believes the three conditions applicable in the terrestrial world also apply in the cyberworld. Leukfeldt and Yar [53] also agreed that RAT is suitable for cybercrime due to the similarities between cyberspace and the terrestrial world.

There are other studies in support of Grabosky's [37] position. For instance, Pratt et al. [75] used RAT to explain Internet Fraud. Hutchings and Hayes [42] used RAT to study and explain phishing victimization. [52] went further to use RAT to explain cybercrime determinants at the national level. [79] also used RAT to explain online victimization. [81] narrowed in by using RAT to analyze and explain insider threats.

The Capable Guardian. This study investigated the lack of digital forensic resources amongst the financial crimes agencies in Nigeria. Looking at the three elements of RAT—motivated offender, a suitable target, and the absence of a capable guardian—the lack of forensic resources amongst law enforcement agencies fit in the context of the absence of a capable guardian. Tseloni et al. [87] define guardianship as the capability of the persons and objects to prevent the crime. The concept of capable guardianship may be applied rather widely. Yar [93] suggests this could be the property owner, custodian, law enforcement, Computer Emergency Response Teams, banks, or any other, whose presence may discourage the occurrence of the crime in question. Bello and Griffiths [15] posited that the awareness of the existence of a capable guardian is a demotivating factor to the criminal.

However, there are challenges in understanding and analyzing RAT in the cyberworld. These challenges are more pronounced when situating law enforcement agencies in the role of capable guardians. For instance, just as in the real world, in cyberspace, the police are likely not to be present at the scene of a crime but needed when the primary guardian fails to effectively deter crime [34, 38]. It is possible to apply RAT despite the challenge posed by the complexities of formal guardianship in cyberspace. Consequently, this theory can shape this study, as previous studies by Bello and Griffiths [15] also showed.

1.7.2 Technology-Organization-Environment Framework

Adoption refers to an individual's decisions to accept, diffuse and mainstream innovation in an integrated manner [82]. As organizations continue to invest large sums in new technologies, it is essential to study technology adoption. Such investments may not yield positive results except the right adoption strategies are put in place [2]. The rapidly evolving and emerging technological landscape has necessitated the need for the study of innovation adoption. Researchers have applied several technology adoption models to study emerging technologies over the last few years [54]. For instance, the Theory of Reasoned Action (TRA) [5], the theory of Planned Behaviors [4], the Technology Acceptance Model (TAM) [22], and the Unified Theory of Acceptance and Use of Technology (UTAUT) [91] have all contributed to perspectives in technology adoption. However, Oliveira and Martins [70] observed that the above models focused more on the individual and suggested that the Technology-Organization-Environment (TOE) framework offers a better explanation of technology adoption at the firm level. Leung et al. [54] noted that an essential feature of the TOE framework is incorporating environmental factors, which help explain technology adoption.

From the name, the TOE framework considers the three critical elements of adoption: technology, organization, and environment. Technological context includes all relevant technologies in the firm. This context comprises existing related tools as well as emerging technologies [2]. Tornatzky et al. [86] describe technological context as internal and external technologies relevant to the firm. While internal technologies have to do with practices and technologies already adopted by the firm, external technologies refer to available technologies in the market. Following this, Leung et al. [54] hold that technological context primarily focuses on technical characteristics in the technology adoption process. Leung et al. [54] summarized the factors in the technological contexts condensed from previous technological adoption studies as perceived direct benefits, indirect benefits, and cross-technology compatibility [18, 45, 77].

From the Organizational context, Leung et al. [54] condensed the factors from previous studies in adoption as financial readiness, technological readiness, and top management support. These organizational factors may impede or facilitate innovation and technological adoption at the firm level [2]. It is possible to apply the components summarized by Leung et al. [54] to this study, which was structured to investigate the lack of forensic resources and digital forensic readiness of financial crime agencies in Nigeria. For instance, financial readiness and technological readiness are two concepts that researchers can use to explain poor technology adoption. Introducing and mainstreaming an emerging technology such as digital forensics technology will be affected or enhanced by organizational factors, which this study is also structured to investigate.

The environment context focuses on the space where the firm or organization conducts its business and extends to external factors presenting either opportunities or constraints for technological innovation [2]. It also encompasses its industry, competitors, and governmental interface and policies [86]. These factors affect the adoption of innovation and technology at the firm level. For instance, Al-Hujran et al. [8] established that the regulatory framework was one of the leading environmental factors that affected adoption. Therefore, the TOE framework is suited for studying technological adoption at the firm level by introducing factors such as the environment.

1.8 Conceptual Framework

This conceptual framework of digital forensic readiness influenced this study. Digital forensic readiness, although a relatively new term, has received a lot of attention in recent times. The term, first used by Tan [84], has two primary objectives: to maximize the usefulness of evidence collected and minimize the cost of investigations. Carrier and Spafford [16] further divided forensic readiness into operational readiness and infrastructural readiness, with the former being concerned with adequate training and equipment and the latter the efficient preservation of data. There are different perspectives on digital forensic readiness like time, cost, training, and technology [28]. To be adequately empowered to investigate Nigeria's growing Internet fraud cases, the country's financial crime agencies will need to attain a considerable level of forensic readiness. This readiness can be measured or assessed using any of the digital forensic readiness frameworks.

Different researchers have come up with other frameworks for Digital Forensic Readiness. For instance, Ngobeni et al. [62] came up with a conceptual model for wireless networks. Makutsoane and Leonard [55] came up with a forensic readiness model for a cloud service provider. Alenezi et al. [9] came up with a framework for measuring an organization's forensic readiness of cloud services. Almarzooqi and Jones' [10] framework for digital forensic readiness narrowed their model to assessing the core capabilities of a digital forensic organization. Garba and Bade [35] proposed a digital forensic readiness model for Nigerian banks. This improved previous research work on Zenith Bank, Nigeria [36]. Englbrecht et al. [29] proposed a capability model for digital forensic readiness. These are several of the available sources in the literature addressing digital forensic readiness models.

Pooe and Labuschagne [74] identified five critical components of a digital forensic readiness model: People, Process, Policy, Technology, and Data. These components shaped this study, and interview questions were structured to reflect them. This research used the five themes to investigate the lack of digital forensic resources in financial crimes agencies. This research used the guiding themes in examining the two major financial crimes agencies.

1.9 Limitations of the Study

While the two agencies chosen as the population for this study are principally responsible for investigating and prosecuting financial crimes in Nigeria, in reality, there are also overlapping roles by other related agencies. For instance, the Office of the National Security Adviser plays a central role in cybercrime investigation, as host to Nigeria's Computer Emergency Response Team [83]. They coordinate the nation's corporate response to cyberattacks and therefore play a role in the fight against Internet fraud. However, this study did not capture them because they are not frontline agencies in financial crime investigation.

Other critical stakeholders also impacted the law enforcement agencies' lack of forensic resources. For instance, the justice system is a crucial stakeholder that is affected by this lack. This study did not capture their perspective on this. Cybercrime incidents happen at a blistering pace, in contrast to the slow wheel of justice. Most of the investigations of financial crimes end up in court. When a technological gap exists within the financial crimes agencies, the justice system, or both, this presents a challenge. This study is limited because it did not consider the lack of digital forensic resources from the perspectives of the justice system.

1.10 Assumptions

The assumption that the financial crime agencies' lack of digital forensic resources was a significant factor in the slow pace of prosecution and the high caseloads of financial crimes and Internet fraud in Nigeria motivated this research. Following the theoretical framework of Routine Activity Theory and particularly capable guardianship, digital forensic readiness of law enforcement plays a role in the volume of caseloads. That is, a lack of digital forensic resources is assumed to be a motivation for Internet fraud. This research assumed that participants spoke freely and sincerely during the interviews. This situation is not always the case, as most law enforcement agents, by their training, may have been conservative with their answers. The researchers informed participants of the role the study's potential outcome could play in both institutions to get their buy-in. Understanding the extent of the lack of forensic resources and the impact on the caseloads could be crucial to developing a roadmap towards building forensic capability and readiness for the agencies.

1.11 Definitions

Cybersecurity: Von Solms and Van Niekerk [92] defined cybersecurity as the collection of tools, policies, security concepts, security safeguards, guidelines, risk management approaches, actions, training, best practices, assurance, and technologies used to protect the cyber environment and organization and user's assets.

Cybercrime: There are several definitions of cybercrime. Different contexts, perspectives, and jurisdictions have influenced different definitions of the term. Sabillon et al. [80] described the term as illegal acts where a digital device or information system is either a tool, target or both. Nigeria's National Information Technology Development Agency [60] defines cyber crime as a criminal activity done using computers and the Internet.

Digital Evidence: Carrier and Spafford [17] define digital evidence of an incident as digital data containing reliable information supporting or refuting a hypothesis about the incident investigated.

Digital Forensics: The Digital Forensics Research Workshop (DFRWS) [23] defines digital forensics as "the use of scientifically derived and proven methods toward the preservation, collection, validation, identification, analysis, interpretation, documentation and presentation of digital evidence derived from digital sources to facilitate or further the reconstruction of events found to be criminal, or helping to anticipate unauthorized actions shown to be disruptive to planned operations."

Digital Forensic Readiness: The term, first used by Tan [84], has two primary objectives: maximizing the usefulness of evidence collected and minimizing investigations' cost. Carrier and Spafford (2004) further divided forensic readiness into operational readiness and infrastructural readiness, with the former being concerned with adequate training and equipment and the latter the efficient preservation of data.

Internet Fraud: The Federal Bureau of Investigation [31] defines Internet fraud as the act of using Internet services or software with Internet connectivity to defraud or take advantage of victims. There are several examples of methods used by Internet fraudsters, including Business Email Compromise (BEC), data breach, Denial of Service (DoS), Phishing, Spoofing, ransomware, and many others.

1.12 Summary

Nigeria has struggled with high caseloads of Internet fraud. The scale and magnitude have been of great concern to the nation and the international community [25, 71]. Over the years, cybercriminals have grown in numbers and sophistication [41]. Disturbingly, the law enforcement agencies have not considerably increased their digital forensic capability to address this scourge. Ehimen and Bola [27], Olayemi [69], and Oraegbunam [73] all pointed to the lack of digital forensic resources of these agencies.

This study investigated this lack of digital forensic resources in great detail, with the EFCC and the Nigeria Police Force as case studies. This chapter introduced the topic, statement of the problem, the purpose of study, research questions, the significance of the study, and the conceptual framework. Chapter 2 is an in-depth literature review of the topic. Some of the issues reviewed include cybercrime, historical perspectives, emerging technologies and cybercrime, Internet fraud, the role of investigative agencies, cybercrime laws, various reforms, digital forensics, digital evidence, digital forensic readiness, and many more.

References

1. Abdul-Rasheed SL, Lateef I, Yinusa MA, Abdullateef R (2016) Cybercrime and Nigeria's external image: a critical assessment. J Pan Afr Stud 9(6):119–133

2. Ahmed I (2020) Technology organization environment framework in cloud computing. TELKOMNIKA 18(2):716–725
3. Ajayi EFG (2016) Challenges to enforcement of cyber-crimes laws and policy. J Internet Inf Syst 6(1):1–12
4. Ajzen I (1991) The theory of planned behavior. Organ Behav Hum Decis Process 50(2):179–211
5. Ajzen I, Fishbein M (1980) Understanding attitudes and predicting social behavior. Prentice Hall, Englewood Cliffs, NJ
6. Akanle O, Adesina JO, Akarah EP (2016) Towards human dignity and the Internet: the cybercrime (yahoo yahoo) phenomenon in Nigeria. Afr J Sci Technol Innov Dev 8(2):213–220
7. Akanle O, Shadare BR (2019) Yahoo-plus in Ibadan: meaning, characterization and strategies. Int J Cyber Criminol 13(2)
8. Al-Hujran O, Al-Lozi EM, Al-Debei MM, Maqableh M (2018) Challenges of cloud computing adoption from the TOE framework perspective. Int J E-Bus Res (IJEBR) 14(3):77–94
9. Alenezi A, Hussein RK, Walters RJ, Wills GB (2017) A framework for cloud forensic readiness in organizations. In: 2017 5th IEEE international conference on mobile cloud computing, services, and engineering (MobileCloud), pp 199–204. https://doi.org/10.1109/MobileCloud.2017.12
10. Almarzooqi A, Jones A (2016) A framework for assessing the core capabilities of a digital forensic organization. In: IFIP international conference on digital forensics, Jan 2016. Springer, Cham, pp 47–65
11. Arshad H, Jantan AB, Abiodun OI (2018) Digital forensics: review of issues in scientific validation of digital evidence. J Inf Process Syst 14(2)
12. Associated Press (2016) Nigerian man charged with hacking Los Angeles county emails. Guardian Newspaper. https://www.theguardian.com/us-news/2016/dec/18/los-angeles-county-email-hack-kelvin-onaghinor
13. Barboza T (2016) L.A. County targeted in phishing cyberattack; private information of 750,000 people compromised. Los Angeles Times. https://www.latimes.com/local/lanow/la-me-ln-county-cyberattack-20161217-story.html
14. Baxter P, Jack S (2008) Qualitative case study methodology: study design and implementation for novice researchers. Qual Rep 13(4):544–559
15. Bello M, Griffiths M (2021) Routine activity theory and cybercrime investigation in Nigeria: how capable are law enforcement agencies? In: Rethinking cybercrime. Palgrave Macmillan, Cham, pp 213–235
16. Carrier B, Spafford E (2004) An event-based digital forensic investigation framework. Digital Investigation. https://dfrws.org/wp-content/uploads/2019/06/2004_USA_paper-an_event-based_digital_forensic_investigation_framework.pdf
17. Carrier BD, Spafford EH (2005, August) Automated digital evidence target definition using outlier analysis and existing evidence. Digital Forensic Research Workshop, New Orleans, LA.
18. Chau PY, Tam KY (1997) Factors affecting the adoption of open systems: an exploratory study. MIS Q 21(1)
19. Choi KS, Lee CS, Louderback ER (2020) Historical evolutions of cybercrime: from computer crime to cybercrime. In: The Palgrave handbook of international cybercrime and cyberdeviance, pp 27–43
20. Cohen LE, Felson M (1979) Social change and crime rate trends: a routine activity approach. Am Sociol Rev 588–608
21. Cross C (2018) Victims' motivations for reporting to the 'fraud justice network.' Police Pract Res 19(6):550–564
22. Davis FD (1989) Perceived usefulness, perceived ease of use, and user acceptance of information technology. MIS Q 319–340
23. Digital Forensics Research Workshop (2001) Defining digital forensic examination and analysis tools. https://www.dfrws.org/sites/default/files/session-files/pres-defining_digital_forensic_examination_and_analysis_tools.pdf
24. Dortmans PJ, Thakur N, Ween A (2015) Conjectures for framing cyberwarfare. Def Secur Anal 31(3):172–184

25. Eboibi FE (2017) A review of the legal and regulatory frameworks of Nigerian Cybercrimes Act 2015. Comput Law Secur Rev 33(5):700–717
26. Economic and Financial Crimes Commission (2023) EFCC secures 3785 convictions in 2022. https://www.efcc.gov.ng/efcc/index.php/news-and-information/news-release/8781-efcc-secures-3785-convictions-in-2022
27. Ehimen OR, Bola A (2010) Cybercrime in Nigeria. Bus Intell J 3(1):93–98
28. Elyas M, Maynard SB, Ahmad A, Lonie A (2014) Towards a systemic framework for digital forensic readiness. J Comput Inf Syst 54(3):97–105
29. Englbrecht L, Meier S, Pernul G (2019) Towards a capability maturity model for digital forensic readiness. Wireless Netw 1–13
30. Farquhar JD (2012) Case study research for business. Sage
31. Federal Bureau of Investigation (n.d.) Internet fraud. www.fbi.gov/scams-and-safety/common-scams-and-crimes/internet-fraud
32. Federal Bureau of Investigation (2019) Business email compromise the $26 billion scam. https://www.ic3.gov/Media/Y2019/PSA190910
33. Federal Bureau of Investigation (2023) Internet crime report. https://www.ic3.gov/Media/PDF/AnnualReport/2022_IC3Report.pdf
34. Felson M (1998) Crime and everyday life. Thousand Oaks
35. Garba AA, Bade AM (2019) A recommended digital forensics readiness framework for Nigerian banks. Int J Dev Res 9(08)
36. Garba AA, Siraj MM (2015) A holistic-based digital forensic readiness framework for Zenith Bank, Nigeria. In: International conference on computational and social sciences, pp 551–560
37. Grabosky PN (2001) Virtual criminality: old wine in new bottles? Soc Leg Stud 10(2):243–249
38. Grabosky P, Smith R (2001) Telecommunication fraud in the digital age: the convergence of technologies. In: Wall D (ed) Crime and the Internet. Routledge
39. Guardian Newspaper (2021) 80% of EFCC's 978 convictions cybercrime related. https://guardian.ng/news/80-of-efccs-978-convictions-cybercrime-related/
40. Guardian Newspaper (2022) NCC puts cybercrime losses in Nigeria at $500m, sets to implement DMS. https://guardian.ng/news/ncc-puts-cybercrime-losses-in-nigeria-at-500m-sets-to-implement-dms/
41. Hinchliffe A (2017) Nigerian princes to kings of malware: the next evolution in Nigerian cybercrime. Comput Fraud Secur 2017(5):5–9
42. Hutchings A, Hayes H (2009) Routine activity theory and phishing victimisation: who gets caught in the 'net'? Curr Issues Crim Just 20(3):433–452
43. ICPC (2012) ICPC establishes forensic laboratory. https://icpc.gov.ng/2012/09/07/icpc-establishes-forensic-laboratory/
44. ICPC (2022) ICPC arraigns impersonator of ex-primate of anglican communion, others over N30.4m fraud. https://icpc.gov.ng/2022/04/10/cpc-arraigns-impersonator-of-ex-primate-of-anglican-communion-others-over-n30-4m-fraud/
45. Iacovou CL, Benbasat I, Dexter AS (1995) Electronic data interchange and small organizations: adoption and impact of technology. MIS Q 465–485
46. International Telecommunication Union (2012) Understanding cybercrime: phenomena, challenges and legal response. http://www.itu.int/ITU-D/cyb/cybersecurity/docs/Cybercrime%20legislation%20EV6.pdf
47. International Telecommunication Union (2020) Statistics. https://www.itu.int/en/ITU-D/Statistics/Pages/stat/default.aspx
48. Interpol (2017) Global cybercrime strategy. https://www.interpol.int/en/Crimes/Cybercrime
49. Interpol (2023) African cyberthreat assessment report cyberthreat trends. www.interpol.int
50. Joffee R (2010) Cybercrime: the global epidemic at your network door. Netw Secur 2010(7):4–7
51. Kigerl A (2020) Spam-based scams. In: Holt T, Bossler A (eds) The Palgrave handbook of international cybercrime and cyberdeviance. Palgrave Macmillan, Cham. https://doi.org/10.1007/978-3-319-78440-3_42
52. Kigerl A (2012) Routine activity theory and the determinants of high cybercrime countries. Social Science Computer Review, 30(4):470–486

53. Leukfeldt ER, Yar M (2016) Applying routine activity theory to cybercrime: a theoretical and empirical analysis. Deviant Behav 37(3):263–280
54. Leung D, Lo A, Fong LHN, Law R (2015) Applying the technology-organization-environment framework to explore ICT initial and continued adoption: an exploratory study of an independent hotel in Hong Kong. Tour Recreat Res 40(3):391–406
55. Makutsoane MP, Leonard A (2014) A conceptual framework to determine the digital forensic readiness of a cloud service provider. In: Proceedings of PICMET'14 conference: Portland international center for management of engineering and technology; infrastructure and service integration, July 2014, pp 3313–3321
56. Manky D (2013) Cybercrime as a service very modern business. Comput Fraud Secur 2013(6):9–13
57. Meyers A (2018) Not your fairy-tale prince: the nigerian business email compromise threat. Computer Fraud & Security, 2018(8):14–16
58. Mihai IC, Pruna Ş, Petrica G (2017) A comprehensive analysis on cyber-threats against elearning systems. ELearn Softw Educ 3:344–351. https://doi.org/10.12753/2066-026X-17-225
59. Mohammed KH, Mohammed YD, Solanke AA (2019) Cybercrime and digital forensics: bridging the gap in legislation, investigation, and prosecution of cybercrime in Nigeria. Int J Cybersecur Intell Cybercrime 2(1):56–63
60. National Information Technology Development Agency (2019) National cybersecurity policy/strategy implementation guidelines for ministries, departments & agencies (MDAs) & private ICT organizations. https://nitda.gov.ng/wp-content/uploads/2020/03/National-Cybersecurity-Strategy-Implementation-GuidelinesFinal.pdf
61. News Agency of Nigeria (2016) Police to create special unit to tackle cybercrime. Guardian Newspaper. https://guardian.ng/news/police-to-create-special-unit-to-tackle-cybercrime/
62. Ngobeni S, Venter H, Burke I (2010) A forensic readiness model for wireless networks. In: Chow K-P, Shenoi S (eds) Advances in digital forensics VI, vol 337. Springer Berlin Heidelberg, pp 107–117. https://doi.org/10.1007/978-3-642-15506-2_8
63. Nigerian Communications Commission (2004) An overview of the Nigerian telecommunications environment. https://www.ncc.gov.ng/archived/speeches/NCC%20CEO%20Presentation%20on%20Overview%20of%20Nigerian%20Telecoms%20Industry.pdf
64. Nigerian Communications Commission (2023) Subscriber data. https://ncc.gov.ng/statistics-reports/subscriber-data#monthly-subscriber-technology-data
65. Nigerian Deposit Insurance Company (2019) NDIC annual report 2018. https://ndic.gov.ng/wp-content/uploads/2019/09/NDIC-2018-ANNUAL-REPORT.pdf
66. Obuah E (2010) Combatting corruption in Nigeria: the Nigerian economic and financial crimes (EFCC). Afr Stud Q 12(1)
67. Office of the National Security Adviser (2021) National cybersecurity policy and strategy. https://cert.gov.ng/ngcert/resources/NATIONAL_CYBERSECURITY_POLICY_AND_STRATEGY_2021.pdf
68. Okolorie GR (2020) Uncovering patterns in complex investigations is no match for Nigeria's Economic and Financial Crimes Commission (EFCC) [Interview]. Cellebrite, 22 Dec 2020. https://www.cellebrite.com/en/uncovering-patterns-in-complex-investigations-is-no-match-for-nigerias-economic-and-financial-crimes-commission-efcc/
69. Olayemi OJ (2014) A socio-technological analysis of cybercrime and cyber security in Nigeria. Int J Sociol Anthropol 6(3):116–125
70. Oliveira T, Martins MF (2011) Literature review of information technology adoption models at firm level. Electron J Inf Syst Eval 14(1):110–121
71. Omodunbi BA, Odiase PO, Olaniyan OM, Esan AO (2016) Cybercrimes in Nigeria: analysis, detection, and prevention. J Eng Technol 1(1):37–42
72. Omotubora AO (2016) Comparative perspectives on cybercrime legislation in Nigeria and the UK—a case for revisiting the "hacking" offences under the Nigerian Cybercrime Act 2015. Eur J Law Technol 7(3)

73. Oraegbunam IK (2015) The Nigerian police and problems of cybercrime investigation: need for adequate training. Niger Law J 18(1):1–28
74. Pooe A, Labuschagne L (2012) A conceptual model for digital forensic readiness. In: 2012 information security for South Africa, Aug 2012. IEEE, pp 1–8
75. Pratt TC, Holtfreter K, Reisig MD (2010) Routine online activity and Internet fraud targeting: extending the generality of routine activity theory. J Res Crime Delinq 47(3):267–296
76. Punch Newspaper (2022) IGP shakes up cybercrime unit. https://punchng.com/igp-shakes-up-cybercrime-unit/
77. Ramdani B, Chevers D, Williams DA (2013) SMEs' adoption of enterprise applications: a technology-organisation-environment model. J Small Bus Enterpr Dev
78. Reed TS (2019) Cybercrime and technology losses: claims and potential insurance coverage for modern cyber risks. Tort Trial Insur Pract Law J 54(1):153–209
79. Reyns BW (2015) A routine activity perspective on online victimisation. J Financ Crime
80. Sabillon R, Cano J, Cavaller V, Serra J (2016) Cybercrime and cybercriminals: a comprehensive study. Int J Comput Netw Commun Secur 4(6)
81. Samonas S (2013) Insider fraud and routine activity theory. LSE Research Online. http://eprints.lse.ac.uk/50344/1/Samonas_Insider_fraud_routine_2013.pdf
82. Straub ET (2009) Understanding technology adoption: theory and future directions for informal learning. Rev Educ Res 79(2):625–649
83. Symantec Corporation and African Union (2016) Cybercrime & cybersecurity trends in Africa. www.thehaguesecuritydelta.com/media/com_hsd/report/135/document/Cyber-security-trends-report-Africa-en.pdf
84. Tan J (2001) Forensic readiness. @ Stake, Cambridge, MA, pp 1–23
85. Tellis W (1997) Application of a case study methodology. Qual Rep 3(3):1–19
86. Tornatzky LG, Fleischer M, Chakrabarti AK (1990) Processes of technological innovation. Lexington Books
87. Tseloni A, Wittebrood K, Farrell G, Pease K (2004) Burglary victimization in England and Wales, the United States and the Netherlands: a cross-national comparative test of routine activities and lifestyle theories. Br J Criminol 44(1):66–91
88. Umar I, Samsudin RS, Mohamed M (2016) Understanding the successes and challenges of Anti-Corruption Agency (ACA) in Nigeria: a case of Economic and Financial Crimes Commission (EFCC). Asian J Multidiscip Stud 4(5):27–33
89. United Nations Office on Drugs and Crime (2013) Comprehensive study on cybercrime https://www.unodc.org/documents/organized-crime/UNODC_CCPCJ_EG.4_2013/CYBERCRIME_STUDY_210213.pdf
90. Vanguard Newspaper (2020) Nigeria police, interpol arrest three suspects over cybercrime. Vanguard Newspaper. https://www.vanguardngr.com/2020/07/nigeria-police-interpol-arrest-3-suspects-over-cybercrime/
91. Venkatesh V, Morris MG, Davis GB, Davis FD (2003) User acceptance of information technology: toward a unified view. MIS Q 425–478
92. Von Solms R, Van Niekerk J (2013) From information security to cyber security. Comput Secur 38:97–102
93. Yar M (2005) The novelty of 'cybercrime': an assessment in light of routine activity theory. Eur J Criminol 2(4):407–427
94. Yin RK (2003) Case study research: design and methods, 3rd edn. Sage, Thousand Oaks, CA
95. Yin RK (2009) Case study research: design and methods, 4th edn. Sage, Thousand Oaks, CA
96. Zainal Z (2007) Case study as a research method. J Kemanusiaan 5(1)

Chapter 2
Cyber Crime in Nigeria—Reviewing the Problems

Abstract This chapter presents a scholarly review of the cybercrime challenge in Nigeria. The chapter starts with a historical background of cybercrime and progresses to the foundational concepts and definitions. This is followed by a review of the growing threat of cybercrime and the factors driving the surge in cybercrime statistics. This chapter also drills into the internet fraud challenge in Nigeria, and the various reforms made to effectively tackle the challenge. The reforms made cover institutional, structural, and legal dimensions. Specifically, the chapter presents various reforms such as the Economic and Financial Crimes Commission (EFCC), the Independent Corrupt Practices Commission (ICPC), the Advanced Fee Fraud and Other Fraud Related Offences Act, the Cybercrime (Prevention, Prohibition, etc.) Act 2015, the Evidence (Amendment) Act 2023, and others. The chapter also presented a review of available literature on technology and cybercrime investigation. The chapter ended by identifying and presenting the gaps in the literature reviewed.

Keywords Cybercrime · Internet fraud · Financial crimes · Independent Corrupt Practices Commission · Nigeria Police Force · Advance Fee Fraud · Evidence Act · 419

2.1 Introduction

Cybercrime is becoming a global menace, affecting nations, with no exception [98]. Nigeria is known to be one of the hotbeds of cybercrime globally, with heavy caseloads of cybercrime incidences [39]. These increased cybercrime activities have had a devastating impact on the country's image and in financial terms. Cybercrimes are a growing threat to the Nigerian economy [96]. The Nigeria Deposit Insurance Company [86] report shows Nigeria lost 15.15 billion Naira (approximately $43 million) to fraud in the banking sector alone. This figure represented an increase of 539% from the 2.37 billion Naira recorded in 2017. Cybercrime accounts for most of these. Recent figures show this trend has continued to increase exponentially. The Nigerian Communications Commission (NCC) puts total annual loss to cybercrime

R. T. Sibe and C. Kaunert, *Cybercrime, Digital Forensic Readiness, and Financial Crime Investigation in Nigeria*, Advanced Sciences and Technologies for Security Applications, https://doi.org/10.1007/978-3-031-54089-9_2

at $500 million. The implication of this is that cybercrime contributes to about 0.08% loss in GDP [50]. The victims cut across the financial sector to other institutions and even individuals across different jurisdictions.

This literature review researched the increasing wave of cybercrimes in Nigeria and the lack of forensic capability of the cybercrime agency. This study examined the lack of digital forensic resources using a case study approach. The study was structured to review the growing wave of cybercrime and Internet fraud in Nigeria and globally. The review highlighted the concept of cybercrime, historical perspectives, threat types, and vectors. This review included critical reforms in the fight against cybercrime, investigation of digital crimes, and digital forensics readiness.

2.2 Article Search

This literature review researched peer-reviewed articles on Internet fraud in Nigeria and the forensic readiness of cybercrime investigation agencies. The search also included challenges of cybercrimes in Nigeria from the law enforcement perspective. Articles published since 2018 were used, except in a few instances to provide context and history, to ensure that peer-reviewed articles were up to date. Digital Forensics is an emerging discipline, and expectedly, there are few peer-reviewed articles on it. Following this, there are also a few peer-reviewed articles on the forensic readiness of cybercrime investigative agencies in Nigeria. The review relied on a combination of peer-reviewed papers from reputable newspapers and government agency websites to fill this gap.

The phrases and search keywords include "digital forensic readiness," "digital forensic readiness framework," "Internet fraud," "cybercrime," and "cybercrime in Nigeria." Others include "forensic resources," "Business Email Compromise," "Nigerian 419", "Nigerian Advanced Fee Fraud," "financial crimes," "Yahoo Yahoo," and "cybersecurity laws in Nigeria." The review relied on the University of the Cumberlands Library and Google Scholar databases. Given this is an emerging issue with few supporting peer-reviewed articles, the study also relied on other sources on the World Wide Web, such as Government Agencies websites and other reliable institutional websites. This review concentrated on the key issues and challenges of Internet fraud and the readiness of the Nigerian investigating agencies to combat this (Table 2.1).

Table 2.1 Research databases used for the review of literature

Search engine	Number of resources obtained
University of the Cumberlands Library	68
Google Scholar	210
Others	227

Note This table shows the various sources of articles cited in this literature review

2.3 Historical Background

Information and Communication Technology is now widely applied in almost all facets of life. In Nigeria, the liberalization of the telecommunication industry in 2001 catalyzed the Nigerian Information Technology industry [1]. In 1999, Nigeria had just about five hundred thousand phone lines [87]. During this era, phones were a luxury item, available in the homes of a few elitist class. During this period, the federal government owned NITEL had a monopolistic grip in the telecommunication sector. The liberalization of the telecommunication sector led to an exponential growth in telecommunication subscriber statistics. As at August 2023, the total number of mobile phone subscribers had risen to over 220 million; translating to a tele-density of 115.63% [90]. This rapid increase also triggered other associated development. While this deepened access and connectivity, it also enabled a new kind of crime—Cybercrime.

The use of the Internet in Nigeria dates back to the mid-nineties. Only a handful of large commercial corporations used it, as the Internet was not freely available to the general public [65]. As of March 2023, the total number of active Internet subscribers (including GSM, fixed, and fixed wireless subscribers) had risen exponentially to over 223 million [90]. While this has deepened access and connectivity, it also enabled a new kind of crime—Cybercrime. The increasing threat of cybercrimes emanating from Nigeria has been disturbing in the last two decades [39, 96]. In responding to the rising cybercrime cases in Nigeria, the country took steps to stem the tide. The actions taken so far by the government have been a combination of institutional, structural, and legal reforms. Nigeria had a long history of military rule, spanning from 1983 to 1999. This period coincided with the era of institutional decay, autocratic rule, and large-scale corruption [38]. Following the return to democracy in 1999, successive administrations made efforts to strengthen institutions in the fight against cybercrimes.

The signing of the EFCC Act 2002 by President Olusegun Obasanjo was one such institutional reform [91]. The EFCC Act was first enacted as Financial Crimes Commission (Establishment) Act 2002, and later re-enacted as Financial Crimes Commission (Establishment) Act 2004 [127]. This institution is primarily responsible for fighting financial crimes, which includes cybercrimes and Internet fraud. Before the passage of the Cybercrime Act, the EFCC Act, while not created exclusively to tackle cybercrime, did serve as the significant legislation for the prosecution of cybercrimes [19]. Also, in 2006, President Olusegun Obasanjo signed into law the Advance Fee Fraud and other Related Offences Act [36]. In 2011, President Goodluck Jonathan signed into law the Evidence Act 2011. Before this, the old Evidence Act, which lasted over a century, did not provide for the admissibility of digital evidence in Nigerian courts. Admissibility of digital evidence is an essential step in the prosecution of Internet fraudsters and cybercriminals, and the amendment of the Evidence Act was, therefore, a significant milestone [78]. Note that the evidence in cybercrime prosecution is largely digital in nature. With this amendment, digital forensic evidence and expert testimonies became admissible in Nigerian courts.

Despite the various institutional and structural reforms embarked upon, Cybercrime in Nigeria continued to rise. One major cause of concern was the lack of central legislation, with cybercrime as its focus. In response, President Goodluck Jonathan signed into law the Cybercrime (Prohibition, Prevention, etc.) Act, 2015. This law aimed to detect, prevent, and prosecute cybercrime in Nigeria [2]. This law provides the main legal framework for combatting Cybercrime in Nigeria. Before this, there was no central legal framework for Cybercrime in Nigeria [94]. This act attempts to regulate the conduct of persons in cyberspace.

2.4 Cybercrime

Information technology has been increasingly deployed in all facets of our life [64, 106]. This has significantly influenced the scope and definition of work, lifestyle, healthcare, education, manufacturing, and in fact all aspects of our lives. The invention of the internet and the revolution of telephony has also catalysed technology adoption in all sectors. Specifically, the last decade has seen a surge in tele-density and internet penetration. In 2022, there were about 5.31 billion unique mobile phone users in the world; representing about 67.1% or more than two-thirds of the world's population. As at the start 2022, total number of global internet users has grown to 4.95 billion, with internet penetration put at 62.5% of the world population (with more than 4% growth rate, when compared to the preceding year) [129].

While this growth in technology adoption has come with a lot of positive influence and optimized efficiency, it has also been exploited by criminals, and birthed a new kind of crime—Cybercrime. Globally, the last 3 decades has seen an increase in technology enabled crime. Holt et al. [54, p. 5] noted the three ways computer and telephony have been exploited by users:

1. As a medium of communicating and promoting subcultures online;
2. As a mechanism to target sensitive information online; and
3. As an incidental device for facilitating crime and provide evidence of criminal activity, both in the digital world and the terrestrial world.

So, what is cybercrime? The next section will answer this.

2.4.1 Definition of Cybercrime

There are many variations of the definition of cybercrime, although the meanings appear consistent [24]. Different contexts, perspectives, and jurisdictions have influenced different definitions of the term. The lack of a global consensus on the definition of cybercrime adds to the growing confusion in the use and application of the term. Wall [128] had attempted what served as one of the earliest typology of cybercrime. This produced the four typologies listed below:

i. Cyber trespass
ii. Cyber deception/thefts
iii. Cyber pornography/obscenity
iv. Cyber violence.

It is noteworthy that Wall's [128] typology above are not specific offences, but a description of a range of behaviours and activities. Two decades later, there is no consensus on the definition, and the rapidly evolving landscape means that new types of cybercrime continue to evolve with the evolving technological landscape.

The United Nations Office on Drugs and Crime [124] argued that no single definition of cybercrime conveys the universal meaning of the word. The institution defined it broadly, including the collection of actions constituting the offense and the modus operandi. Sabillon et al. [111] described the term as illegal acts where a digital device or information system is either a tool, target or both.

Also, different jurisdictions have attempted to define the term for purposes of clarity. For instance, Nigeria's National Information Technology Development Agency [82] defines cyber crime as criminal activity committed using computers and the Internet. The Nigerian Cybercrimes (Prohibition, Prevention, etc.) Act [88], although did not explicitly define it, however captures it as the use of computer technology to perpetrate crimes such as:

1. unlawful access;
2. system interference;
3. interception of electronic messages and money transfers;
4. tampering with critical national infrastructure;
5. willful misdirection or electronic messages;
6. unlawful interceptions;
7. computer-related forgery;
8. computer related fraud;
9. theft of electronic devices;
10. unauthorized modification of computer systems, network data and system interference;
11. fraudulent issuance of e-instructions;
12. child pornography and related offences;
13. child pornography;
14. cyber terrorism;
15. cyberstalking;
16. cybersquatting.

The United States Department of Justice [123] defines cybercrime as "any violations of criminal law that involve a knowledge of computer technology for their perpetration, investigation, or prosecution." The Association of Chief Police Officer of England, Wales, and Northern Ireland [119] define electronic crime as networked computers or Internet technology to commit or facilitate a crime. Although these definitions read differently, they all point in the same direction.

It is noteworthy that the term, cybercrime, is often used interchangeably with other words, such as computer crime, electronic crime, digital crime, and computer-related crime [111]. However, Ajayi [11] and McGuire and Dowling [74] argued against the interchangeable use of computer crime and cybercrime, positing that the terms have distinct meanings. The former is crimes committed using the computer, while the latter is an umbrella term that captures both cyber-dependent and cyber-enabled crimes.

In their study proposing cybercrime taxonomy, Chandra and Snowe [31] broke down cybercrime into two broad classifications. They are pure technology crime and cyber-advanced crime. This study classified pure technology crime as those targeting computer systems, related technologies, and networked systems. The impact of this is usually to undermine the three cardinal pillars of information security—confidentiality, integrity, and availability. Cyber-advanced crime targets natural persons, property (other than those classified under pure technology crime), and government. They target these assets or entities to deprive and disrupt, and in the process, compromise or damage the assets.

The Convention on cybercrime, put together by subject experts from member states of Council of Europe [34] and some non-member states categorizes from substantive criminal law point of view:

1. Offences against the confidentiality, integrity and availability of computer data and systems—This includes the following:

    i. Illegal access
    ii. Illegal interception
    iii. Data interference
    iv. System interference
    v. Misuse of devices

2. Computer-related offences

    Computer-related forgery
    Computer-related fraud

3. Content-related offences

    i. Offences related to child pornography

4. Offences related to infringement of copyrights and related rights
5. Attempt and aiding or abetting.

While there is yet a consensus on the definition of cybercrime—and there may never be given the various factors influencing and shaping definition—there is an understanding of what constitutes a cybercrime. These definitions may be syntactically and semantically different but all point in same direction, and leaves little ambiguity of what constitutes cybercrime.

2.4.2 Historical Perspective of Cybercrime

What is now known as cybercrime has been around for decades; albeit, not known by this name. Some threat types and vectors now classified as cybercrime have been around for decades. The first reported case of cybercrime was in the 1960s. However, because mainframe computers at the time where not networked, they were not known as cybercrime. At the time, this was mainly referred to as computer crime; a name coined in reflection of the tool and object of crime—the computer. The earliest known taxonomy of computer crime was credited to Parker [102]. Parker [102] defined computer crime as one where the computer is:

1. The object of crime;
2. The environment where crime occurs;
3. The instrument used to commit crime;
4. The symbol of crime.

Parker's [102] definition showed the computer switching roles, but remain a key role in this crime taxonomy.

The early computer crimes were largely insider activities, since they were isolated mainframes [23, 130]. This continued in the 70s, when there were reported cases of hacking using social engineering [49]. In 1973, there was a reported case of a bank teller defrauding the bank by manipulating computer records [72]. There was also the case of sending of spam mail through the ARPANET distribution list [111]. Although the different cybercrime-related activities were in existence for decades, Sussman and Heuston coined the term cybercrime in 1995 [111, 112]. The application of this term has expanded over the years, with increased sophistication and impact. Also, emerging technologies and the evolving threat landscape continue to expand the scope of the definition.

Beyond computer crime, several other related terminologies were used, all of which are now all classified under the term cybercrime. For instance, Sabeil et al. [110] define digital crime as "any criminal activity which involves the use of computers and networks or any other digital devices". Karyda and Mitrou [67] define electronic crime "as an illegal act that is carried out using a computer or electronic media". The Internet Crime Complaint Centre define Internet crime to include any illegal activity involving one or more components of the Internet, such as websites, chat rooms, and/or email. Internet crime involves the use of the Internet to communicate false or fraudulent representations to consumers. These crimes may include, but are not limited to, advance-fee schemes, non-delivery of goods or services, computer hacking, or employment/business opportunity schemes (Table 2.2).

These definitions have been limited over the years, particularly with emerging technologies and the increasing scope of technology enabled crime. This book uses these terminologies interchangeably or broadly classified as cybercrime.

Table 2.2 Cybercrime taxonomy and reference to definitions reviewed

S. No.	Taxonomy	Reference to definitions reviewed
1.	Cybercrime	Wall [128], United Nations Office on Drugs and Crime [124], Sabillon et al. [111], National Information Technology Development Agency [82], Nigerian Cybercrimes (Prohibition, Prevention, etc.) Act [88], United States Department of Justice [123], Association of Chief Police Officer of England, Wales, and Northern Ireland [119], Chandra and Snowe [31], Council of Europe [34], Sabillon et al. [111] and Sarmah et al. [112]
2.	Computer crime	Parker [102], Brenner [23], Yang (130), Yang [130] and Fell [49]
3.	Digital crime	Sabeil et al. [110]
4.	Electronic crime	Karyda and Mitrou [67]
5.	Internet crime	Internet Crime Complaint Centre

Note This table shows the various cybercrime taxonomy and references reviewed

2.4.3 The Growing Threat of Cybercrime

Over the years, cybercrime has taken different dimensions. The scale and extent have increased over time. The exponential growth in the use of computers in almost all spheres increased the attack surface and catalyzed the growing threat of cybercrime. Computers are now central to all human endeavors [64, 106]. This centralized role had become a significant attraction to criminals to take advantage of the increasing vulnerabilities in the cyber world [17, 26]. Interpol [61] described cybercrime as the fastest growing transnational crime. It is now a significant concern globally.

There are several factors behind the rapid growth of cybercrime. This book presents some of the key factors behind the rising case of cybercrime, synthesised from available literature.

1. **Increased Connectivity**

A significant driver behind the increase of cybercrime is the exponential increase in connectivity [124]. The International Telecommunication Union [59] put the total number of persons using the Internet at 4.1 billion. This figure translates to 53.6% of the global population. In Nigeria, Internet connectivity had grown exponentially from just a few exclusive access in 1999 [87], to 220 million by June 2023; translating to a tele-density of 115.30%. This has catalyzed the growth in internet connectivity to 194 million active internet subscribers in Nigeria [90]. With a large pool of connected users, cybercriminals have a lot more probability of success. With such exponential growth in connectivity, there is also a higher propensity that more persons will turn to cybercrime.

2. **Virtual Anonymity of the Cyberspace**

Another incentive is the virtual anonymity of cyberspace [106]. Cybercriminals derive additional comfort from their seeming anonymous criminal activities online. They can commit industrial scale virtual heist, while being anonymously behind their computer screens. The growing sophistication of anti-forensics tools and tactics further emboldens the cybercriminal to engage in cybercrime. These tools, most of which are now readily available in the cyberspace for an affordable fee, further empowers the cybercriminal to wreak havoc and cover his trail and identity.

3. **Borderless Nature of Cybercrime**

Also, the borderless nature of cyberspace is a motivation for cybercrime, as they have a limitless range in addition to their virtual anonymity. Cybercriminals could potentially commit Internet fraud in different countries from their base in a foreign country. This cross-border nature of cybercrime presents complex jurisdictional roadblocks to law enforcement agencies [61]. Cybercriminals exploit this challenge to escape without prosecution or conviction. To arrest and prosecute a suspect in another country requires a lot of complicated international diplomacy, collaborations, and sometimes frustrating extradition processes, which are mostly slower compared to the fast pace of cybercrime [58]. This position aligns with Bello and Griffiths [22] submission that multiple laws and jurisdictions, and the lack of collaboration, were a significant challenge in cybercrime prosecution. Mohammed et al. [78] also supported this view, noting a need to bridge existing gaps between all stakeholders.

4. **"Bloodless" Nature of Cybercrime**

Furthermore, for the perpetrator, cybercrime is relatively less risky than other crimes involving dangerous field operations. Cybercrime operations are typically bloodless [37]. For instance, a cybercriminal in his apartment could defraud a bank of millions of dollars without any physical danger to his life. In contrast, traditional bank robbery, for example, could be bloody and fatal. The perpetrators of armed robbery will need to go through a complicated planning process of overcoming the physical security barriers, complex logistics involved in robbing and transportation of loot, and in keeping the Police away from the trail. These are dangerous operations that could easily be fatal. In contrast, hackers have committed serious online bank heists from the comfort of their homes. This convenience, comfort, less risk, and bloodless characterization are behind the growing threat of cybercrime.

5. **Crimeware-as-a-Service**

Also, the increasing number, scope, and sophistication of specialist hacking tools, powerful malware, and anti-forensic techniques make tracking down a cybercrime complex and challenging. These tools are increasingly accessible and are even sold and leased in cyberspace. Thus, people with less sophisticated skills can now procure these tools and deploy same to vulnerable and unsuspecting people. This model is now increasingly sophisticated and evolved to Cybercrime-as-a-service or crimeware as a Service [72, 77]. The proliferation of cybercrime-as-a-service is a major driving force behind the increase in cybercrime, opening the cybercrime space to both the experienced and inexperienced. Today, a rookie cybercriminal can easily procure dangerous tools for as little as $20 dollars, with full instruction on how to deploy it, and in some cases money-back guarantee.

6. **Emerging Technologies and Cybercrime**

Emerging technologies such as cloud computing, the Internet of Things, Social Media, and Blockchain have increased the number of Internet users, and by extension, vulnerabilities. These emerging complexities have increased the attack surface and the range of threat vectors [77]. The technical complexity of emerging technologies brings new sets of vulnerabilities which cybercriminals can easily exploit. These comes with the unintended (and intended in some cases) consequences of making investigation a lot more complicated. Bello and Griffiths [22] support this position, noting that the constantly evolving technological landscape gives cybercriminals the edge over cybercrime investigators. These vulnerabilities introduced by emerging technologies have led to an exponential rise in the number of threat types and vectors, with new concerns such as identity theft, Business Email Compromise, malware attacks, Distributed Denial of Service (DDoS), and many more [28].

7. **Remote Work**

In addition to this, the changes in the workplace may have also contributed to the growing scale of cybercrime. COVID-19 pandemic saw a lot of institutions transiting to online and hybrid work mode. The pandemic forced the rapid switch to telework. Companies that started the year without planning for teleworking switched abruptly switched [20]. This increasing switch to remote working, teleworking, and even other policies such as "Bring Your Own Device" (BYOD) have thrown in more significant vulnerabilities and increased the cyber risk [44]. Sirineni [114] identified three ways that cybercriminals took advantage of the abrupt switch to remote work: they took advantage of less security monitors at home to evade detection, the cybercriminals exploited shared devices at home with known vulnerabilities and less security controls; companies resorted to outsourcing to other jurisdictions to drive down cost, and this came with cybersecurity challenges.

8. **The Speed of Cybercrime Versus the Speed of Cybercrime Investigation**

Cybercrime incidents happen at a blistering pace, in contrast to the slow wheel of justice. This wide gap in speed gives cybercriminals an edge [71]. In reinforcing this position, Hadlington et al. [51] also pointed out the widening gap between the speed of cybercrime and the speed of investigation as a significant challenge. The painfully slow investigation process and prosecution of digital crimes put cybercriminals ahead in terms of numbers. In some countries, the justice system is still undergoing reforms to catch up with the growing cybercrime. For instance, it was not until 2015 that

Nigeria signed the Cybercrime act [78]. As at today, there are still countries with no dedicated cybercrime law. These gaps between the cybercrime world and the justice system—both in speed and technological capability—give cybercriminals further impetus.

9. **Panic and Despair**

Finally, cybercrime thrives in an atmosphere of panic and despair, such as the recent COVID-19 pandemic [10], [52], [81]. The COVID-19 pandemic has forced the rapid switch to telework. Companies that started the year without planning for teleworking switched abruptly [20]. Teleworking increases the attack surface and the possibility of cybercrime. Cybercriminals thrive in panic and chaos, and they have taken advantage of the rapid switch and the uncertainty occasioned by the pandemic. McAfee [73] reported 375 threats per minute, a 71% increase in mobile malware, a 689% increase in new PowerShell malware, and an increase of 58% for new malware, recorded during the first quarter of 2020. In recognition of the spike in cybercrimes and Internet fraud during the COVID-19 pandemic, the Central Bank of Nigeria [29] issued cybercrime warning and advisory to Nigerian banks and the public. This press release was to proactively warn commercial banks and their customers in the wake of a potential spike in cyber attacks. Eboibi's [40] study of what he called the "cyber pandemic" in Nigeria further underscores how cybercriminals took advantage of the pandemic situation in Nigeria and the rest of the world to launch more cyber attacks.

2.5 The Rising Cost of Cybercrime

Cybercrime originated from an online perspective, but the scale goes beyond online transactions, extending to the physical. While it had an online root, the impact could be far-reaching on the physical world. An estimated $26 billion was lost by BEC victims between 2016 and 2019, in a total of 166,349 cases reported to the Internet Crime Complaint Centre [48]. Between 2018 and 2022, the Internet Crime Complaint Centre [60] received a total of 3.26 million complaints, with a total loss of $27.6 billion. It is noteworthy that the loss for 2022 alone was put at $10.3 billion (Fig. 2.1).

Most victims do not report cybercrime cases; therefore, this figure is only indicative [35]. From a Nigerian perspective, the rising scale of Internet fraud has also been of significant concern. In 2018, the Nigerian Deposit Insurance Company [86] reported a staggering 539% increase in the cost of fraud to the Nigerian economy compared to the previous year. This amount translates to 15.15 billion Naira, with Internet fraud representing a sizeable amount of this. This exponential increase in Internet fraud in Nigeria has called to question the measures to prevent, investigate and prosecute cybercrimes.

In 2022, the Nigerian Communications Commission estimated an annual loss of $500 million to cybercrime. This contributes to about 0.08% loss of GDP [6]. This is even more so, given that Nigerians have continued to embrace e-transactions. A

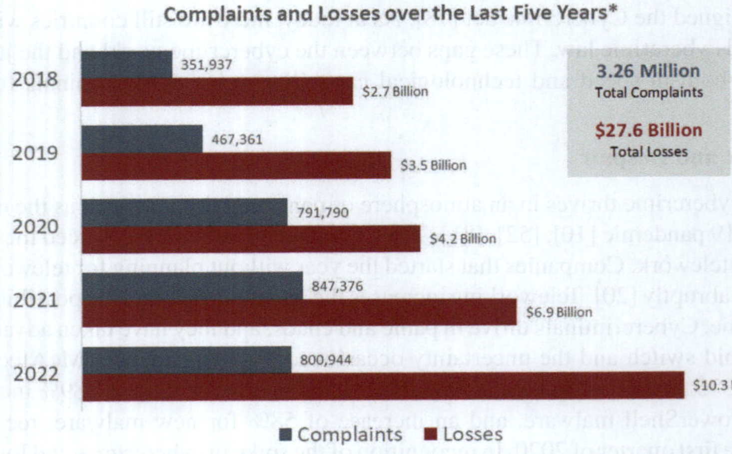

Fig. 2.1 Cybercrime complaints and losses over the last five years. *Credit* Internet Crime Complaint Centre [60]

recent report shows that the NIBSS Instant Payment Platform (NIP) recorded a total of N271.5 trillion in the first 9 months of the year 2022 [7]. With such high level of technology adoption in the financial sector, the potential for criminals to take advantage of the wider attack surface and increasing vulnerabilities will be more pronounced.

2.6 Internet Fraud (419) in Nigeria

The Federal Bureau of Investigation [46] defines Internet fraud as "the use of Internet services or software with Internet access to defraud victims or otherwise take advantage of them." Cybercriminals commit internet fraud using several sophisticated methods, such as Business Email Compromise (BEC), phishing, spoofing, Denial of Service (DoS), Distributed Denial of Service (DDoS), malware, data breach, ransomware, and many more. Like any other fraud, Internet fraud is driven mainly by financial gains [26, 35]. Internet fraud evolved out of Advance Fee Fraud. The fraudulent scheme is said to have its history in West Africa, particularly Nigeria [68]. Globally, this scheme is most associated with Nigeria, which has influenced its naming—"419" and "Yahoo Yahoo" [14, 13, 70]. The illicit scheme got its "419" name from Nigeria's criminal code for fraud (419). Apart from averaging the highest loss per victim, Nigerian "419" scams are the second most reported cybercrime [33]. Therefore, it is of significant concern to the country.

Nigeria has been battling the scourge of cybercrimes over the last two decades. The country is one of the cybercrime hotbeds in the world; and the highest in Sub-Saharan Africa [39]. Internet fraud in Nigeria has continued to increase in exponential proportions and has attracted global attention. Suleiman [117] showed 55% of youths sampled in a study were involved in Internet fraud, 30% aged between 23 and 45 years were also involved. This was further corroborated in studies by Abdulkadir and Abdulkadir [2], noting that while cybercrime cuts across different age strata, majority of perpetrators in Nigeria are the youths. A lot of the youths involved do this largely for economic reasons. The army of young recruits is a significant factor behind the upsurge of Internet fraud in Nigeria. They often leverage the experience of their older scammers. A good number of them live extravagantly from the proceeds of their crime [53]. While there may have been some success in combating cybercrimes, the caseloads of Internet fraud continue to increase due to the vast army of recruits and many other factors.

The advent of new cybercrime tools and improvements in cybercrime investigation forced Nigerian Internet fraudsters to retool and evolve. The scheme has grown from flooding cyberspace with spam emails of a prince looking for love to a more sophisticated Business Email Compromise (BEC) [75]. The poorly written emails with elementary grammatical errors have since given way for well written scam emails. They are now more deliberate and precise in their current operations. In Business Email Compromise, also known as Email Account Compromise, the Internet fraudster targets businesses and individuals engaged in legitimate transfers. An estimated $26 billion was lost by BEC victims between 2016 and 2019, in a total of 166,349 cases reported to the Internet Crime Complaint Centre [48]. Most victims of cybercrime never report, therefore, this figure is only suggestive [35]. Internet fraudsters take control of victims' corporate email, using schemes such as social engineering, spoofing, and others to defraud their victims.

Symantec Corporation and African Union [118] reported that out of a large pool of email addresses used by online scammers, 46% were Nigerian Internet Protocol (IP) addresses. Internet fraudsters have metamorphosed from the stage of sending bulk emails to unsuspecting victims to carrying out spear-phishing attacks that compromise their corporate email accounts. They have grown in technological sophistication, using sophisticated malware tools with greater efficiency [53]. This increased sophistication has become an incentive for more attacks.

Beyond using "419" mails, malware, and Business Email Compromise, Nigerian Internet fraudsters also engage in spoofing and impersonation of legitimate corporate websites. Over time, they have improved in proficiency and skills to clone websites and spoof emails to trick victims [53]. The rising scale of Internet fraud in Nigeria is now of great concern. In 2018, the Nigerian Deposit Insurance Corporation [89] reported a staggering 539% increase in the cost of fraud to the Nigerian economy compared to the previous year. This amount translates to 15.15 billion Naira, with Internet fraud representing a sizeable amount of this. This exponential increase in Internet fraud in Nigeria has called to question the measures to prevent, investigate and prosecute cybercrimes.

2.7 Internet Fraud Investigation in Nigeria

The primary investigating agency for Internet fraud in Nigeria is the Economic and Financial Crimes Commission (EFCC). Set up by the Economic and Financial Crimes Commission (EFCC) Act 2004, the commission's mandate extends beyond Internet fraud to other financial crimes [4], [63], [91, 122]. In the early years, the numbers of successfully investigated cybercrime cases was not much. The commission investigated 15,124 petitions, securing only 568 convictions between 2010 and 2015 [100]. As early as 2009, the EFCC announced the successful shutdown of about eight hundred websites allegedly related to cybercrime gangs [69]. Since then, the commission has continued to record exponential breakthroughs showing the rising caseloads.

However, other agencies often play overlapping roles, specifically investigating Internet fraud. For instance, the Nigerian Police Force has a dedicated cybercrime unit with a mandate to crack down on cybercrime [83]. This unit investigates and prosecutes Internet fraud [126]. Also, the Office of the National Security Adviser plays a central role in cybercrime investigation, as host to Nigeria's Computer Emergency Response Team [22, 118]. They coordinate the nation's corporate response to cyber attacks.

2.7.1 *Institutional Reforms*

Since the Fourth Republic (which began in 1999), Nigeria has embarked on critical reforms to establish institutions and rework the laws to give impetus to the fight against Internet fraud. For instance, the EFCC Act 2004 was enacted, which set up a body for the sole purpose of investigating and prosecuting financial crimes [4], [63], [91, 122]. Before the EFCC act, there was the Independent Corrupt Practices Commission (ICPC) in 2000. While the mandate of the Independent Corrupt Practices Commission restricted them to investigating official corruption, the Economic and Financial Crimes Commission had a broader mandate to investigate and prosecute "any person, corporate body, or organization" suspected of economic crimes [122]. Between 2010 and 2015, the Economic and Financial Crimes Commission investigated a total of 15,124 petitions. Out of this, the commission filed 2460 cases in court, with only 568 convictions [100].

In 2006, the Advance Fee Fraud and other Related Offences Act became law. This law focused on advanced fee fraud. Another key landmark was the amendment of the Evidence Act in 2011. With this amendment, digital evidence is now admissible in Nigerian jurisprudence. Beyond this, another important milestone was the enactment of the Cybercrimes (Prevention, Prohibition, etc.) Act 2015. This law is the primary legal framework for combatting cybercrime in Nigeria [8], [9], [93], [12]. Over time, these steps have given impetus to the fight against cybercrimes in Nigeria.

The primary institution prosecuting cybercrime in Nigeria is the EFCC, established by the Economic and Financial Crimes Commission (Establishment) Act 2004 [78]. Before this, the Nigerian Police Force Fraud unit was mainly responsible for prosecuting financial crimes, including cybercrime. However, following the enactment of the Cybercrime (Prevention, Prohibition, etc.) Act 2015, the expanded definition of cybercrime extends beyond financial crimes, and by extension, the scope and the mandate of the Economic and Financial Crimes Commission. In addition to the EFCC and the Nigerian Police Force, other agencies in the fight against cybercrime include the Independent Corrupt Practices Commission and the Department of State Services [118].

As mentioned above, the Independent Corrupt Practices and Other Related Offences Commission (ICPC) also investigates cybercrime related offences. Although the establishment act predates the Cybercrime Act 2015, and did not specifically mention cybercrime, however, specific sections of the Establishment Act, such as sections 15 and 43 did make reference to investigating computer related crimes. Therefore, while the commission is focused on investigating corruption, they also investigate the intersection of computers and digital technology used for perpetrating crime—and this falls within the context of cybercrime.

2.7.2 EFCC

The Economic and Financial Commission was established by an act of parliament in 2002, and was later amended in 2004. The commission was tasked to combat economic crimes, by preventing, investigating, prosecuting economic and financial crimes. The EFCC was formed in response to pressure from the Financial Action Task Force (FATF) on Money Laundering, otherwise known by the French name Groupe d'action financière (GAFI). GAFI, an initiative of G7 (consisting of Canada, France, Germany, Italy, Japan, United Kingdom, and the United States of America) was formed in 1989, with the key objective of combatting money laundering [43]. To give the commission more operational and legal impetus, the commission is tasked with the responsibility of executing the provisions of other related laws. Specifically, section 7(2) of the Economic and Financial Crimes Commission (Establishment) Act 2004 states that the Commission is charged with the responsibility of enforcing the provisions of:

a. The Money Laundering Act 2004; 2003 No. 7 1995 No. 13;
b. The Advance Fee Fraud and Other Fraud Related Offences Act 1995;
c. The Failed Banks (Recovery of Debts) and Financial Malpractices in Banks Act 1994, as amended;
d. The Banks and other Financial Institutions Act 1991, as amended; and the Miscellaneous Offences Act;
e. Any other law or regulations relating to economic and financial crimes, including the Criminal code of penal code.

While there is no mention of the word "cybercrime" in the Economic and Financial Crimes Commission (Establishment) Act 2004, it has clear provisions enabling it to tackle it. Specifically, in defining the responsibilities of the commission, section 6(b) of the Economic and Financial Crimes Commission (Establishment) Act 2004 states that the commission shall be responsible for the investigation of all financial crimes including advance fee fraud, money laundering, counterfeiting, illegal charge transfers, futures market fraud, fraudulent encashment of negotiable instruments, computer credit card fraud, contract scam, etc. The commission continues to be the leading prosecution agency for combatting cybercrime in Nigeria.

Also, with impressive figures (prosecution success rate of 98.93% in 2021 and an improvement of 70.5% in total number of convictions) by the EFCC, one is not surprised by the growing number of convictions. For instance, in 2020, the commission recorded 976 convictions. Out of this number, 345 are listed as cybercrime and 4 listed as computer related fraud (Economic and Financial Crimes Commission 2020). In 2021, the number of convictions increased to 2220. Out of this number, 394 are listed as cybercrime and 13 listed as computer related fraud (Economic and Financial Crimes Commission 2021). In 2022, the number of convictions rose to 3785. Out of this number, 747 are listed as cybercrime and 83 listed as computer related fraud [43]. It is noteworthy to mention that there are possibilities that there are other convictions showing other crime typologies which may have elements of cybercrime but listed differently. For instance, there are several prosecutions listed as OBT (obtaining by tricks), impersonation, etc., which in reality may have relied on the use of computers or an electronic device.

2.7.3 Nigeria Police Force

Cybercrime is a crime; therefore, expectedly, it falls within the mandate of the Police to investigate and prosecute this. In Nigeria, the Nigeria Police Force is the major law enforcement agency in the country. The origins of the Nigeria Police Force can be traced to 1861, when a 30-man Consular Guard was set up in Lagos [85]. Several operational and legal restructuring his since taken place since then. The 1999 Constitution (as amended) provided a legal basis for the Nigeria Police Force. Specifically, section 214 of the 1999 Constitution (as amended) stated that: "There shall be a Police Force for Nigeria, which shall be known as the Nigeria Police Force, and subject to the provisions of this section, no other police force shall be established for the Federation or any part thereof".

Also, the Nigeria Police Act 84 also further reinforces the establishment, composition and duties of the Nigeria Police Force.

Section 4 of the Nigeria Police Act 84 states that "the Police Force shall:

a. Prevent and detect crimes, and protect the rights and freedom of every person in Nigeria as provided in the Constitution, the African Charter on Human and Peoples rights and any other law;

b. Maintain public safety, law and order;
c. Enforce all laws and regulations without prejudice to the enabling Acts of other security agencies;
d. Collaborate with other agencies to take necessary action and provide the required assistance or support to persons in distress, including victims of road accidents, fire disasters, earthquakes, and flood;
e. Facilitate the free passage and movement on highways, roads, and streets open to the public;
f. Adopt community partnership in the discharge of its responsibilities under this Act or any other law; and
g. Vet and approve the registration of private detective schools and private investigative outfits".

Although there was no mention of cybercrime, the Police Act 2020 clearly empowers the Police to prevent and detect crimes; and that includes cybercrime. The Nigeria Police Force has a dedicated cybercrime unit with a mandate to crack down on cybercrime [83]. This unit investigates and prosecutes Internet fraud [126]. In 2022, the Inspector General of Police announced a merger of all cybercrime related departments, under the newly formed Nigeria Police Force National Cyber-crime Centre, currently under the Force Criminal Investigations Department, Force Headquarters, Abuja [105]. This was to give way for focused unit for better efficiency in investigating and prosecuting cybercrime.

2.7.4 ICPC

The Independent Practices and other related offences Commission was established by the Corrupt Practices and other related Offences Act 2000. Section 6 (a–f) of the ICPC Act 2000 sets out the duties of the Commission as paraphrased in the following:

a. To receive and investigate complaints from members of the public on allegations of corrupt practices and in appropriate cases, prosecute the offenders.
b. To examine the practices, systems and procedures of public bodies and where such systems aid corruption, to direct and supervise their review.
c. To instruct, advise and assist any officer, agency, or parastatal on ways by which fraud or corruption may be eliminated or minimized by such officer, agency or parastatal.
d. To advise heads of public bodies of any changes in practice, systems or procedures compatible with the effective discharge of the duties of public bodies to reduce the likelihood or incidence of bribery, corruption and related offences.
e. To educate the public on and against bribery, corruption and related offences.
f. To enlist and foster public support in combating corruption.

As mentioned above, the Independent Corrupt Practices and Other Related Offences Commission (ICPC) also investigates cybercrime related offences.

Although the establishment act predates the Cybercrime Act 2015, and did not specifically mention cybercrime, however, specific sections in the Establishment Act, such as sections 15 and 43 did make reference to investigating computer related crimes. For instance, section 15 of the Act states that:

"Any person who, with intent to defraud or conceal a crime or frustrate the Commission in its investigation of any suspected crime of corruption under this Act or under any other law:

a. destroys, alters, mutilates, or falsifies, any book, documents, valuable security, account, computer system, diskette, computer printout or other electronic device which belongs to or is in the possession of his employer, or has been received by him on account of his employment, or any entry in any such book, document, accounts or electronic device, or is privy to any such act; or
b. makes, or is privy to making any false entry in any such book, document, account or electronic record; or
c. omits, or is privy to omitting, any materials particular from any such book, document, account or electronic record; is guilty of a felony, and shall on conviction be liable to seven (7) years imprisonment".

The reference to "diskette", "computer printout" and "electronic device" in section 15 cited above and section 43 (particularly with respect to the intent and object of crime) can fall under the broad classification of cybercrime. Therefore, while the commission is focused on investigating corruption, they also investigate the intersection of computers and digital technology used for perpetrating crime—and this falls within the context of cybercrime. For instance, in 2022, the ICPC busted a cybercrime syndicate in connection to a N30.4 million fraud [56]. To boost their investigative capacity, the commission had in 2012 set up a digital forensic laboratory [56].

2.7.5 *Structural Reforms*

Despite these critical steps, the country has continued to witness increasing cases of cybercrime. While there are many other reasons for this, one of the primary reasons for this is a lack of technical capability and forensic resources [22, 32, 78, 120]. While Nigeria may have made some improvements, this has not been sufficient to meet one of the highest cybercrime caseloads in the world. The current system is limited in scope with infrastructure and a lack of forensic investigators, which leaves it dependent on other countries' cybercrime agencies for support. Apart from the lack of forensic technology, there is also a shortage of investigators (who are stretched, themselves) with forensic capabilities [95, 101]. These limitations have necessitated the need for structural reforms.

In 2015, the Cybercrime Act was passed into law, to give more impetus to the fight against cybercrime. The law is the central legislation for combatting cybercrime in Nigeria. Section 41 of the Cybercrime (Prohibition, Prevention, etc.) Act

2015 empowers the Office of the National Security Adviser (ONSA) to play the coordinating role for national cybersecurity. In accordance with this provision, the National Security Adviser is saddled with the responsibility of establishing the National Cybersecurity Coordination Centre (NCCC) to champion and implement the nation's cybersecurity programme [92].

The ONSA, in exercise its responsibilities as contained in the Cybercrime (Prohibition, Prevention, etc.) Act 2015 releases periodically, the national cybersecurity policy and strategy. The last edition which was released in 2021 also outlined structural measures in line with the extant provisions. For instance, the National Computer Emergency Response Team, also known as the Nigeria Computer Emergency Response Team (ngCERT), the focal point of the nation's cyber incident response management is now domiciled under the National Cybersecurity Coordination Centre (NCCC). Also, to be domiciled under the NCCC is the National Digital Forensic Laboratory (NDFL), to provide the requisite tools and facilities for investigation and intelligence gathering of cyber related issues. Also, in reflection of the growing call for the amendment of the Cybercrime (Prohibition, Prevention, etc.) Act 2015, the Cybersecurity Advisory Council (CAC) is charged with the responsibility of driving the process for the amendment [92]. As at the time of writing this, the Nigerian Senate was conducting public hearing for the amendment.

2.7.6 *Legal Reforms*

In combatting the scourge of cybercrime and Internet fraud, the Nigerian government has made critical legal reforms. Before the enactment of Cybercrime (Prevention, Prohibition, etc.) Act 2015, there was no central legislation to confront Cybercrime [94]. Before this, the laws were not specific to cybercrime and only derived by inference. Mu'azu-Abdullahi [80] blamed the rising threat of cybercrime on the absence of a coherent framework that tackles the scourge. Other laws, such as the Advance Fee Fraud and other Fraud Related Offences Act, 1996, did not cover electronic channels. In the last two decades, new laws were either created or amended to address these legal challenges. The principal legal milestones are:

1. Advance Fee Fraud Act and Other Related Offences Act 2006;
2. Evidence Act 2023;
3. Cybercrime (Prevention, Prohibition, etc.) Act 2015.

2.7.7 *Advance Fee Fraud Act and Other Related Offences Act 2006*

The amended Advanced Fee Fraud and Other Fraud Related Offences 2006, while it captures telecommunications-related fraud, did not cover the expansive view of the modern definition of Cybercrime [80]. For instance, it had no mention of Internet fraud, credit card fraud, etc. However, the amendment was a significant improvement in the national push against cybercrime.

The amendment introduced a new part (Part 1A) that dealt with "Electronic Telecommunication Offences". It outlines the duty of the service provider to obtain subscriber's information, and penalties for none compliance. The act also outlines the specific demands (such as registration with EFCC) from Internet Service Providers (Café's, etc.), and the responsibility they have to take reasonable steps to ensure their service is not exploited or utilised to perpetrate crime.

This amendment, although addressed an important issue of the duty of care from the service provider's point of view, however, does not capture the current realities. Majority of Nigerian internet users do so via the GSM networks. Precisely, as at March 2023, there were about 225 million internet (this is about 99.85% of all internet subscribers from all sources in the country) subscribers connecting via GSM [90].

Therefore, the operating environment and landscape is not exactly the same as that of the 2007 Internet Service Providers. Beyond this, the static fine alternatives have proved insufficient over the years, when juxtaposed with the inflationary pool, loss of value of the Naira and currency differential. For instance, section 12(1)(2) of the Advanced Fee Fraud and other related offences Act 2006 states that "Any customer or subscriber who

(a) fails to furnish, the information specified in subsection (1) of this section; or
(b) with the intent to deceive, supplies false information or conceals or disguises the information required under this section, commits an offence and is liable on conviction to imprisonment for a term of not less than three years or a fine of N100,000."

Here's the challenge with provisions such as this: In 2006, ₦100,000 was about $776.52 (at ₦128.78 to $1 exchange rate). Today, ₦100,000 has lost value colossally and is now only worth $125.32 (at the official rate of N797.98 to a dollar) [121]. Figure 2.2 shows a historical performance of the Nigerian Naira against the US Dollar. Also, if you look at this from an inflationary point of view, in October 2006, inflation in Nigeria was at 6.10%, as at October 2023, inflation had risen to 27.33% [30]. Therefore, the penalty has shrunk in value, and is now an incentive for Advance Fee Fraud Criminals since they can easily pay this amount. Setting static penalty options in a country with volatile monetary and macroeconomic parameters have proved counterproductive and in fact an incentive to the criminals. Figure 2.3 shows Nigeria's inflation rate over the last 25 years.

2.7.8 Evidence (Amendment) Act 2023

Another critical amendment that happened in Nigeria affecting the fight against cybercrime was the amendment of the Evidence Act of 2011 [99], [125]. This amendment paved the way for the admissibility of digital evidence in Nigerian courts. This development was a significant landmark in Nigeria's fight against cybercrime. Prior

Fig. 2.2 Performance of the Naira against the US Dollar. *Note* This figure shows the historical performance of the Nigerian Naira against the US Dollar [121]

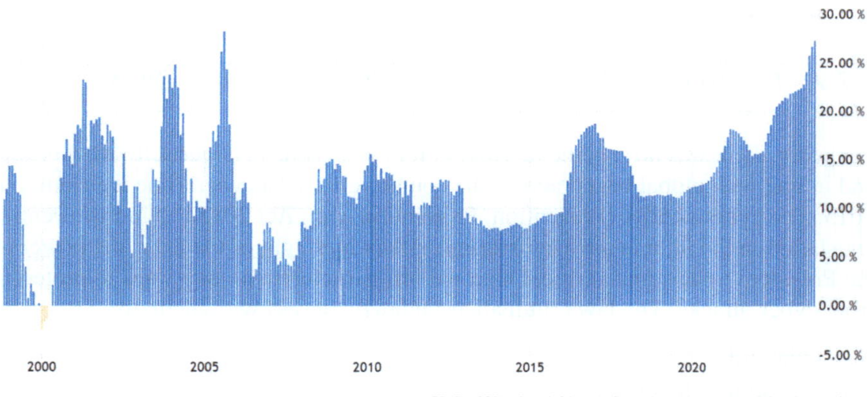

Fig. 2.3 Inflation rate over the last 25 years. *Note* This figure shows the inflation rate over the last 25 years. *Source* Trading Economics/National Bureau of Statistics

to this, digital evidence was not admissible in Nigerian courts. However, despite this laudable milestone, there were calls for the amendment in reflection of emerging realities. The Act as it was, did not reflect the emerging technologies, therefore, needed amendment.

On the 12th of June 2023, President Bola Tinubu signed the amendment to law. This law, now cited as Evidence (Amendment) Act did not repeal the Evidence Act 2011, but merely made amendments in reflection of the evolving technological landscape and in new innovations. This amendment contained sections that brought clarity and would undoubtedly strengthen prosecution of cases involving digital evidence. Specific amendments include the expansion of the scope to include "electronic records", as can be seen in Section 84(a), (b), (c), (d), and (e). Section 84 specifically made records in a computer admissible, as long as it satisfies conditions stated in the Act. Section 84C recognized the use of/authentication of digital signature or electronic signature. The amendment also introduced electronic oath taking and the electronic gazettes.

In reflection of the possible confusion the emerging technological terminologies might introduce, the amendment introduced new definitions such as "audio-visual communication", "cloud computing", "digital signature", "electronic record", "electronic signature", "magnetic media" and "optical media". Perhaps, in reflection of the fast-paced technological landscape, section 255(1) gave the Minister of Justice a blanket responsibility for making "regulations generally prescribing further conditions with respect to admissibility of any class of evidence that may be relevant under this Act". While this appeared a positive provision in good faith, however, concerns might be raised on such strong powers given to a political appointee (in Nigeria, the Minister of Justice is a political appointee that can be hired or fired at the President's pleasure). In all, this amendment is a positive addition to Nigeria's jurisprudence, particularly as it concerns the admissibility of digital evidence.

2.7.9 *Cybercrime (Prevention, Prohibition, etc.) Act 2015*

For years, there was no specific legislation for cybercrime in Nigeria. To fill this gap, and in line with global best practice, the country enacted a cybercrime legislation in 2015. The cybersecurity (Prevention, Prohibition, etc.) Act 2015 is Nigeria's central legislation in the fight against cybercrime. A key highlight of the act is the power of the President to designate critical national infrastructure and take steps to protect it from cyber-attacks. The law criminalizes unlawful access with intent to:

1. unlawful access;
2. system interference;
3. interception of electronic messages and money transfers;
4. tampering with critical national infrastructure;
5. willful misdirection or electronic messages;
6. unlawful interceptions;
7. computer-related forgery;
8. computer related fraud;
9. theft of electronic devices;
10. unauthorized modification of computer systems, network data and system interference;
11. fraudulent issuance of e-instructions;
12. child pornography and related offences;
13. cyber terrorism;
14. cyberstalking;
15. cybersquatting.

Following the Cybercrime Act, Nigeria established the Nigerian Computer Emergency Response Team (ngCERT). The Office of the National Security Adviser manages this team [22, 118]. The primary responsibility of ngCERT is to centrally monitor, coordinate and mitigate against cyber attacks directed at the country's national infrastructure. Nigeria set up a national computer forensic laboratory as part of the plan to have a well-equipped Computer Emergency Response Team. There have been questions as to the proper funding and sustainable running of the ngCERT. For instance, Kademi [65] noted that apart from the initial budget of $9.3 million, there has not been any sustainable funding structure. Rufai et al. [109] also stated that despite the central role played by ngCERT, they are broadly unpopular, as most stakeholders are not even aware of its existence.

While Cybercrime (Prevention, Prohibition, etc.) Act 2015 has received commendations as a bold step towards combatting cybercrime; there has been a contrary position that the act has been primarily ineffective despite improvements. For instance, Mohammed et al. [78] submitted there had been no landmark judgment that shows the effectiveness of the law. Omotubora [97] faults the act for fundamentally failing to criminalize basic hacking. Eboibi [40] submitted that the Cybercrime Act 2021 suffers from a lack of implementation. These gaps undermine the success of the battle against Internet fraud in Nigeria.

Ajayi [11] argued that the prescribed penalties in the law were not enough to serve as a deterrent. Mohammed et al. [78] submitted that the justice system had been rather too slow to adjust, retool and upgrade, to face the fast, dynamic world of cybercrime. Brown [25] corroborated this position by noting that the stakeholders in Nigeria's criminal justice system have not grasped fundamental aspects of cybercrime. Defense lawyers of cybercrime suspects often exploit the gaps between the letters of the Cybercrime act and enforcement procedures to win their cases on technicalities [12]. This challenge is made more complicated with the jurisdictional impediments relating to cybercrime.

In examining Ajayi's [11] position of the inadequate penalties for cybercrime in Nigeria, this study reviewed the Cybercrime (Prevention, Prohibition, etc.) Act 2015 closely, and summarized the key findings on the extent of the penalties. Table 2.3 summarises the offence categories and the penalties.

Although many would argue that penalties and punishments may never be sufficient deterrents in themselves, however, such should be reasonable and commensurate. As was the case of Advance Fee Fraud, the cybercrime Act did make provision for options of fines. Therefore, it suffers from the eroded currency value over time. In 2015 when the Act was passed, the exchange rate of dollar to Naira was about ₦186 to $1. Today, the Naira now exchanges with the dollar at official rate of ₦797.98 to a dollar [121]. Recall that most of the cybercriminals get their proceeds in dollars. Therefore, the Nigerian cybercriminal has technically had his fine reduced by over 329% from 2015 to 2023. Clearly, those who crafted this law may not have contemplated a rollercoaster macroeconomic indices in so short a time.

Table 2.3 Summary of penalties in the Cybercrime Act 2015

Category	Section	Penalty
Crimes against critical national information infrastructure	5	Penalty ranges from not more than 10 years imprisonment to life imprisonment without an option of fine
Unlawful access to computer	6	Penalty ranges from ₦5 to ₦7 million, and/or ₦1 to ₦7 million
Non-compliance to registration of cyber cafes	7	Penalty ranges from ₦1 to ₦2 million and/or 3 years imprisonment
System interference	8	Penalty ranges from a term of not more than 2 years or a fine of not more than ₦5,000,000.00, or both fine and imprisonment
Intercepting electronic messages, emails electronic money transfers	9	Liable to imprisonment for 7 years in the first instance and upon second conviction shall be liable to 14 years imprisonment
Tampering with critical infrastructure	10	Liable to a fine of ₦2,000,000.00 or imprisonment for 3 years
Willful misdirection of electronic messages	11	Liable to imprisonment for three years or a fine of ₦1,000,000.00 or both
Unlawful interception	12	Penalty ranges from 1 to 2 years imprisonment and/or ₦1–₦5 million fine
Computer related forgery	13	Liable on conviction to imprisonment for a term of not less than 3 years or to a fine of not less than ₦7,000,000.00 or both
Computer related fraud	14	Penalty ranges from 3 to 7 years imprisonment and/or ₦5–₦10 million
Theft of electronic devices	15	Penalty ranges from 1 to 7 years imprisonment and/or a fine of ₦1–₦10 million
Unauthorized modification of computer systems, network data and system interference	16	Penalty ranges from 2 to 3 years imprisonment and/or a fine of ₦5–₦7 million
Electronic signatures	17	Liable on conviction to imprisonment for a term of not more than 7 years or a fine of not more than ₦10,000,000.00 or to both fine and imprisonment
Cyber terrorism	18	Liable to life imprisonment
Exceptions to financial institutions, posting and authorized options	19	Liable to payment of a fine of ₦1 million or seven years imprisonment or both

(continued)

Table 2.3 (continued)

Category	Section	Penalty
Fraudulent issuance of instructions	20	Liable to imprisonment for 7 years
Reporting of cyber threats	21	Liable to denial of internet services and in addition, pay a mandatory fine of ₦2,000,000.00 into the National Cyber Security Fund
Identity theft and impersonation	22	Penalty ranges from 5 to 7 years imprisonment and/or a fine of ₦5–₦7 million
Child pornography and related offences	23	Penalty ranges from 5 to 10 years imprisonment and/or a fine of ₦10–₦25 million
Cyberstalking	24	Penalty ranges from 3 to 10 years imprisonment and/or a fine of ₦7–₦25 million
Cybersquatting	25	Liable on conviction to imprisonment for a term of not more than 2 years or a fine of not more than ₦5,000,000.00 or to both fine and imprisonment
Racist and xenophobic offences	26	Liable on conviction to imprisonment for a term of not more than 5 years or to a fine of not more than ₦10,000,000.00 or both such fine and imprisonment
Attempt, conspiracy, aiding and abetting	27	Liable on conviction to imprisonment for a term of not more than 7 years and shall in addition, refund the stolen money or forfeit any property to which it has been converted to the bank, financial institution or the customer
Importation and fabrication of E-tools	28	Penalty ranges from 2 to 5 years imprisonment and/or a fine of ₦5–₦10 million
Breach of confidence by service providers	29	If corporate organization be guilty of an offence and is liable to a fine of ₦5,000,000.00 and forfeiture of further equivalent of the monetary value of the loss sustained by the consumer If the offender is a natural person, he commits an offence and shall be liable on conviction to imprisonment for a term of not more than 7 years and to a fine of not more than ₦5,000,000.00 or to both imprisonment and fine
Manipulation of ATM/POS terminals	30	Liable on conviction to five years imprisonment or ₦5,000,000.00 fine or both
Employees responsibility	31	Liable on conviction to 3 years imprisonment or ₦3,000,000.00 or both
Phishing, spamming, spreading of computer virus	32	Liable upon conviction to 3 years imprisonment or a fine of ₦1,000,000.00 or both
Electronic cards related fraud	33	For an individual, penalty ranges from 3 to 7 years imprisonment and/or a fine of ₦500,000–₦7 million For an institution, penalty ranges from ₦1 to ₦10 million

(continued)

Table 2.3 (continued)

Category	Section	Penalty
Dealing in card of another	34	Liable on summary conviction to 3 years imprisonment or to a fine of one ₦1,000,000.00 and shall further be liable to repayment in monetary terms the value of loss sustained by the cardholder or forfeiture of the assets or goods acquired with the funds from the account of the cardholder
Purchase or sale of card of another	35	Liable on summary conviction to a fine of ₦500,000.00 and shall further be liable to payment in monetary terms the value of loss sustained by the card holder or forfeiture of the assets or goods acquired with the funds from the account of the cardholder
Use of fraudulent device or attached E-mails and websites	36	Liable to imprisonment for a period of 3 years or to a fine of ₦1,000,000.00 and shall further be liable to payment in monetary terms the value of loss sustained by the cardholder or forfeiture of the assets or goods acquired with the funds from the account of the cardholder

Note This table presents the penalties in the Cybercrime Act 2015

2.8 Current Situation of Cybercrime in Nigeria

Cybercrime in Nigeria continues to grow at an exponential rate. The reach is of international dimensions and has earned the country a bad reputation. The Federal Bureau of Investigation [47] ranked Nigeria at 19th on the list of global cybercrime victims. Nigeria's "419" scams were ranked the 3rd most committed Internet crime globally. The authorities traced a breach involving confidential health records of over 750,000 persons in Los Angeles to Nigerian cybercriminals [18, 21]. Even during a global pandemic, Nigerian Internet fraudsters were reportedly sending phishing attacks. Palo Alto Networks Unit 42 reportedly tracked COVID-19 phishing attacks to a Nigerian cybercrime and Business Email Compromise group, known by the codename "SilverTerrier" [107]. The impact of Nigerian cybercrime stretched even beyond financial implications to institutional attacks and reputational damage. For instance, on the eve of Nigeria's 2015 National elections, the Independent National Electoral Commission's website was attacked and defaced. A Nigerian hacktivist group known as Nigerian Cyber Army claimed responsibility [3, 16]. In the 2023 elections, there were reported cyberattacks directed at the country. Specifically, the Ministry of Communication and Digital Economy put the figures at about 12 million attacks during the Presidential Elections [76]. This attack underpins the audacious scale and the extent the Nigerian cybercriminals are willing to stretch their impact.

The rising caseloads of cybercrime continue to be a thing of concern to law enforcement agencies in Nigeria. Eboibi [39] submitted that Law enforcement agencies in Nigeria continue to struggle with the cybercrime caseloads. Chigozie-Okwum et al. [32] also noted that the rapidly increasing caseloads of cybercrime put a more significant burden on investigators in Nigeria. There are several reasons suggested as the top reasons behind the surge of cybercrime caseloads in Nigeria. Interestingly, the top reasons from literature mostly seem to be social and economic factors. For instance, Oni et al. [98] think the rising cybercrime cases are due to unemployment and greed. Chigozie-Okwum et al. [32] suggested that unemployment, poverty, and the relatively lower risk of cybercrime serve as an incentive behind the increasing figures. Adesina [8[also aligns with this position, stating that Nigerian youths turn to cybercrime due to poverty.

The last two decades have witnessed key reforms—legal, institutional and structural. Despite these reforms, the cybercrime rate continues to go high. To date, there is no celebrated cybercrime conviction in Nigeria; the convicted has been largely young and unknown cybercriminals [78]. There have been genuine concerns raised on the effectiveness of the Cybercrime Act, and this calls for a rejig of the law [11, 97]. There is a need to revamp the rules, the justice system, and the investigative capacities of the cybercrime law enforcement agencies. For a nation with one of the highest caseloads of cybercrime in the world, there are genuine questions of the digital investigative and forensic capabilities of the nation's financial crimes agency. So far, most of the high profile conviction of Nigerian cybercriminals have been in other jurisdictions.

Cybercrime is of international dimension, and this poses several challenges. Cybercriminals could simultaneously commit Internet fraud in different countries without traveling. This borderless nature of cybercrime presents complex jurisdictional roadblocks to law enforcement agencies during investigation and prosecution. To arrest and prosecute a suspect in another country requires a lot of complex international diplomacies, collaborations, and sometimes frustrating extradition processes, which are mostly slower compared to the fast pace of cybercrime [58, 61]. Bello and Griffiths [22] held that multiple laws and jurisdictions and a lack of collaboration were significant challenges in cybercrime prosecution. Mohammed et al. [78] also supported this view, noting the need to bridge existing gaps between stakeholders such as security professionals, law enforcement agents, and prosecutors.

Interestingly, despite jurisdictional roadblocks, there have been increased handshakes and technical collaborations between Nigerian law enforcement and their international counterparts. This development has led to several collaborations leading to high-profile arrests. This success is a positive development, given the international dimension of cybercrime. For instance, in 2013, the British law enforcement agency donated digital forensic equipment to the EFCC [41]. Also, in 2018 the National Crime Agency of the United Kingdom donated digital forensic equipment worth over £500,000 to the EFCC forensic laboratory [42]. There have also been training collaborations to build staff capacity in digital evidence acquisition and forensic analysis.

2.9 Technology and Cybercrime Investigation

Digital technology is increasingly playing more significant roles in all spheres of human endeavors and generating enormous data in the process. Today, these devices capture human vitals, footprints, and intricate details such as spatial location, heartbeat, biometric features, financial transactions, and many more [27]. This information holds vital clues to reconstruct events, and therefore answer many forensic questions that could potentially solve a crime. Analyzing digital forensics data could provide clues such as where a suspect was at the time of the crime, revealing a document's metadata, revealing the IP address of an intruder, exposing user footprints in a system or network, and many more.

Cybercrime completely disrupted the crime space and the scope of crime investigation. It broadened the dimension of evidence and the acquisition thereof. Before the advent of digital crimes, the concept of evidence largely revolved around physical items. However, with digital crimes came the idea of digital evidence and admissibility in court. The good old principle in criminology—the Locard's Exchange Principle—guides cybercrime investigation. The exchange principle states that a criminal must leave something at the crime scene and take something from the crime scene. This principle is the foundation of forensic science, applied in both physical and digital evidence [104], [15, 55].

2.10 Emerging Technologies and Cybercrime Investigation

The technological landscape continues to evolve with emerging technologies. This dynamic nature of the technology space brings in specific challenges. Mihai et al. [77] held that emerging technologies increased the attack surface and possible vulnerabilities. Bello and Griffiths [22] also submitted that the rapidly evolving technological landscape gives cybercriminals the edge over cybercrime investigators. There is also the challenge of the complications of forensic investigation of the ever-evolving emerging technologies. Karie and Venter [66] identified emerging technologies as one of the technical challenges facing digital forensics.

The advent of emerging technologies such as Big Data, Blockchain, the Internet of Things (IoT), and Cloud Technologies have increased the digital space and exponentially increased the likely sources of digital evidence [5]. Digital devices have flooded the technology landscape with a torrent of digital evidence all over the place. The big data challenge is one that significantly affects the digital forensics space. In 2018, an estimated 22 billion Internet of Things IoT (IoT) connected devices existed worldwide. This number will potentially increase to 38.6 billion connected IoT devices [115]. These devices are in a constant handshake with other devices and generating data. International Data Corporation [57] estimates that the connected IoT devices will potentially generate about 79.4 ZB of data in 2025.

Buried in this torrent of data are potential sources of digital evidence. The more data floods the space, the more difficult it is to analyze data to detect crime footprints [132]. The increasing volume of data, structure, diversity, and velocity makes it even more difficult to analyze data forensically [27]. Globally, most digital forensic laboratories struggle to keep pace with the volume of data to process [79, 113]. The increased availability and affordability of digital devices and associated evidence and the increasing role in modern criminal investigation are significant reasons behind the popularity of Digital Forensics both as a science and a discipline [55]. The more this trend continues, the more likely digital evidence will feature more in courtrooms.

Other complexities also affect digital forensics. For instance, modern systems are becoming increasingly secure. The advancement in complex encryption, cryptography, secure network communication, and anonymous routing continue to pose increasing difficulties to digital forensics examiners in terms of access [62]. Ricci et al. [108] also noted that encrypted drives are more difficult to analyze and acquire. Other emerging technologies, such as the Internet of Things (IoT) and cloud computing, also have unique complexities affecting the digital forensic investigation. Stoyanova et al. [116] outlined some of the challenges faced during a forensic analysis of IoT.

On the challenges with cloud computing, Pichan et al. [103] noted that one key challenge with cloud computing is jurisdictional complexities. Most institutions contract their cloud services to offshore service providers. Different jurisdictions have different regulatory requirements and data privacy rules that may affect digital forensic investigations. Montasari and Hill [79] noted that there are also other technical challenges associated with cloud technology concerning digital forensics. These challenges include the lack of standardization across cloud service providers, varying service level agreements, and others.

2.11 Gaps in Literature

Nigeria's primary Internet fraud agency is the Economic and Financial Crimes Commission [78, 91, 122]. However, other agencies appear to have overlapping functions. For instance, the Nigerian Police Force set up a dedicated cybercrime unit [83]. Recently, the Nigeria Police Cybercrime Unit, in a joint operation with the Interpol National Central Bureau (NCB), made arrests of Internet fraud suspects [126]. Also, the Office of the National Security Adviser plays a central role in cybercrime investigation. The Office of the National Security Adviser hosts Nigeria's Computer Emergency Response Team, created by the Cybercrime (Prevention, Prohibition, etc.) Act 2015 [118]. Despite these overlapping roles, there is a noticeable lack of available literature examining these overlapping and sometimes duplicitous functions, potentially creating a chaotic cybercrime investigation landscape.

The Nigerian Cybercrime Act (Prevention, Prohibition, etc.) Act 2015 is the central legislation for cybercrime [94]. The act expands the definition of cybercrime beyond Internet fraud. No studies robustly examined the other cybercrime taxonomies contained in the act and a clear assignment of roles to investigating agencies within the Nigerian context. The studies available are limited to Internet fraud or "419". Perhaps the overwhelming caseloads of Internet fraud may have influenced the concentration of studies in that area at the expense of other types of cybercrime.

A few studies suggested the lack of forensic capabilities of the Nigerian cybercrime investigative agencies and the justice system, but none studies this in great detail. Specifically, no studies examine that particular skills gap and resources needed in Nigeria's financial crimes agencies. It is vital to get a proper resource inventory and capabilities to confront the growing threat of financial crimes successfully. This process would involve measuring the forensic readiness of the agencies and identifying gaps. The absence of a detailed study on this is a gap in research.

Over the years, there have been many reforms to tackle cybercrime in Nigeria. Nigeria enacted the primary cybercrime legislation for cybercrime, the Nigerian Cybercrime Act (Prevention, Prohibition, etc.) Act 2015 [94]. There are also noticeable gaps in this legislation. For instance, Omotubora [97] observed the cybercrime act failed to criminalize basic hacking. For a law central to the fight against cybercrime, gaps such as this need to be resolved. The law did not also capture emerging technologies.

2.12 Summary

Nigeria continues to struggle with the rising cases of Internet fraud. Despite several reforms and efforts at curbing this, the numbers continue to rise [39, 96]. Computers have become a central part of our lives, and connectivity continues to improve, and this has become an attraction to cybercriminals [17, 26, 64, 106, 124]. Also, emerging technologies such as the Internet of Things, Cloud computing, Blockchain, Social Media, Big Data, and others widen the attack surface and vulnerabilities [28, 77]. Beyond these, there is also the challenge of a lack of forensic resources for financial crimes agencies in Nigeria.

This study established the lack of forensic resources in the Nigerian financial crime agencies and made recommendations. This chapter examined this challenge, starting from the historical perspectives of cybercrime. The study also reviewed emerging technologies and the role they play in the rising caseloads of cybercrime. The chapter examined Internet fraud and the role of investigative agencies. The review also discussed the various reforms in dealing with the growing threat of Internet fraud in Nigeria.

The review involved a qualitative analysis of the various cybercrime-related laws in Nigeria and their interplay in the coordinated war against Internet fraud. The chapter also examined the vital concept of technology and cybercrime investigation. The chapter also considered crucial considerations such as digital evidence and the admissibility of scientific evidence. In chap. 3, the review progressed to narrow into digital forensics—history, Daubert standard, digital forensics investigation process models, digital forensics readiness, and the digital forensic readiness of Nigeria's financial crime agencies.

This research investigated the lack of digital forensic resources in Nigerian financial crime agencies. This study examined the digital forensic readiness of the agencies, identifying specific gaps and resource needs in the process. Case studies are exploratory research that allows a close examination to deepen understanding of a particular issue within a defined context [131], [45]. The research population is the Nigerian financial crimes agencies, identified from this review to be the Economic and Financial Crimes Commission (EFCC) and the Cybercrime Unit of the Nigeria Police Force.

Chapter 3 presents the important concepts of Digital Evidence, Digital Forensics, and Digital Forensic Readiness, while Chap. 4 presents the study design and methodology. The study involved conducting interviews with personnel of the EFCC and the Nigerian Police Force. The researchers used Sony digital recorder during the interview sessions. The study relied on the qualitative software—NVIVO—to analyze the data collected. Other sources of data included available publications, press releases, and reports.

References

1. Abdul-Rasheed SL, Lateef I, Yinusa MA, Abdullateef R (2016) Cybercrime and Nigeria's external image: a critical assessment. J Pan Afr Stud 9(6):119–133
2. Abdulkadir AB, Abdulkadir AO (2019) Cybercrimes act in Nigeria: experimenting compliance with internationally recognized human rights provisions. J Int Stud 15:117–132
3. Abimboye M (2015) INEC website hacked. Premium Times. www.premiumtimesng.com/news/top-news/179539-inec-website-hacked.html
4. Achimugu H, Muhammed U, Ogirima II (2020) Economic and financial crimes commission (EFCC) and the challenge of public service corruption in nigeria [Conference session]. The International Seminar on Regional Politics, Administration and Development 2020, STISIPOL Raja Haji, Riau, Indonesia
5. Adedayo OM (2016) Big data and digital forensics. In: 2016 IEEE international conference on cybercrime and computer forensic (ICCCF), pp 1–7. https://doi.org/10.1109/ICCCF.2016.7740422
6. Adepetun A (2022a) NCC puts cybercrime losses in Nigeria at $500m, sets to implement DMS. The Guardian Newspaper, Apr 2022. https://guardian.ng/news/ncc-puts-cybercrime-losses-in-nigeria-at-500m-sets-to-implement-dms/
7. Adepetun A (2022b) Cybercrimes raise concerns for N30.2tr monthly e-payments. The Guardian Newspaper, Nov 2022. https://guardian.ng/news/cybercrimes-raise-concerns-for-n30-2tr-monthly-e-payments/
8. Adesina OS (2017) Cybercrime and poverty in Nigeria. Canadian social science, 13(4):19–29
9. Adeyoju A (2019) Cybercrime and cybersecurity: finTech's greatest challenges. Available at SSRN 3486277
10. Ahmad T (2020) Corona virus (COVID-19) Pandemic and work from home: challenges of cybercrimes and cybersecurity. Soc Sci Res Netw https://doi.org/10.2139/ssrn.3568830
11. Ajayi EFG (2016) Challenges to enforcement of cyber-crimes laws and policy. J Internet Inf Syst 6(1):1–12

12. Ajetunmobi RA, Uwadia CO, Oladeji FA (2016) Computer forensic guideline: a requirement for fighting cyber crime in Nigeria now? In: UNILAG research conference 2016, Nigeria. https://ir.unilag.edu.ng/handle/123456789/5833
13. Akanle O, Adesina JO, Akarah EP (2016) Towards human dignity and the internet: the cybercrime (yahoo yahoo) phenomenon in Nigeria. Afr J Sci Technol Innov Dev 8(2):213–220
14. Akanle O, Shadare BR (2019) Yahoo-plus in Ibadan: meaning, characterization and strategies. Int J Cyber Criminol 13(2)
15. Al-Khateeb H, Epiphaniou G, Daly H (2019) Blockchain for modern digital forensics: the chain-of-custody as a distributed ledger. In: Jahankhani H, Kendzierskyj S, Jamal A, Epiphaniou G, Al-Khateeb H (eds) Blockchain and clinical trial. Springer International Publishing, pp 149–168. https://doi.org/10.1007/978-3-030-11289-9_7
16. Alade A (2015) INEC website hacked. Vanguard Newspaper. www.vanguardngr.com/2015/03/inec-website-hacked/
17. Arshad H, Jantan AB, Abiodun OI (2018) Digital forensics: review of issues in scientific validation of digital evidence. J Inf Process Syst 14(2)
18. Associated Press (2016) Nigerian man charged with hacking Los Angeles county emails. Guardian Newspaper. https://www.theguardian.com/us-news/2016/dec/18/los-angeles-county-email-hack-kelvin-onaghinor
19. Awhefeada UV, Bernice OO (2020) Appraising the laws governing the control of cybercrime in Nigeria. J Law Crim Justice 8(1):30–49
20. Baert S, Lippens L, Moens E, Weytjens J, Sterkens P (2020) The COVID-19 crisis and telework: a research survey on experiences, expectations and hopes. https://www.econstor.eu/bitstream/10419/216771/1/GLO-DP-0532.pdf
21. Barboza T (2016) L.A. County targeted in phishing cyberattack; private information of 750,000 people compromised. Los Angeles Times. https://www.latimes.com/local/lanow/la-me-ln-county-cyberattack-20161217-story.html
22. Bello M, Griffiths M (2021) Routine activity theory and cybercrime investigation in Nigeria: how capable are law enforcement agencies? In: Rethinking cybercrime. Palgrave Macmillan, Cham, pp 213–235
23. Brenner SW (2010) Cybercrime: criminal threats from cyberspace. Bloomsbury Publishing USA
24. Broadhead S (2018) The contemporary cybercrime ecosystem: a multi-disciplinary overview of the state of affairs and developments. Comput Law Secur Rev 34(6):1180–1196
25. Brown CS (2015) Investigating and prosecuting cyber crime: forensic dependencies and barriers to justice. Int J Cyber Criminol 9(1):55
26. Button M, Nicholls CM, Kerr J, Owen R (2014) Online frauds: learning from victims why they fall for these scams. Aust N Z J Criminol 47(3):391–408
27. Casey E (2019) The chequered past and risky future of digital forensics. Aust J Forensic Sci 51(6):649–664
28. Caviglione L, Wendzel S, Mazurczyk W (2017) The future of digital forensics: challenges and the road ahead. IEEE Secur Priv 15(6):12–17
29. Central Bank of Nigeria (2020) Alert! Beware of COVID-19 cyber-attacks, fraud. https://www.cbn.gov.ng/Out/2020/CCD/CBN%20Press%20release%20-%20COVID-19%20-%20Cyber%20Security.pdf
30. Central Bank of Nigeria (2023) Inflation rates (percent). https://www.cbn.gov.ng/rates/inflrates.asp?year=2023
31. Chandra A, Snowe MJ (2020) A taxonomy of cybercrime: theory and design. Int J Account Inf Syst 38:100467
32. Chigozie-Okwum C, Ugboaja S, Micheal D, Osuo-Genseleke M (2017) Proliferation of cyber insecurity in Nigeria: a root cause analysis. AFRREV STECH Int J Sci Technol 6(2):53–60
33. Choi KS, Lee CS, Louderback ER (2020) Historical evolutions of cybercrime: from computer crime to cybercrime. In: The Palgrave handbook of international cybercrime and cyberdeviance, pp 27–43
34. Council of Europe (2001) Convention on cybercrime. https://rm.coe.int/1680081561

35. Cross C (2018) Victims' motivations for reporting to the 'fraud justice network.' Police Pract Res 19(6):550–564
36. Danjuma MH, Sarki ZM, Lalu AU (2018) Forensic science, electronic evidence and cybercrime prosecution in Nigeria. In: Ndubueze PN (ed) Cyber criminology and technology-assisted crime control: a reader. Ahmadu Bello University Press, pp 367–382
37. Dortmans PJ, Thakur N, Ween A (2015) Conjectures for framing cyberwarfare. Def Secur Anal 31(3):172–184
38. Ebegbulem JC (2012) Corruption and leadership crisis in Africa: Nigeria in focus. Int J Bus Soc Sci 3(11)
39. Eboibi FE (2017) A review of the legal and regulatory frameworks of Nigerian Cybercrimes Act 2015. Comput Law Secur Rev 33(5):700–717
40. Eboibi FE (2021) Cybercriminals and coronavirus cybercrimes in Nigeria, the United States of America and the United Kingdom: cyber hygiene and preventive enforcement measures. Commonw Law Bull 47(1):113–142
41. Economic and Financial Crimes Commission (2013) UK government donates forensic equipment to EFCC. https://efccnigeria.org/efcc/news/576-uk-government-donates-forensic-equipment-to-efcc
42. Economic and Financial Crimes Commission (2018) UK to support EFCC's anti-corruption fight with digital forensic technology. https://efccnigeria.org/efcc/news/3328-uk-to-support-efcc-s-anti-corruption-fight-with-digital-forensic-technology
43. Economic and Financial Crimes Commission (2023) History of EFCC. https://www.efcc.gov.ng/efcc/about-us-new/history-of-efcc
44. Eriksen-Jensen M (2013) Holding back the tidal wave of cybercrime. Comput Fraud Secur 2013(3):10–16
45. Farquhar JD (2012) Case study research for business. Sage
46. Federal Bureau of Investigation (n.d.) Internet fraud. https://www.fbi.gov/scams-and-safety/common-scams-and-crimes/internet-fraud
47. Federal Bureau of Investigation (2017) Internet crime report. https://www.ic3.gov/Media/PDF/AnnualReport/2017_IC3Report.pdf
48. Federal Bureau of Investigation (2019) Business email compromise the $26 billion scam. https://www.ic3.gov/Media/Y2019/PSA190910
49. Fell J (2017) Cyber crime-history: hacking through history. Eng Technol 12(3):30–31
50. Guardian Newspaper (2022) NCC puts cybercrime losses in Nigeria at $500m, sets to implement DMS. https://guardian.ng/news/ncc-puts-cybercrime-losses-in-nigeria-at-500m-sets-to-implement-dms/
51. Hadlington L, Lumsden K, Black A, Ferra F (2021) A qualitative exploration of police officers' experiences, challenges, and perceptions of cybercrime. Policing J Policy Pract 15(1):34–43
52. Hawdon J, Parti K, Dearden TE (2020) Cybercrime in america amid COVID-19: the initial results from a natural experiment. Am J Crim Justice 1–17
53. Hinchliffe A (2017) Nigerian princes to kings of malware: the next evolution in Nigerian cybercrime. Comput Fraud Secur 2017(5):5–9
54. Holt TJ, Bossler AM, Seigfried-Spellar KC (2022) Cybercrime and digital forensics: an introduction. Routledge
55. Horsman G (2017) Can we continue to effectively police digital crime? Sci Justice 57(6):448–454. https://doi.org/10.1016/j.scijus.2017.06.001
56. ICPC (2012) ICPC establishes forensic laboratory. https://icpc.gov.ng/2012/09/07/icpc-establishes-forensic-laboratory/
57. International Data Corporation (2019) The growth in connected IoT devices is expected to generate 79.4ZB of data in 2025. https://www.idc.com/getdoc.jsp?containerId=prUS45213219
58. International Telecommunication Union (2012) Understanding cybercrime: phenomena, challenges and legal response. http://www.itu.int/ITU-D/cyb/cybersecurity/docs/Cybercrime%20legislation%20EV6.pdf

59. International Telecommunication Union (2020) Statistics. https://www.itu.int/en/ITU-D/Statistics/Pages/stat/default.aspx
60. Internet Crime Complaint Centre (2023) Internet crime report 2022. https://www.ic3.gov/Media/PDF/AnnualReport/2022_IC3Report.pdf
61. Interpol (2017) Global cybercrime strategy. https://www.interpol.int/en/Crimes/Cybercrime
62. Irons A, Lallie HS (2014) Digital forensics to intelligent forensics. Future Internet 6(3):584–596
63. Jamo IA (2021) Economic and financial crimes commission (EFCC) and anti-corruption crusade in Nigeria: success and challenges. Gusau international J Manag and Soc Sci 4(2):13–13.
64. Joffee R (2010) Cybercrime: the global epidemic at your network door. Netw Secur 2010(7):4–7
65. Kademi AMA (2018) Strengthening strategic approach to counter cyberspace threats in Nigeria. In: Proceedings of the international conference on cyber warfare & security, Mar 2018, pp 328–337
66. Karie NM, Venter HS (2015) Taxonomy of challenges for digital forensics. J Forensic Sci 60(4):885–893
67. Karyda M, Mitrou L (2007) Internet forensics: legal and technical issues. In: Second international workshop on digital forensics and incident analysis (WDFIA 2007), Aug 2007. IEEE, pp 3–12
68. Kigerl A (2020) Spam-based scams. In: Holt T, Bossler A (eds) The Palgrave handbook of international cybercrime and cyberdeviance. Palgrave Macmillan, Cham. https://doi.org/10.1007/978-3-319-78440-3_42
69. Kshetri N (2019) Cybercrime and cybersecurity in africa. J glob inf technol manage 22(2):71–81
70. Lazarus S, Okolorie GU (2019) The bifurcation of the Nigerian cybercriminals: narratives of the Economic and Financial Crimes Commission (EFCC) agents. Telematics Inform 40:14–26
71. Li JX (2017) Cybercrime and legal countermeasures: a historical analysis. Int J Crim Justice Sci 12(2):196–207
72. Manky D (2013) Cybercrime as a service very modern business. Comput Fraud Secur 2013(6):9–13
73. McAfee (2020) McAfee labs COVID-19 threat report. https://www.mcafee.com/enterprise/en-us/assets/reports/rp-quarterly-threats-july-2020.pdf
74. McGuire M, Dowling S (2013) Cybercrime: a review of the evidence. https://assets.publishing.service.gov.uk/government/uploads/system/uploads/attachment_data/file/246749/horr75-summary.pdf
75. Meyers A (2018) Not your fairy-tale prince: the Nigerian business email compromise threat. Comput Fraud Secur 2018(8):14–16
76. Michael C (2023) INEC server records 12m cyberattacks during presidential poll. Business Day Newspaper. https://businessday.ng/news/article/inec-serverrecords-12m-cyberattacks-during-presidential-poll-pantami/
77. Mihai IC, Pruna Ș, Petrica G (2017) A comprehensive analysis on cyber-threats against elearning systems. ELearn Softw Educ 3:344–351. https://doi.org/10.12753/2066-026X-17-225
78. Mohammed KH, Mohammed YD, Solanke AA (2019) Cybercrime and digital forensics: bridging the gap in legislation, investigation, and prosecution of cybercrime in Nigeria. Int J Cybersecur Intell Cybercrime 2(1):56–63
79. Montasari R, Hill R (2019) Next-generation digital forensics: challenges and future paradigms. In: 2019 IEEE 12th international conference on global security, safety and sustainability (ICGS3), Jan 2019. IEEE, pp 205–212
80. Mu'azu-Abdullahi S (2016) An overview of the legal framework of advanced fee fraud and cybercrime in Nigeria. Hasanuddin Law Rev 2(2):195–212
81. Naidoo R (2020) A multi-level influence model of COVID-19 themed cybercrime. Eur J Inf Syst 1–16

82. National Information Technology Development Agency (2019) National cybersecurity policy/strategy implementation guidelines for ministries, departments & agencies (MDAs) & private ICT organizations. https://nitda.gov.ng/wp-content/uploads/2020/03/National-Cybersecurity-Strategy-Implementation-GuidelinesFinal.pdf
83. News Agency of Nigeria (2016) Police to create special unit to tackle cybercrime. Guardian Newspaper. https://guardian.ng/news/police-to-create-special-unit-to-tackle-cybercrime/
84. Nigeria Police Act (2020) https://placng.org/i/wp-content/uploads/2020/09/Police-Act-2020.pdf
85. Nigeria Police Force (2023) History of the nigeria police force. https://www.npf.gov.ng/aboutus/History_Nigeria_Police.php
86. Nigeria Deposit Insurance Company (2019) NDIC annual report 2018. https://ndic.gov.ng/wp-content/uploads/2019/09/NDIC-2018-ANNUAL-REPORT.pdf
87. Nigerian Communications Commission (2004) An overview of the Nigerian telecommunications environment. https://www.ncc.gov.ng/archived/speeches/NCC%20CEO%20Presentation%20on%20Overview%20of%20Nigerian%20Telecoms%20Industry.pdf
88. Nigerian Cybercrimes (Prohibition, Prevention, etc) Act (2015). https://cert.gov.ng/ngcert/resources/CyberCrime__Prohibition_Prevention_etc__Act__2015.pdf
89. Nigerian Deposit Insurance Company (2019) NDIC annual report 2018. https://ndic.gov.ng/wp-content/uploads/2019/09/NDIC-2018-ANNUAL-REPORT.pdf
90. Nigerian Communications Commission (2023) Subscriber data. https://ncc.gov.ng/statistics-reports/subscriber-data#quarterly-subscriber-operator-data-3
91. Obuah E (2010) Combatting corruption in Nigeria: the Nigerian economic and financial crimes (EFCC). Afr Stud Q 12(1)
92. Office of the National Security Adviser (2021) National cybersecurity policy and strategy. https://cert.gov.ng/ngcert/resources/NATIONAL_CYBERSECURITY_POLICY_AND_STRATEGY_2021.pdf
93. Ojukwu SD, Agu OC (2020) Legality of the cybercrimes (Prrohinition, Prevention, etc) act as an instrument for internet crimes control in Nigeria. J Commercial and Property Law 7(2)
94. Oke O (2015) An appraisal of the Nigerian cybercrime (prohibition, prevention etc.) act, 2015 (SSRN scholarly paper ID 2655593). Soc Sci Res Netw. https://doi.org/10.2139/ssrn.2655593
95. Olayemi OJ (2014) A socio-technological analysis of cybercrime and cyber security in Nigeria. Int J Sociol Anthropol 6(3):116–125
96. Omodunbi BA, Odiase PO, Olaniyan OM, Esan AO (2016) Cybercrimes in Nigeria: analysis, detection, and prevention. J Eng Technol 1(1):37–42
97. Omotubora AO (2016) Comparative perspectives on cybercrime legislation in Nigeria and the UK—a case for revisiting the "hacking" offences under the Nigerian Cybercrime Act 2015. Eur J Law Technol 7(3)
98. Oni S, Berepubo KA, Oni AA, Joshua S (2019) E-government and the challenge of cybercrime in Nigeria. In: 2019 sixth international conference on eDemocracy & eGovernment (ICEDEG), Apr 2019. IEEE, pp 137–142
99. Onoja EO (2018) Issues on exclusionary rules of evidence under the evidence act 2011. Afr J Law Hum Rights 2
100. Onyema E, Roy P, Oredola H, Ayinla S (2018) The EFCC and the politics of (in) effective implementation of Nigeria's anti-corruption policy. https://eprints.soas.ac.uk/31283/1/ACE-WorkingPaper007-EFCC-Nigeria.pdf
101. Oraegbunam IK (2015) The Nigerian police and problems of cybercrime investigation: need for adequate training. Niger Law J 18(1):1–28
102. Parker D (1976) Crime by computer. Scribner, New York
103. Pichan A, Lazarescu M, Soh ST (2018) Towards a practical cloud forensics logging framework. J Inf Secur Appl 42:18–28
104. Prayudi Y, Priyambodo TK (2015) Secure and trusted environment as a strategy to maintain the integrity and authenticity of digital evidence. Int J Secur Appl 9(6):299–314. https://doi.org/10.14257/ijsia.2015.9.6.28

105. Punch Newspaper (2022) IGP shakes up cybercrime unit. https://punchng.com/igp-shakes-up-cybercrime-unit/
106. Reed TS (2019) Cybercrime and technology losses: claims and potential insurance coverage for modern cyber risks. Tort Trial Insur Pract Law J 54(1):153–209
107. Renals P (2020) SilverTerrier: new COVID-19 themed business email compromise schemes. https://unit42.paloaltonetworks.com/silverterrier-covid-19-themed-business-email-compromise/
108. Ricci J, Baggili I, Breitinger F (2019) Blockchain-based distributed cloud storage digital forensics: where's the beef? IEEE Secur Priv 17(1):34–42
109. Rufai A, Modi S, Wadata B (2020) A survey of cyber-security practices in Nigeria. International research J Adv Eng Sci 5(3):222–226
110. Sabeil E, Manaf AA, Ismail Z (2012) Development of Malaysian digital forensics investigator competency identification methods. In: Advanced machine learning technologies and applications: first international conference, AMLTA 2012, Cairo, Egypt, 8–10 Dec 2012. Proceedings 1. Springer Berlin Heidelberg, pp 554–565
111. Sabillon R, Cano J, Cavaller V, Serra J (2016) Cybercrime and cybercriminals: a comprehensive study. Int J Comput Netw Commun Secur 4(6)
112. Sarmah A, Sarmah R, Baruah AJ (2017) A brief study on cybercrime and cyber laws of India. Int Res J Eng Technol (IRJET) 4(6):1633–1640
113. Shaw A, Browne A (2013) A practical and robust approach to coping with large volumes of data submitted for digital forensic examination. Digit Investig 10(2):116–128
114. Sirineni G (2022) Remote work has led to a cybercrime boom—here's how to stop it. https://www.forbes.com/sites/forbesbusinesscouncil/2022/03/07/remote-work-has-led-to-a-cybercrime-boom-heres-how-to-stop-it/?sh=6150d97e2f6a
115. Statista (2020) Number of Internet of Things (IoT) connected devices worldwide in 2018, 2025 and 2030. https://www.statista.com/statistics/802690/worldwide-connected-devices-by-access-technology/
116. Stoyanova M, Nikoloudakis Y, Panagiotakis S, Pallis E, Markakis EK (2020) A survey on the Internet of Things (IoT) forensics: challenges, approaches, and open issues. IEEE Commun Surv Tutor 22(2):1191–1221
117. Suleiman AO (2019) The impulsive upsurge of yahoo-yahoo in the 21st century in Nigeria: Islamic perspective. Afr J Criminol Justice Stud 12(1)
118. Symantec Corporation and African Union (2016) Cybercrime & cybersecurity trends in Africa. www.thehaguesecuritydelta.com/media/com_hsd/report/135/document/Cyber-security-trends-report-Africa-en.pdf
119. The Association of Chief Police Officer of England, Wales and Northern Ireland (2009) ACPO e-crime strategy. http://library.college.police.uk/docs/acpo/Ecrime-Strategy-2009.pdf
120. Tonye WS (2018) Cyber forensic and data collection challenges in Nigeria. Glob J Comput Sci Technol 18(3)
121. Trading Economics (2023) Nigerian Naira. https://tradingeconomics.com/nigeria/currency
122. Umar I, Samsudin RS, Mohamed M (2016) Understanding the successes and challenges of Anti-Corruption Agency (ACA) in Nigeria: a case of Economic and Financial Crimes Commission (EFCC). Asian J Multidiscip Stud 4(5):27–33
123. United States Department of Justice (2007) Prosecuting computer crimes. https://www.justice.gov/sites/default/files/criminal-ccips/legacy/2015/03/26/prosecuting_ip_crimes_manual_2013.pdf
124. United Nations Office on Drugs and Crime (2013) Comprehensive study on cybercrime. https://www.unodc.org/documents/organized-crime/UNODC_CCPCJ_EG.4_2013/CYBERCRIME_STUDY_210213.pdf
125. Urhibo K (2021) Combating and addressing the menace of cybercrime in Nigeria: an overview of applicable laws. Afr J Crim Law Jurisprud 6
126. Vanguard Newspaper (2020) Nigeria police, Interpol arrest three suspects over cybercrime. Vanguard Newspaper. https://www.vanguardngr.com/2020/07/nigeria-police-interpol-arrest-3-suspects-over-cybercrime/

127. Viko IJ (2021) Analysis of the legal and institutional framework for fighting cybercrime in Nigeria. Int J Comp Law Legal Philos (IJOCLLEP) 3(2)
128. Wall DS (2001) Cybercrimes and internet. In: Wall DS (ed) Crime and the internet. Routledge, pp 1–17
129. We Are Social (2022) Digital 2022 global overview report. https://wearesocial.com/uk/blog/2022/01/digital-2022-another-year-of-bumper-growth-2/
130. Yang Z (2011) A survey of cybercrime. https://www.cse.wustl.edu/~jain/cse571-11/ftp/crime/#Brenner10
131. Zainal Z (2007) Case study as a research method. Jurnal Kemanusiaan 5(1)
132. Zawoad S, Hasan R (2015) Digital forensics in the age of big data: challenges, approaches, and opportunities. In: 2015 IEEE 17th international conference on high performance computing and communications, 2015 IEEE 7th international symposium on cyberspace safety and security, and 2015 IEEE 12th international conference on embedded software and systems, pp 1320–1325. https://doi.org/10.1109/HPCC-CSS-ICESS.2015.305

Chapter 3
Digital Evidence, Digital Forensics, and Digital Forensic Readiness

Abstract This chapter presents a scholarly review of the concepts of digital evidence, digital forensics, and digital forensic readiness. The chapter starts by introducing definitions, foundational concepts of digital evidence, and its relevance in crime investigations. The chapter examines the admissibility of digital evidence, both in Nigeria and other jurisdictions. The chapter analyses Nigeria's Evidence Act, in relation to the admissibility of digital evidence in the Nigerian justice system. The chapter also presents important principles in the United States justice system, such as the Federal Rules of Evidence, Frye Standard, Daubert Standard, and other important principles of the admissibility of evidence. This chapter also presents digital forensics—definition, principles, and investigation models. The chapter also analyses the concept of digital forensic readiness. The chapter ends by reviewing available literature on digital forensic readiness of law enforcement agencies in Nigeria.

Keywords Cybercrime · Digital evidence · Evidence admissibility · Evidence Act · Digital forensics · Digital forensic readiness · Forensic investigation models

3.1 Introduction

Digital evidence is very crucial to solving cybercrime cases. However, it's application in policing and crime investigation goes beyond just cybercrime investigation. Given the increased technology adoption and ubiquity of digital devices, it is difficult for a modern day crime not to have a digital dimension [11, 21]. There is always a likelihood that a digital device was used to plan the crime, used to facilitate the crime; present at the crime scene; used to attempt to conceal the crime; or used to distribute the proceeds of the crime. For instance, consider a robbery incident at a bank. Ordinarily, this is a physical crime involving humans and weapons. However, there are several potential sources of digital evidence that could prove vital to this case.

R. T. Sibe and C. Kaunert, *Cybercrime, Digital Forensic Readiness, and Financial Crime Investigation in Nigeria*, Advanced Sciences and Technologies for Security Applications, https://doi.org/10.1007/978-3-031-54089-9_3

For instance, the armed robbers may have relied on their phones and computers for planning and reconnaissance. They may have done keyword searches on their devices to get more information about the bank. They may have been in contact with a malicious insider who gave them hints on the security configuration of the building. All of these can be unearthed forensically if the right suspect is in custody. The electronic device of the armed robber may also have been used as an accessory at the scene of crime. There is the possibility that they carried at least one phone to communicate with their gang members should they need cover or reinforcement. Unbeknownst to them, Call Detail Record (CDR) analysis and cell forensics can reveal the mobile devices present at the crime scene. The robbers may have also worn a smart watch, which will have geolocation data and handshakes with the local WiFi. After the robbery, they may also have relied on their phones to coordinate their escape and share proceeds of the crime. All these would leave digital footprints that can be extracted forensically and help solve the crime. Therefore, digital evidence is not only useful in cracking cybercrime cases, but they also place crucial role in investigating many real-world crimes.

It is the job of the digital forensic expert to identify, collect, preserve, and analyse these digital footprints in a forensically sound manner and legally defensible [11]. It is noteworthy that digital evidence can be abstract and volatile in nature. Meaning that it can be susceptible to change and manipulation. This is why digital forensics is a very methodical and ethical discipline and requires specialist tools and skillset. Admissibility of evidence is an important consideration before it can play any role in the case. This chapter introduced the concept of digital evidence, admissibility of digital evidence, digital forensics, digital forensic investigation models, and digital forensic readiness.

3.2 Digital Evidence

There are several definitions of digital evidence. However, they all appear to point in same direction. For instance, the Standard Working Group on Digital Evidence (SWGDE) defines digital evidence as any information of probative value that is either stored or transmitted in a digital form. The National Justice Institute defines digital evidence as the information stored or transmitted in binary form that may be relied on in court. Digital evidence includes computer evidence, evidence from mobile devices such as phones, drones, video camera, smart devices, and many other digital devices.

Digital evidence is ubiquitous and found in most common devices, such as computers, mobile phones, flash drives, routers, the Internet, and many more [47]. With the rising number of cybercrime cases and the growing number of connected devices, digital evidence continues to feature prominently in criminal investigations. Cybercrime investigations involve investigating digital devices. Just as criminals in the terrestrial world leave traces of their presence at the crime scene, in digital crimes, criminals also leave digital footprints. While the collection and preservation of physical evidence could be relatively straight forward, doing same for digital evidence could be a little more complex.

There are several reasons why collection, preservation, and analysis of digital evidence could prove daunting. One major challenge of digital evidence is volatility. Most digital evidence is volatile and relatively easier to tamper with [46]. The process of digital evidence acquisition requires complex toolkit, expert skill, and delicate analysis which can be challenging. The other significant challenges are the complexity of acquiring data at the lowest level, the growing volume and sources of digital evidence, the challenge of timelining, and the complexities of digital forensic tools [51]. Investigating digital crimes requires careful acquisition, analysis, and presentation of digital evidence [50]. These delicate and expert requirements constitute a significant challenge and disruption to the normal crime investigation process.

Beyond the complicated process of collection, preservation, and analysis of digital evidence in a forensically sound manner, a significant challenge before investigators is the complexity of tendering digital evidence in court. Apart from the stated reasons, there are several reasons why tendering digital evidence could be daunting. First, is the legal hurdle of admissibility, which is presented in the next section. The abstract nature of digital forensics makes it quite technical and difficult to understand and comprehend. Even in the Information Technology community, digital forensics is a specialist area requiring specialist skillset. This constitutes a major challenge.

This is even more of a challenge to the legal community. The abstract nature of digital evidence, and the difficulties of understanding the associated terminologies by the justice community makes it a challenge in the court room. Lawyers and Judges are not forensic experts, therefore, they often struggle with the high level of technicalities. This complexity throws in the challenge for digital evidence to be presented in a clear and understandable manner. Given this challenge, it is important for judges to have an underlying knowledge of digital forensics and associated technologies [61]. Unfortunately, this is not always the case. In addition to this, technology is evolving at a fast pace, greater than the speed of prosecution, and ultimately justice, and it becomes increasingly difficult to keep pace with emerging technologies. Therefore, this leaves the challenging of constantly updating protocols and procedures governing collection, preservation, and analysis of digital evidence. All of these are major challenges digital evidence face in the courtroom, particularly in developing economies with relatively low technological adoption in the justice system.

3.2.1 Admissibility of Digital Evidence in Nigeria

Like other physical evidence, there is always the question of admissibility for digital evidence. For digital evidence to be admissible in court, it must meet certain legal and technical requirements [11]. The expansion of the scope and definition of evidence, to include digital evidence, was not without its challenges. While other forensic sciences got a relatively more straightforward route to acceptance in the courtroom, it took quite some debate for digital evidence to be generally accepted [1]. In most jurisdictions, digital evidence was not admissible in court years after digital forensics became mainstream. For instance, Nigeria only amended the Evidence Act to allow for the admissibility of digital evidence in 2011. The old Evidence Act of 1945 and the Evidence Act, Cap E14 Laws of the Federation of Nigeria 2004 did not expressly recognize the admissibility of digital evidence and left a lot of conflicting judgments on admissibility of computer generated documents [32, 59]. This amendment fundamentally transformed the Nigerian justice system that relied previously on an evidence act with no clear provision for admissibility of digital evidence [5]. Specifically, section 84 of the Act now makes provision for the admissibility of digital evidence, as well as the guidelines governing admissibility.

A classic example where the court in Nigeria relied entirely on digital evidence to sentence a suspect was the tragic case of *State v. Lawal Segun and Ors*, in 2012. This is said to be the first case in Nigeria where the court completely relied on digital evidence. In this case, four students of University of Port Harcourt were gruesomely murdered by a mob in Aluu, a neighbouring village to the university. The four victims, popularly referred to as the "Aluu Four" were students of the University of Port Harcourt, Rivers State, Nigeria. Unbeknownst to the killers, someone in the crowd had secretly recorded the barbaric scenes with his mobile phone and uploaded it to the internet, via YouTube. In the ensuing prosecution, the prosecution team downloaded the horrific video from YouTube, and stored in a compact disk. This was tendered and admitted by the court, and subsequently, the gruesome scenes were displayed via a projector in court. The landmark admissibility of the internet generated evidence relied on the provisions of Sections 84 and 258(1) of the Evidence Act, 2011. This was a novel case were a court in Nigeria relied exclusively on electronic evidence, with no eyewitness or circumstantial evidence [44].

In summary, the conditions for the admissibility of digital evidence in Nigeria can be found in Section 84(2) of the evidence act, and it is reproduced below:

(a) *That the document containing the statement was produced by the computer during a period over which the computer was used regularly to store or process information for the purposes of any activities regularly carried on over that period, whether for profitor not, by anybody, whether corporate or not, or by any individual;*
(b) *That over that period there was regularly supplied to the computer in the ordinary course of those activities information of the kind contained in the statement or of the kind from which the information so contained is derived;*
(c) *That throughout the material of that period the computer was operating properly or, if not that in any respect in which it was not operating properly or was out of operation during that part of that period was not such as to affect the production of the document or the accuracy of its contents; and*
(d) *That the information contained in the statement reproduces or is derived from information supplied to the computer in the ordinary course of those activities.*

One of the issues frequently raised in court had to do with the authenticity of the electronic evidence tendered. This is because, electronic evidence can be altered or tampered with. To address this, the evidence Act makes provision for the authentication of digital evidence. Specifically, section 84(4) outlines the steps for authentication of a digital evidence. The steps include identifying the document evidence and describing how it was produced; outlining the particulars of the device involved in the production; duly signed by a person authorized or responsible for the production. Section 84(4) is reproduced below:

In any proceeding where it is desired to give a statement in evidence by virtue of this section, a certificate

(a) *Identifying the document containing the statement and describing the manner in which it was produced;*
(b) *Giving such particulars of any device involved in the production of that document as may be appropriate for the purpose of showing that the document was produced by a computer;*

    i. *dealing with any of the matters to which the conditions mentioned in subsection (2) above relate, and purporting to be signed by a person occupying a responsible position in relation to the operation of the relevant device or the management of the relevant activities, as the case may be, shall be evidence of the matter stated in the certificate; and for the purpose of this subsection it shall be sufficient for a matter to be stated to the best of the knowledge and belief of the person stating it.*

That is, Section 84(4) basically requires a certificate proving the authenticity of the document and the state of the device that generated it. Nwafor [59] submits that the coming provisions of sections 84(2) and 84(4) can be termed evidentiary frontiers, since they form the foundation and governs the admissibility of evidence. Nwafor [59] further posits that digital evidence must satisfy four evidential frontiers, listed below:

1. The document must be pleaded;
2. Relevance to the case;
3. The document must be admissible in law (Section 84(2));
4. Must satisfy the requirements of authentication (Section 84(4)).

It is noteworthy that admissibility merely allows evidence to be accepted as part of proceedings, it does not confer an automatic weight to it. That is, the fact that in a proceeding, digital evidence was admissible, does not mean that evidence automatically assign a weighty probative value to it. For digital evidence to be admissible in the Nigerian court, it simply means it satisfied the provisions of section 84 of the evidence act. Therefore, it is incumbent on the person tendering digital evidence to properly lay the foundation for its admissibility, using section 84. It is the duty of the court to now consider the reliability, credibility, and persuasive nature of the evidence to take a decision as to the weight in relation to the case, in line with section 34 of the Evidence Act [60].

While the enactment of the Evidence Act 2011 was a significant achievement, there were immediate calls for the amendment. Anyebe [12] argued that the provisions of the Act were not sufficient, and there was a need to amend the law. Similarly, Erugo [39] posited that while the Act was a landmark legislation in terms of the admissibility of digital evidence, however, the provisions were inadequate and therefore problematic in implementation. Beyond the technicalities of law and the challenges, from a technological standpoint, the Act clearly was not comprehensive. The Act, although makes provision for the admissibility of digital evidence, seemed worded in terminologies not reflective of the emerging technological landscape.

In response to this, the Nigerian National Assembly reviewed the Act. On the 12th of June 2023, President Bola Tinubu signed the amendment to the evidence act. This law, now cited as Evidence (Amendment) Act 2023 did not repeal the Evidence Act 2011, but merely made amendments in reflection of the evolving technological landscape and new innovations. This amendment contained sections that brought clarity and would undoubtedly strengthen prosecution of cases involving digital evidence. Specific amendments include the expansion of the scope to include "electronic records", as can be seen in Section 84(a), (b), (c), (d), and (e). The amendment provided clarity for areas with hitherto hazy deductions. Section 84 specifically made records in a computer admissible, as long as it satisfies conditions stated in the Act. Section 84C recognized the use of authentication of digital signature or electronic signature. The amendment also introduced electronic oath taking and the electronic gazettes.

The Evidence (Amendment) Act 2023 made important additions labelled Sections 84A, 84B, 84C, and 84D which is reproduced below:

Information in Electronic Form

84A. *Where any law provides that information or any other matter shall be in writing or in the typewritten or printed form, then, notwithstanding anything contained in such law, such requirement shall be deemed to have been satisfied if such information or matter is*

(a) *Rendered or made available in an electronic form; and*
(b) *Accessible so as to be usable for a subsequent reference.*

Records in a Computer to Be Admissible

84B. *Notwithstanding anything contained in this Act, any information contained in an electronic record which is printed on a paper, stored, recorded or copied in optical or magnetic media or cloud computing or database produced by a computer shall be deemed to also be a document, if the conditions mentioned in this section are satisfied in relation to the information and the computer in question and shall be admissible in any proceeding, without further proof or production of the original, as evidence or any contents of the original or any fact stated in it of which direct evidence would be admissible.*

Authentication of Electronic Record

84C. (1) *Subject to the procisions of this section any person may authenticate an electornic record by affixing his digital signature on it.*

(2) *A person may authenticate any electronic record by such digital signature or electronic authentication technique which*
(a) *is considered reliable; or*
(b) *may be specified by this Act.*

(3) *For the purpose of this subsection (2), any digital signature or electronic authentication technique will be considered reliable if*
(a) *the signature creation data or the authentication data are, within the context in which they are used, linked to the signatory or, as the case may be, the authenticator and of no other person;*
(b) *any alteration to the digital signature made after affixing such signature is detectable;*
(c) *any alteration to the information made after its authentication by the digital signature is detectable; and*
(d) *it fulfills such other conditions which may be prescribed.*

Proof of Digital Signature

84D. (1) *Except in the case of a secure digital signature, if the digital signature of any person is alleged to have been affixed to an electronic record, the fact such digital signature is the digital signature of the person must be proved.*

(2) *A digital signature is deemed to be secure if the signature creation data*
(a) *at the time of affixing the signature, was under the exclusive control of the signatory and no other person; and*
(b) *was stored and affixed in such exclusive manner as may be prescribed.*

In reflection of the possible confusion the emerging technological terminologies might introduce, the amendment introduced new definitions such as "audio-visual communication", "cloud computing", "digital signature", "electronic record", "electronic signature", "magnetic media" and "optical media". Perhaps, in reflection of the fast paced technological landscape, section 255(1) gave the Minister of Justice a blanket responsibility for making "regulations generally prescribing further conditions with respect to admissibility of any class of evidence that may be relevant under this Act". While this appeared a positive provision in good faith, however, concerns might be raised on such strong powers given to a political appointee (in Nigeria, the Minister of Justice is a political appointee that can be hired or fired at the President's pleasure). In all, this amendment is a positive addition to Nigeria's jurisprudence, particularly as it concerns the admissibility of digital evidence and the fight against cybercrime.

3.2.2 *Admissibility of Digital Evidence in Other Jurisdictions (Case Study: USA)*

It is difficult to discuss digital forensics and digital evidence without discussing the United States of America, given the remarkable contribution they have made to the subject and discipline. Therefore, this section is dedicated to the admissibility of digital evidence in the USA. In the United States of America, the Federal Rules of Evidence (FRE) governs the admissibility of evidence in federal court proceedings. The judge decides admissibility, based on different standards and mechanisms for evaluating relevance and reliability [45]. FRE 401–403 defines relevance and FRE 901 specifies the important task of identifying and authenticating evidence. These sections are reproduced below (as amended April 26, 2011).

Rule 401. Test for Relevant Evidence

Evidence is relevant if:

(a) *It has any tendency to make a fact more or less probable than it would be without the evidence; and*
(b) *The fact is of consequence in determining the action.*

It is incumbent on the proponent to prove the authenticity of the evidence being pleaded. FRE 901 defines and gives the condition for authenticity, and it is reproduced below (as amended April 26, 2011):

Rule 402. General Admissibility of Relevant Evidence

Relevant evidence is admissible unless any of the following provides otherwise:

- *The United States Constitution;*
- *A federal statute;*
- *These rules; or*
- *Other rules prescribed by the Supreme Court.*

Irrelevant evidence is not admissible.

Rule 403. Excluding Relevant Evidence for Prejudice, Confusion, Waste of Time, or Other Reasons

The court may exclude relevant evidence if its probative value is substantially outweighed by a danger of one or more of the following: unfair prejudice, confusing the issues, misleading the jury, undue delay, wasting time, or needlessly presenting cumulative evidence.

Rule 901. Authenticating or Identifying Evidence

(a) *IN GENERAL. To satisfy the requirement of authenticating or identifying an item of evidence, the proponent must produce evidence sufficient to support a finding that the item is what the proponent claims it is.*

(b) *EXAMPLES. The following are examples only—not complete list—of evidence that satisfies the requirement:*

(1) *Testimony of a Witness with Knowledge. Testimony that an item is what it is claimed to be.*
(2) *Nonexpert Open about Handwriting. A nonexpert opinion that handwriting is genuine, based on a familiarity with it that was not acquired for the current litigation.*
(3) *Comparison by an Expert Witness of the Trier of Fact. A comparison with an authenticated specimen by an expert witness or the trier of fact.*
(4) *Distinctive Characteristics and the Like. The appearance, contents, substance, internal patterns, or other distinctive characteristics of the item, taken together with all the circumstances.*
(5) *Opinion about a Voice. An opinion identifying a person's voice—whether heard firsthand or through mechanical or electronic transmission or recording—based on hearing the voice at any time under the circumstances that connect it with the alleged speaker.*
(6) *Evidence about a Telephone Conversation. For a telephone conversation, evidence that a call was made to the number assigned at the time to:*
   (a) *A particular person, if circumstances, including self-identification, show that the person answering was the one called; or*
   A particular business, if the call was made to a business and the call related reasonably transacted over the phone.
(7) *Evidence about Public Record: Evidence that:*
   (a) *A document was recorded or filed in a public office as authorized by law; or*
   (b) *A purported public record or statement is from the office were items of this kind are kept.*
(8) *Evidence about Ancient Documents or data Compilations. For a document or data compilation, evidence that:*
   (a) *Is in a condition that creates no suspicion about the authenticity;*
   (b) *Was in a place where, if authentic, it would likely be; and*
   (c) *Is at least 20 years old when offered.*
(9) *Evidence about a Process or System. Evidence describing a process or system and showing that it produces an accurate result.*
(10) *Methods Provided by a Statute or Rule. Any method of authentication or identification allowed by a federal statute or a rule prescribed by the Supreme Court.*

The above rules are for admissibility of evidence—whether physical or digital. In the United States of America, the landmark ruling in the civil case of *Lorraine v. Markel American Insurance Company* established the guidelines for the admissibility and authentication of digital evidence. In this case, Jack Lorraine and Beverly Mack owned a yacht which was damaged by lightning. Both sued the Markel American Insurance Company for damages covered by the insurance policy. In this case, electronic evidence (consisting of emails) put forward was not admissible, and the judge established the five evidentiary considerations when assessing the admissibility of digital evidence [45]. The five evidentiary considerations are: relevance, authenticity, not hearsay or admissible hearsay, original writing rule, and not duly prejudicial.

Excerpt of that ruling of *Lorraine v. Markel American Insurance Company* [52] is shared below:

> Whenever ESI is offered as evidence, either at trial or in summary judgment, the following evidence rules must be considered: (1) is the ESI relevant as determined by Rule 401 (does it have any tendency to make some fact that is of consequence to the litigation more or less probable than it otherwise would be); (2) if relevant under 401, is it authentic as required by Rule 901(a) (can the proponent show that the ESI is what it purports to be); (3) if the ESI is offered for its substantive truth, is it hearsay as defined by Rule 801, and if so, is it covered by an applicable exception (Rules 803, 804 and 807); (4) is the form of the ESI that is being offered as evidence an original or duplicate under the original writing rule, of if not, is there admissible secondary evidence to prove the content of the ESI (Rules 1001-1008); and (5) is the probative value of the ESI substantially outweighed by the danger of unfair prejudice or one of the other factors identified by Rule 403, such that it should be excluded despite its relevance.

Beyond the general rules for admissibility of evidence discussed above, in the United States of America, there are specific standards for the admissibility of scientific evidence. Casey [21] identifies the stages of the scientific method as: Observation, hypothesis, prediction, experimentation, and conclusion. Casey [21] further showed how the digital forensic process can be situated within the scientific method. First, is the observation stage. An event would have transpired which through **observation** was brought to notice. Following this, the digital forensic examiner formulates a **hypothesis**. For instance, the digital forensic examiner might form a hypothesis that the attack was an SQL injection. Based on his knowledge of digital forensics, the examiner can then **predict** where the likely artifacts of interest can be found. With these predictions, the digital forensic examiner will then use specialist tools to carry out digital forensic examination/analysis (**experimentation**). The outcome of this experimentation is carefully observed and documented, using expert knowledge, and without any bias. A **conclusion** is reached and presented, which will either support or refute the hypothesis. Figure 3.1 presents this.

In the United States of America, three standards are traditionally used for the admissibility of scientific evidence. These standards are the Frye Standard, the Daubert Standard, and FRE 702. Both the Frye Standard and the Daubert Standard have gone on to inspire similar rulings or standards in other jurisdictions around the world [45].

3.2.3 The Frye Standard

This is a landmark ruling on admissibility of expert witness and scientific evidence, reached exactly 100 years ago. In the case of Frye v. United States [40], the defendant, James Alphonso Frye, who had been earlier convicted of second-degree murder,

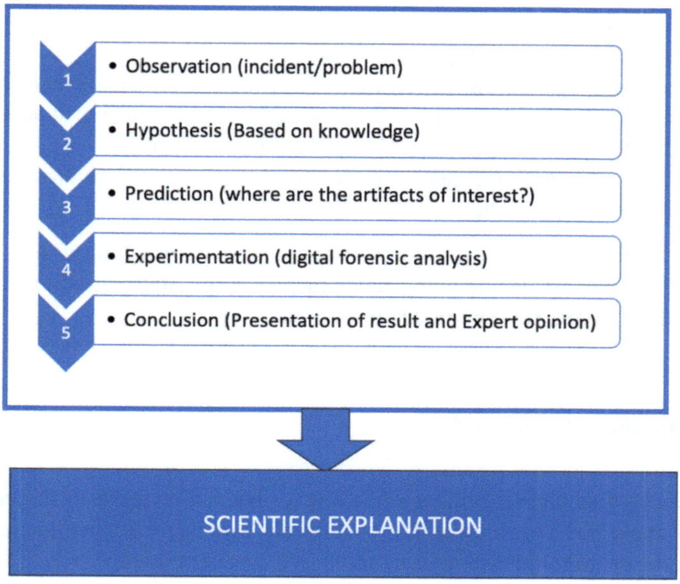

Fig. 3.1 Digital forensic process [21]. *Note* This figure shows how the digital forensic process can be situated within the scientific method

appealed his conviction. The defense council sought to provide expert witness on the basis of a systolic blood pressure test, which is the precursor to the polygraph or lie detector test. This theory was predicated on the postulation that a rise in blood pressure is the evidence that the subject was lying [45]. However, the prosecutor argued that the court should not rely on an unproven method that is not generally accepted.

In the ruling of the case of Frye v. United States [40], the District of Columbia Court agreed with the argument of the prosecutor. Specifically, the court held that:

> Just when a scientific principle or discovery crosses the line between the experimental and demonstrable stages is difficult to define. Somewhere in this twilight zone the evidential force of the principle must be recognized, and while courts will go a long way in admitting expert testimony deduced from a well-recognized scientific principle or discovery, the thing from which the deduction is made must be sufficiently established to have gained general acceptance in the particular field in which it belongs.

In other words, to pass the Frye test, the party pushing for it will have to assemble a collection of experts who will testify on the general acceptability of the principle under review, by the scientific community. While the Frye Standard was a landmark pronouncement on scientific evidence, it was not without many criticisms. Borders Jr. [17] categorized the points raised by the critics under 5 headings:

1. Court's inconsistent characterization of proofs as scientific evidence needing the Frye test;
2. Difficulty by courts to define the relevant scientific fields;

3. The ruling did not specify the percentage of people in the scientific community that must accept the technique under review;
4. Could often result in the deprivation of reliable and outcome-determinative evidence. The test does not reflect the fast pace innovative landscape. The implication is that the court will always lag behind science;
5. The focus on general acceptance seems to obscure critical challenges with the use of the technique under review.

In view of these criticisms, many courts and states have either modified or rejected the use of the Frye test. While many states in the United States are divided between this, the federal courts rely on the Daubert Standard [10].

3.2.4 Daubert Standard

The accuracy of scientific evidence has always been a concern in the courtroom. Therefore, there have been efforts to ensure that forensic evidence is credible and reliable in the criminal justice system and based on exact science [13]. The Daubert Standard is an important legal principle that governs the admissibility of scientific evidence [29]. It originated from the Supreme Courts' decision in Daubert v. Merrell Dow Pharmaceuticals in [27] [49]. In the United States, this principle and the Federal Rules of Evidence provide a guiding benchmark for the admissibility of scientific evidence. This principle is also applicable to digital forensic analysis and is the basis for expert testimonies. It gives five items to be considered by the trial judge to determine if a methodology is valid [48], and is illustrated in Fig. 3.2.

This ruling in Daubert v. Merrell Dow Pharmaceuticals (1993), basically overruled the Frye standard in federal courts. The court in this case ruled that "general

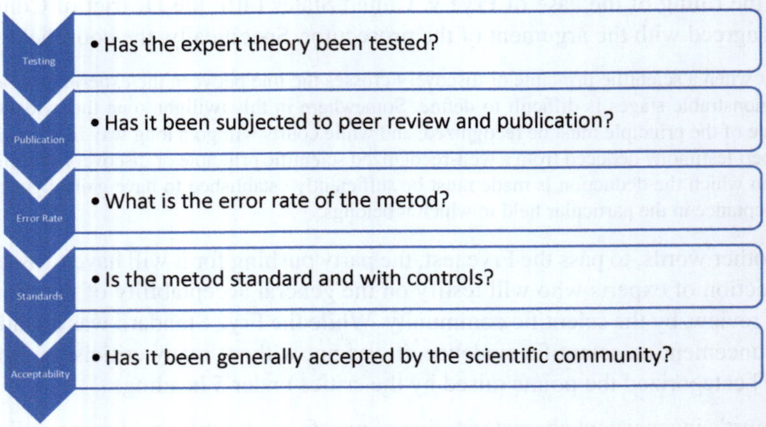

Fig. 3.2 Daubert Standard

acceptance" is not a precondition for admissibility, and it is inconsistent with the evidentiary rule FRE 702 in the federal rules of evidence. The ruling further underlined the gate keeping responsibility of the court [10]. The Daubert Standard held that scientific expert testimony presented in court should undergo reliability test. The Daubert Standard essentially liberalized the admission of expert witness, instead underscoring the importance for cross examining witnesses, rather than just relying on general acceptance in the scientific community. The court as the "gatekeeper" ought to arrive at an informed decision factoring in the conditions stated above, rather than outsourcing that decision to a statistic of the scientific community.

Despite this, some still argue that the Daubert Standard is not exhaustive. Beyond this, there may be other reasons why scientific evidence or testimony may not be admissible. For instance, no matter how accurate, scientific evidence or testimony may not be admissible if it is not relevant to the case [13]. Ryan and Shpantzer [72] summarized two cardinal checks for the admissibility of digital evidence: it must be relevant and derived from a scientific method. Beyond this, a major challenge with the Daubert is that there is not an exact prescription of weight to be given to each of the five criteria listed in the ruling [10].

3.3 Best Practice in Handling Digital Evidence

Cybercrime investigations do end up in court. One of the areas defense counsels do target is technicalities such as if procedures were followed or not. To avoid these pitfalls, different jurisdictions have guidelines for handling evidence. For instance, the National Institute of Justice [57] released the Digital Evidence Policies and Procedures Manual. The United States Department of Justice [81] also released "Forensic Examination of Digital Evidence: Guide for Law Enforcement". Documents such as this serve as guide to ensure that evidence collection, preservation, and forensic analysis is done in a forensically sound manner. One of these principles for handling cybercrime scene that is quite popular is the Association of Chief Police Offices [14], summarized:

> **Principle 1**: No action taken by law enforcement agencies, persons employed within those agencies or their agents should change data which may subsequently be relied upon in court.
>
> **Principle 2**: In circumstances where a person finds it necessary to access original data, that person must be competent to do so and be able to give evidence explaining the relevance and the implications of their actions.
>
> **Principle 3**: An audit trail or other record of all processes applied to digital evidence should be created and preserved. An independent third party should be able to examine those processes and achieve the same result.
>
> **Principle 4**: The person in charge of the investigation has overall responsibility for ensuring that the law and these principles are adhered to.

These principals can guide law enforcement agencies to avoid some of the pitfalls of evidence contamination and responsibility.

3.4 Digital Forensics

3.4.1 History of Digital Forensics

Digital forensics has grown into an established science, having been around for decades. There are different accounts as to the timelines of the early days. For instance, Garfinkel [43] traced the history of digital forensics to the 1970s. While the earliest accounts were about data recovery, the skillset falls under the broad classification of digital forensics. Horsman [46] and Sommer [74] traced the history of forensics to the 1980s when some police outfits in different countries started setting up specialist Computer Crime Units. Casey [20] traced the history of digital forensics to the late 1980s, when law enforcement agencies developed capabilities in this area. Despite the variance in dates, one thing that is common to the different historical accounts is the role of law enforcement at the beginning.

At the onset, digital forensics was not considered a forensic science [20]. This classification would later change in the 1990s when it became recognized as a forensic discipline. However, some argue that traditional forensic sciences are ahead of digital forensic sciences in terms of precision, despite the common classification. For instance, Overill and Silomon [64] submitted that the accuracy of other forensic sciences—such as fingerprint matching—is far ahead of that of digital forensics. Today, most justice systems across the world still struggle with the concept of digital forensics while accepting the other established forensic sciences.

A lot of events have since happened that shaped and contributed to the standardization of the field. Some of the key events that helped strengthen and standardize the digital forensic field include the establishment of the International Organization on Computer Evidence (IOCE) in the 1990s with the mandate to standardize methods and harmonize principles among nations. Others are the Forensic Information Technology Working Group, established in 1998 by the European Network of Forensic Sciences Institute (ENFSI), the Scientific Working Group for Digital Evidence (SWGDE), and many others [20]. A lot has since happened in the development of the field. Garfinkel [43] classifies 1999–2007 as the "Golden Age" of digital forensics. Within this period, a lot happened in technology and capability in data recovery, network forensics, memory forensics, and many more.

3.4.2 *Definition of Digital Forensics*

Over the years, there have been many different definitions of digital forensics, many of which are fundamentally alike. The Digital Forensics Research Workshop (DFRWS) [28] defines digital forensics as:

> The use of scientifically derived and proven methods toward the preservation, collection, validation, identification, analysis, interpretation, documentation, and presentation of digital evidence derived from digital sources for the purpose of facilitating or furthering the reconstruction of events found to be criminal or helping to anticipate unauthorized actions shown to be disruptive to planned operations. (p. 3)

The United States Computer Emergency Response Team [80] defined computer forensics as the discipline that combines elements of law and computer science to collect and analyze data from computer systems, networks, wireless communications, and storage devices in a way that is admissible as evidence in a court of law. Over the years, the term computer forensics has proved to be limiting as digital evidence has increased across other devices. Today, digital evidence is ubiquitous: in mobile phones, routers, Global Positioning System (GPS), and many others [29]. Therefore, the term digital forensics is preferred by many, who feel it is more encompassing and not limiting in scope.

3.4.3 *Principles of Digital Forensics*

Forensics is a very methodical discipline that is rooted in science. Similarly, digital forensics is very methodical and ethical, requiring utmost care, precision, and strict adherence to standards. As a digital forensic examiner, it is important to always note that your report might end up in court, and it will be robustly scrutinized; therefore, it is important that evidence acquisition and analysis must be forensically sound and legally defensible. To ensure that there is a uniform standard and protocol, scholars and organizations have proposed good practice and principles for digital forensics. For instance, Casey's [21] principles of digital forensics summarized below captures this.

i. ***Evidence Exchange***—One of the foundational principles of forensic science is the Locard's Theory of Exchange. Dr. Edmond Locard, a French criminologist had proposed that, "the perpetrator of a crime will bring something to the crime scene and will leave with something from it." Over the years, this has proven to be true, not only in the terrestrial world, but also in the digital world. The same way a burglar leaves his fingerprint or hair at the crime scene is the same way a hacker leaves digital footprints on the system. These footprints can be found in the file system, registry, memory, system logs, network logs, and many other possibilities. Therefore, the job of a digital forensic examiner is to collect and analyse digital artifacts to look for these footprints.

ii. ***Evidence Characteristics***—Casey [21] noted that exchanges between the individual and crime scene will result in trace evidence, belonging to either of (1) evidence with attributes that fit in the group called *class characteristics* and (2) evidence with attributes that fall in the category called *individual characteristics.* In the digital world, evidence exchange leaves traces of both class characteristics and individual characteristics that could be crucial to solving a case.
iii. ***Forensic Soundness***—Evidence must be collected and preserved in a scientific manner. It is the responsibility of the digital forensic examiner or first responder to collect and preserve evidence in a manner that is considered forensically sound. For instance, if an examiner wants to acquire evidence from a hard drive, there are certain protocols expected, such as use of write blockers to protect the integrity of the drive.
iv. ***Authentication***—In simple terms, authentication is the process of ensuring that the acquired data is the same as that which was seized. While this can be easily verified in certain devices like a hard drive through methods such as hashing, it is not always the case with all devices. For instance, network logs are transient and always changing; memory captures show only the state of the memory at that time, and there is no other time a capture will produce same image, etc. Therefore, in legal terms, the simple definition of authentication above might be problematic. Casey [21] defines authentication for legal terms as process of determining whether the evidence is worthy.
v. ***Chain-of-Custody***—An important aspect of authentication is documenting the state and whereabout of the evidence item. At every given time, evidence must be accounted for—where it was sent to, who received it, who dispatched it, what time was it dispatched, etc. The chain of custody captures this and is a documentary proof that evidence was handled transparently. A good investigation might be lost in court once there are gaps in chain-of-custody, therefore, this is very important.
vi. ***Evidence Integrity***—This is the process of ensuring that evidence was not tempered with. Once evidence is tampered with, it could easily ruin the case being investigated. One important method of checking for integrity is through the use of massage digests and cryptographic hashing. Common algorithms for calculating message digests in digital forensics are MD5, SHA-1, SHA-2 [21]. Every device has a unique hash. The hash of the copied drive is compared with the original to see if it has changed. The minutest alteration on the device will lead to a change in the hash.
vii. ***Objectivity***—An important cornerstone of forensic science is objectivity [21]. It is the responsibility of the forensic examiner to report findings objectively, without any bias. A forensic examiner is not supposed to input his feelings in the report. As it is commonly said, it is better to let the evidence speak for itself.
viii. ***Repeatability***—An important feature of forensic science is repeatability. Analysis and observations made must be repeatable to allow for verifiability [21]. In other words, an analysis done by a forensic examiner, should be repeatable

and produce the same results. There are instances where a forensic examiner is called upon to repeat the forensic examination to verify findings of another examiner. This is one of the reasons why it is expected that a forensic examiner should document every step and process taken.

3.4.4 Digital Forensics Investigation Process Models

There have been several attempts to standardize the digital forensics investigation process. This has motivated several organizations to come up with formal investigative approaches and guidelines, known as forensic framework or models [29]. A formalized and methodical approach to investigation is good to serve as a guide for thorough and efficient investigation [21]. Casey and Schatz [22] traced the origin of the digital forensic process model to McKemmish's [54] definition of forensic computing. The steps identified in the definition—identification, preservation, analysis, and presentation—form the basis of the digital forensics investigation process model. Other scholars have built on this to propose other investigative models. There are different reasons which may inform the choice of any of these models; therefore, it is important to have a good knowledge of each, to have an informed decision. While it is impossible to exhaust all the models, a few have been considered and reviewed in this book.

Computer Forensic Process

The Computer Forensic Investigative Process was proposed in the year 1985. This model was patterned and mapped to the regular process of admission of documentary evidence in court [66]. It is a 4-step process consisting of the following steps: Acquisition, Identification, Evaluation and Admission [84]. While this model looks relatively straightforward, in practice, a modern-day digital investigation could be a lot more complex and dynamic. The computer forensic process is illustrated in Fig. 3.3.

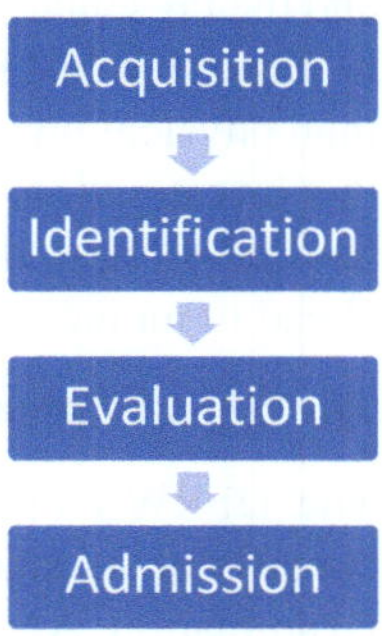

Fig. 3.3 Computer forensic process

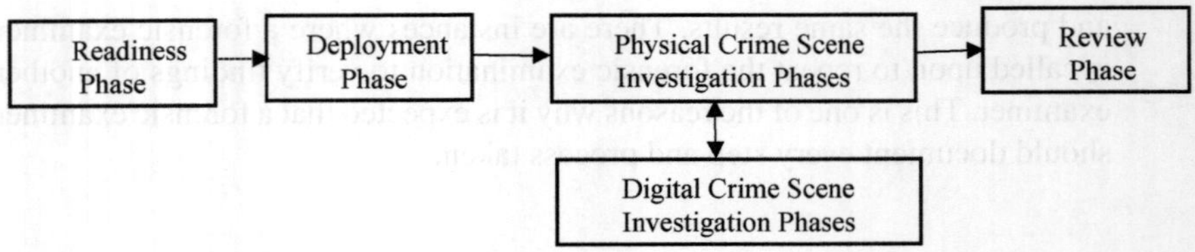

Fig. 3.4 Integrated digital investigation process

Physical Model

Carrier and Spafford [18] proposed an Integrated Digital Investigation Process Model derived from techniques and processes used in physical investigations. The model views the computer as a crime scene and Locard's exchange principle as the guiding theory. The model argues for the adoption of the sequence followed in a physical investigation in forensic investigations. The Integrated Digital Investigation Process model has 17 phases, grouped into five phases:

1. Readiness Phases
2. Deployment Phases
3. Physical Crime Scene Investigation Phases
4. Digital Crime Scene Phases
5. Review Phase.

Again, this is more oriented towards the physical crime scene, and may not suit our investigation in modern digital crimes. The integrated digital investigation process is showed in Fig. 3.4.

Event-Based Digital Forensics Investigation Framework

In arriving at this framework, Carrier and Spafford [18] simplified their Integrated Digital Investigation Process. The model has five primary phases, with possibilities of additional subphases. The five phases are: Readiness Phase, Deployment Phase, Physical Crime Scene Investigation phase, Digital Crime Scene Investigation phase and the Presentation Phase. The event-based digital forensic investigation framework is illustrated in Fig. 3.5. This model is more inclined towards digital investigation than physical investigation [3]. While there are aspects of this model that would suit this investigation, however, it is more suited for institutional teams. For instance, the readiness phase deals with getting the right equipment and training the personnel ahead of an incident happening.

The Digital Forensic Research Workshop (DFRWS) Framework

The DFRWS Framework was proposed in 2001 [29]. This investigative model consists of six standard steps, identified as: Identification, Preservation, Collection, Examination, Analysis and Presentation. Given its standardized nature, it became of

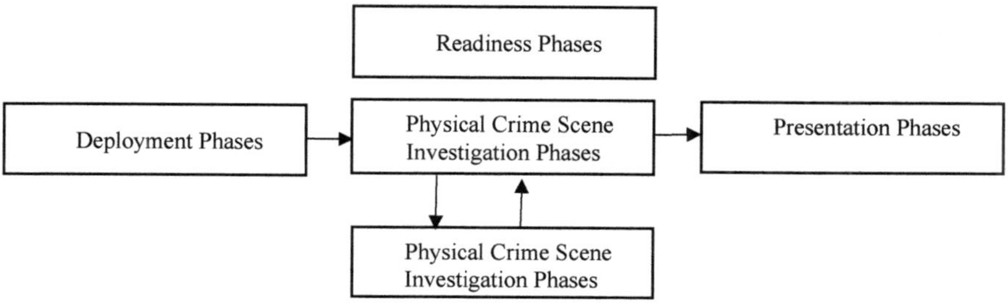

Fig. 3.5 Event-based digital forensics investigation framework

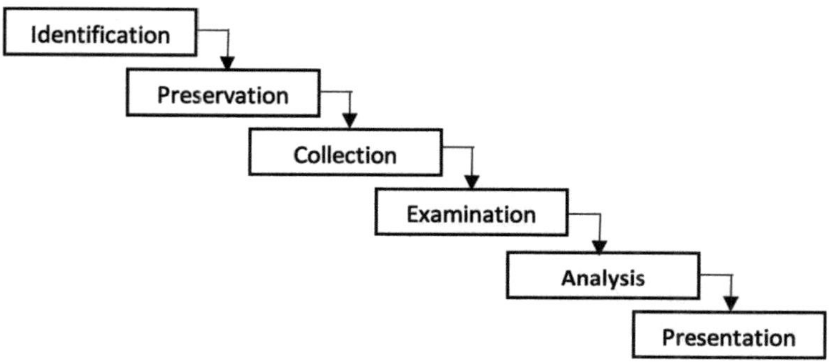

Fig. 3.6 DFRWS [28] investigative model

central interest to researchers that sort to improve on it [76]. This method is standard and straightforward and therefore can be considered for its simplicity. This framework is illustrated with Fig. 3.6.

Abstract Digital Forensic Model

The Abstract Digital Forensics Model was proposed by Reith et al. [69]. This model is essentially an improvement on the DFRWS Investigative Model. It captures all the aspects of the DFRWS Investigation, as well as the addition of new features. For instance, there is a possibility of an iteration between the Analysis and Examination processes, depending on the discoveries in the analysis. A major improvement of note (from the DFRWS Model) is the fact that it has a comprehensive pre and post-investigation procedure [76]. For instance, this model has a provision for returning the evidence, which is very important in this investigation. In view of the detailed nature of this model, including pre and post-investigation process, this model was adopted for this investigation. The abstract digital forensic model is captured in Fig. 3.7.

Others

The Law Enforcement Process Model captures five phases: preparation, collection, examination, analysis, and reporting [18]. Beebe and Clark's 15 Subphase Model

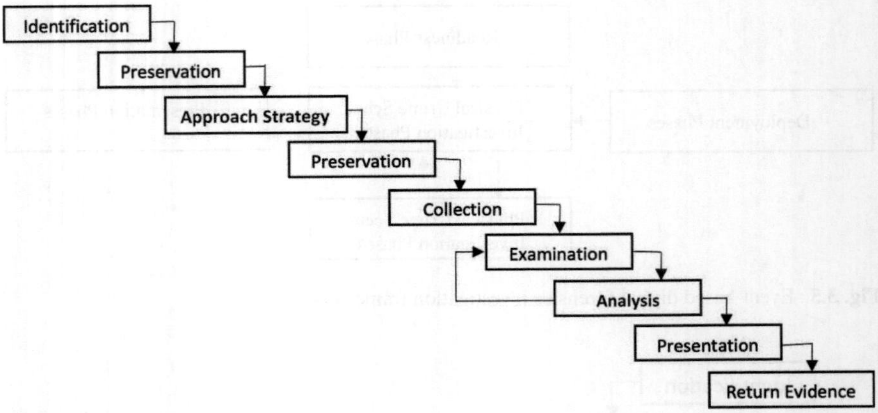

Fig. 3.7 Abstract digital forensic model

adopted a multilayered framework that incorporated phases present in other models and added a subphase with defined objectives [22]. Ciardhuáin's (2004) Evidence Flow Model extends beyond just the technical steps in digital forensic investigation to the non-technical measures, such as notification and transportation of evidence and defense of hypothesis [22]. Beyond these, many other digital forensic investigation models, such as the Harmonized Digital Forensic Investigation Process Model, attempted to harmonize existing models [82]. These models ensure the standardization of digital forensic investigations.

3.5 Digital Forensic Readiness

Although a relatively new term, digital forensic readiness has received a lot of attention in recent times. Digital forensic readiness is now an important terminology in the cybersecurity space. Pooe and Labuschagne [68] noted that research has proved that a comprehensive digital forensic strategy will provide organisations increased ability to respond to cybersecurity incidents, while maintaining the integrity of evidence and keeping the costs low. The term has grown beyond a consideration in risk management and incident response to an important regulatory issue in certain sectors. For instance, in Nigeria, the Central Bank of Nigeria (CBN) [24] released the Risk Based Cybersecurity Framework and Guidelines. In the document, the CBN recommended to the deposit money banks and Payment Service Providers in Nigeria to have "a forensic laboratory equipped with specialized forensic tools to support incident response investigation efforts". The framework also recommends constant training for the "the IR (digital forensic experts are usually a key member of incident response team) team on how to respond, report cyber-incidents, and conduct trend analysis to thwart future occurrence". In essence, the CBN is encouraging banks to build their level of digital forensic readiness.

Used first used by Tan [77], the term is defined as the organisation's readiness to minimise the cost of digital forensics, while maximizing the capability of an organization to collect evidence in a legally defensible manner. Pangalos and Katos [65] viewed it from the perspective of having relevant control to facilitate digital forensic investigation, defining forensic readiness as "the state of the organization where certain controls are in place in order to facilitate the digital forensic processes and to assist in the anticipation of unauthorized actions shown to be disruptive to planned operations". Similarly, Mohay (2005) define digital forensic readiness as "the extent to which computer systems or computer networks record activities and data in a manner such that the records are sufficient in their extent for subsequent forensic purposes, and such that the records are acceptable in terms of their perceived authenticity as evidence in subsequent forensic investigations."

From these definitions, the concept of digital forensic readiness has two primary objectives: to maximize the usefulness of evidence collected; and minimize the cost of investigations. Carrier and Spafford [18] further divided forensic readiness into operational readiness and infrastructural readiness, with the former being concerned with adequate training and equipment and the latter the efficient preservation of data. Rowlingson [71] defined digital forensic readiness as the ability of an organisation to maximise its potential to use digital evidence whilst minimising the costs of an investigation. However, Rowlingson [71] was also quick to observe the exclusion of prevention and recovery from this definition, and the assumption that this definition holds through with a competent Computer Incident Response Team (CSIRT).

It is instructive to note that digital forensics readiness has been studied from different perspectives. Therefore, you may find many literatures looking at it from the various perspectives. For instance, Elyas et al. [37] viewed digital forensic readiness from perspectives such as time, cost, training, and technology. Tan [77] identified the factors affecting the digital forensic readiness as:

- How logging is done
- What is logged
- Intrusion Detection System (IDS)
- Forensic Acquisition
- Evidence Handling.

Tan's [77] break down of the factors above appear limiting to network operations and forensic analysis. Digital Forensic readiness goes beyond just these aspects. Yasinsac and Manzano [83] viewed it from broader enterprise policies that could help an organization prevent and respond to cyber-attacks. The outlined policies are:

- Retaining Information
- Planning the Response
- Training
- Accelerating the Investigation
- Preventing Anonymous Activities
- Protecting the Evidence.

Elyas et al. [36] did a fantastic review of some of the perspectives that forensic readiness has been applied using groupings. These includes resourcing consideration [70], technology use and selection [19], training [19] [71], legal investigations [23], incident response [6], [73], [78] and policy formulation [83]. Elyas et al. [36] concluded that while these research works discussed digital forensic readiness from the respective perspective, it did not treat the topic holistically.

Also, the reviews from literature did not have anything in-depth for digital forensic readiness from a law enforcement point of view. The definitions of digital forensics reviewed and the literature presented appear constrained to the ability of an organization to minimise her digital forensic resources for incidents targeted at them. The challenge is that law enforcement agencies do more than respond to cyber-attacks targeted at them. They also conduct digital forensic examination for criminal investigations from citizens and the general public. Therefore, from a law enforcement point of view, this book synthesizes previous definitions to come up with a definition of digital forensic readiness as the ability of law enforcement agencies to efficiently maximise its investigative capabilities, both internally and externally, through the efficient use of digital forensic resources at minimal cost to the organization. Note that this definition captures their readiness to respond to internal incidents as well as perform their cybercrime investigative duties to the public.

3.5.1 Digital Forensics Readiness Frameworks

Different researchers have come up with many frameworks for Digital Forensic Readiness. For instance, Ngobeni et al. [58] came up with a conceptual model for wireless networks. Makutsoane and Leonard [53] came up with a forensic readiness model for a cloud service provider. Alenezi et al. [8] came up with a framework for measuring an organization's forensic readiness of cloud services. Almarzooqi and Jones' [9] framework for digital forensic readiness narrowed their model to assessing the core capabilities of a Digital Forensic Organization. Garba and Bade [41] proposed a Digital Forensic Readiness model for Nigerian banks. This improved previous research work with Zenith Bank, Nigeria, as a case study [42]. Englbrecht et al. [38] proposed a capability model for digital forensic readiness. There is available literature on existing digital forensics frameworks, leaving the forensic expert with many choice models.

3.5.2 Digital Forensic Readiness of the Nigerian Financial Crimes Agencies

Nigerian investigative agencies will need to attain a considerable level of digital forensic readiness to investigate Internet fraud and online financial crimes efficiently.

In Nigeria, the primary law enforcement agency for cybercrimes is the EFCC, and a complementary role by the Cybercrime division of the Nigerian Police [4, 7]. It is noteworthy to mention that some other agencies and institutions play a critical role in combatting cybercrime. For instance, the Office of the National Security Adviser plays a central role in cybercrime investigation, as host to Nigeria's Computer Emergency Response Team [16, 75]. They coordinate the nation's corporate response to cyber attacks. The scope of this research is limited to the investigative agencies—the EFCC and the Nigerian Police.

There is no available literature that exhaustively handles the digital forensic readiness of Nigeria's financial crimes agencies. However, notable works looked at digital forensic readiness elements of Nigeria's law enforcement agencies, such as technological readiness and personnel readiness. Previous studies only pointed to a lack of forensic resources as a significant setback to cybercrime investigation without investigating specific details [16, 62, 63]. In terms of accessible tools, available literature points to a noticeable gap. Ehimen and Bola [35], Olayemi [62], Oraegbunam [63], Chigozie-Okwum et al. [25], Tonye [79], Mohammed et al. [55], and Bello and Griffiths [16] all submitted that Nigeria's cybercrime agencies lacked digital forensic tools. Specifically, Tonye [79] supports this position, noting that the lack of digital forensic tools was a common challenge affecting the efficiency of the investigative process. Bello and Griffiths [16] also align with this position, stating that the agencies had expired software licenses due to funding challenges. Olayemi [62] also supports this position, noting that the Nigerian Police did not even have a digital forensic laboratory. This gap in available digital forensic tools is a significant setback to cybercrime investigation in Nigeria. The surge in cybercrime cases has further compounded the situation.

From the perspective of personnel adequacy and capability, available literature also points to a gap in resources. For instance, Bello and Griffiths [16], Mohammed et al. [55], Tonye [79], Chigozie-Okwum et al. [25] all agree that there was a gap in the adequacy and capability of talented human resources. Particularly, Chigozie-Okwum et al. [25] stressed the lack of officers with technological skills as a significant concern and the root cause behind Nigeria's rising status as a haven for cybercriminals. This position is consistent with Eboibi [31], who argued that Nigeria lacks technologically savvy personnel and cyber forensic investigators. Olayemi [62] also supports this position that there is an inadequate number of trained personnel. Mohammed et al. [55] also submitted that Researchers generally accept Nigerian cybercrime investigators' lack of forensic capacity.

Analyzing available literature shows the need for constant training of cybercrime investigators, given the reported gap in technological capability. Olayemi [62] submitted that the lack of training opportunities meant a shortage of adequately trained personnel, which impacted the prosecution of financial crimes in Nigeria. To address these gaps, Oraegbunam [63], Chigozie-Okwum et al. [25], Abu et al. [2], and Eboibi [31] all pointed to the need for continuous training for cybercrime investigators and digital forensics experts in Nigeria's financial crimes agencies.

Nigeria has upgraded investigative and enforcement agencies' digital forensics laboratory and technical capability to combat the growing cybercrime challenges.

While some of the efforts at boosting the digital forensic capacity of the law enforcement agencies have been through national initiatives, others have been through technical collaborations with international allies. For instance, in 2013, the British law enforcement agency donated digital forensic equipment to the EFCC [33]. Also, in 2018 the National Crime Agency of the United Kingdom donated digital forensic equipment worth over £500,000 to the EFCC forensic laboratory of the principal cybercrime agency, the Economic and Financial Crimes Commission [34]. There have also been training collaborations to build staff capacity in digital evidence acquisition and forensic analysis. These were some of the efforts put in place to improve the Digital Forensic Readiness of the cybercrime agency.

References

1. Abhulimhen-Iyoha A (2020) Criminal matters and admissibility of electronic evidence in Nigeria. Afr J Crim Law Jurisprud 5. http://journals.ezenwaohaetorc.org/index.php/AFJCLJ/article/viewFile/983/987
2. Abu SO, Lateef OM, Echobu J (2018) Determinants of cyber fraud investigation in Nigeria. Account Tax Rev 2(2)
3. Abulaish M (2018) Advances in digital forensics frameworks and tools: a comparative insight and ranking. Int J Digit Crime Forensics 10(2)
4. Adesina OS (2017) Cybercrime and poverty in Nigeria. Can Soc Sci 13(4):19–29
5. Agwu SK (2019) Appraisal of electronic evidence in Nigerian Courts. Soc Sci Res Netw. https://doi.org/10.2139/ssrn.3592650
6. Ahmed I, Obermeier S, Naedele M, Richard III GG (2012) Scada systems: challenges for forensic investigators. Computer 45(12):44–51
7. Ajetunmobi RA, Uwadia CO, Oladeji FA (2016) Computer forensic guideline: a requirement for fighting cyber crime in Nigeria now? In: UNILAG research conference 2016, Nigeria. https://ir.unilag.edu.ng/handle/123456789/5833
8. Alenezi A, Hussein RK, Walters RJ, Wills GB (2017) A framework for cloud forensic readiness in organizations. In: 2017 5th IEEE international conference on mobile cloud computing, services, and engineering (MobileCloud), pp 199–204. https://doi.org/10.1109/MobileCloud.2017.12
9. Almarzooqi A, Jones A (2016) A framework for assessing the core capabilities of a digital forensic organization. In: IFIP international conference on digital forensics, Jan 2016. Springer, Cham, pp 47–65
10. Anjelica Cappellino JD (2022) Daubert vs. Frye: navigating the standards of admissibility for expert testimony. Expert Institute. www.expertinstitute.com/resources/insights/daubert-vs-frye-navigating-the-standards-of-admissibility-for-expert-testimony/
11. Antwi-Boasiako A, Venter H (2017) A model for digital evidence admissibility assessment. In: Advances in digital forensics XIII: 13th IFIP WG 11.9 international conference, Orlando, FL, 30 Jan–1 Feb 2017. Revised selected papers 13. Springer International Publishing, pp 23–38
12. Anyebe PA (2019) Appraisal of admissibility of electronic evidence in legal proceedings in Nigeria. J Law Policy Glob 92:1
13. Arshad H, Jantan AB, Abiodun OI (2018) Digital forensics: review of issues in scientific validation of digital evidence. J Inf Process Syst 14(2)
14. Association of Chief Police Offices (2012) Forensic examination of digital evidence: a guide for law enforcement. https://nij.ojp.gov/library/publications/forensic-examination-digital-evidence-guide-law-enforcement

15. Beebe NL, Clark JG (2005) A hierarchical, objectives-based framework for the digital investigations process. Digital Investigation 2(2):147–167
16. Bello M, Griffiths M (2021) Routine activity theory and cybercrime investigation in Nigeria: how capable are law enforcement agencies? In: Rethinking cybercrime. Palgrave Macmillan, Cham, pp 213–235
17. Borders Jr JD (1988) Fit to be Fryed: Frye v. United States and the admissibility of novel scientific evidence. Ky Law J 77:849
18. Carrier B, Spafford E (2004) An event-based digital forensic investigation framework. Digit Investig. https://dfrws.org/wp-content/uploads/2019/06/2004_USA_paper-an_event-based_digital_forensic_investigation_framework.pdf
19. Carrier B, Spafford EH (2003) Getting physical with the digital investigation process. Int J digital evid 2(2):1–20
20. Casey E (2019) The chequered past and risky future of digital forensics. Aust J Forensic Sci 51(6):649–664
21. Casey E (2011) Digital evidence and computer crime: forensic science, computers, and the internet. Academic Press
22. Casey E, Schatz B (2011) Conducting digital investigations. In: Casey E (ed) Digital evidence and computer crime: forensic science, computer and the internet, 3rd edn, pp 187–227
23. Casey E (2005) Case study: network intrusion investigation–lessons in forensic preparation. Digital Investigation 2(4):254–260
24. Central Bank of Nigeria (2018) Risk-based cybersecurity framework and guidelines for deposit money banks and payment service providers. https://www.cbn.gov.ng/out/2018/bsd/risk%20based%20cybersecurity%20framework%20exposure%20draft%20june.pdf
25. Chigozie-Okwum C, Ugboaja S, Micheal D, Osuo-Genseleke M (2017) Proliferation of cyber insecurity in Nigeria: a root cause analysis. AFRREV STECH Int J Sci Technol 6(2):53–60
26. Ciardhuáin, S. Ó. (2004). An extended model of cybercrime investigations. International Journal of Digital Evidence, 3(1), 1–22.
27. Daubert v, Merrell Dow Pharmaceuticals (1993) https://nij.ojp.gov/sites/g/files/xyckuh171/files/media/document/frye-v-US.pdf
28. Digital Forensics Research Workshop (2001) Defining digital forensic examination and analysis tools. https://www.dfrws.org/sites/default/files/session-files/pres-defining_digital_forensic_examination_and_analysis_tools.pdf
29. Easttom C (2019) System forensics, investigation, and response, 3rd edn. Jones & Bartlett Learning
30. Eboibi FE (2017) A review of the legal and regulatory frameworks of Nigerian Cybercrimes Act 2015. Comput Law Secur Rev 33(5):700–717
31. Eboibi FE (2021) Cybercriminals and coronavirus cybercrimes in Nigeria, the United States of America and the United Kingdom: cyber hygiene and preventive enforcement measures. Commonw Law Bull 47(1):113–142
32. Eboibi FE, Mac-Barango I (2020) Law and judicial application of digital forensic evidence in Nigeria. J Law Policy Glob 96:61–75
33. Economic and Financial Crimes Commission (2013) UK government donates forensic equipment to EFCC. https://efccnigeria.org/efcc/news/576-uk-government-donates-forensic-equipment-to-efcc
34. Economic and Financial Crimes Commission (2018) UK to support EFCC's anti-corruption fight with digital forensic technology. https://efccnigeria.org/efcc/news/3328-uk-to-support-efcc-s-anti-corruption-fight-with-digital-forensic-technology
35. Ehimen OR, Bola A (2010) Cybercrime in Nigeria. Bus Intell J 3(1):93–98
36. Elyas M, Ahmad A, Maynard SB, Lonie A (2015) Digital forensic readiness: expert perspectives on a theoretical framework. Comput Secur 52:70–89
37. Elyas M, Maynard SB, Ahmad A, Lonie A (2014) Towards a systemic framework for digital forensic readiness. J Comput Inf Syst 54(3):97–105
38. Englbrecht L, Meier S, Pernul G (2019) Towards a capability maturity model for digital forensic readiness. Wireless Netw 1–13

39. Erugo S (2020) Admissibility of electronic evidence in Nigeria: some contending issues. Benson Idahosa Univ Law J 2:22
40. Frye v United States (1923) https://nij.ojp.gov/sites/g/files/xyckuh171/files/media/document/frye-v-US.pdf
41. Garba AA, Bade AM (2019) A recommended digital forensics readiness framework for Nigerian banks. Int J Dev Res 9(08)
42. Garba AA, Siraj MM (2015) A holistic-based digital forensic readiness framework for Zenith Bank, Nigeria. In: International conference on computational and social sciences, pp 551–560
43. Garfinkel SL (2010) Digital forensics research: the next 10 years. Digit Investig 7:S64–S73. https://doi.org/10.1016/j.diin.2010.05.009
44. Godwins RN (2023) Fundamentals of criminal prosecutions. TND Press
45. Holt TJ, Bossler AM, Seigfried-Spellar KC (2022) Cybercrime and digital forensics: an introduction. Routledge
46. Horsman G (2017) Can we continue to effectively police digital crime? Sci Justice 57(6):448–454. https://doi.org/10.1016/j.scijus.2017.06.001
47. Kao D-Y, Wu N-C, Tsai F (2019) The governance of digital forensic investigation in law enforcement agencies. In: 2019 21st international conference on advanced communication technology (ICACT), pp 61–65. https://doi.org/10.23919/ICACT.2019.8701995
48. Koehler JJ (2018) How trial judges should think about forensic science evidence. Judicature 102:28
49. Kwong L (2019) Scientific evidence admissibility: improving judicial proceedings to decrease erroneous outcomes. Themis Res J Just Stud Forensic Sci 7(1):5
50. Leppänen A, Kankaanranta T (2017) Cybercrime investigation in Finland. J Scand Stud Criminol Crime Prev 18(2):157–175
51. Lillis D, Becker B, O'Sullivan T, Scanlon M (2016) Current challenges and future research areas for digital forensic investigation. arXiv: [Cs]. http://arxiv.org/abs/1604.03850
52. Lorraine v. Markel American Insurance Company (2007) https://www.govinfo.gov/content/pkg/USCOURTS-mdd-1_06-cv-01893/pdf/USCOURTS-mdd-1_06-cv-01893-0.pdf
53. Makutsoane MP, Leonard A (2014) A conceptual framework to determine the digital forensic readiness of a cloud service provider. In: Proceedings of PICMET'14 conference: Portland international center for management of engineering and technology; infrastructure and service integration, July 2014, pp 3313–3321
54. McKemmish R (1999) What is forensic computing? In: Trends and issues in crime and justice, pp 1–6. https://pdfs.semanticscholar.org/5c95/45d29c7fff482c9d70c1e3161df3e0683f4e.pdf
55. Mohammed KH, Mohammed YD, Solanke AA (2019) Cybercrime and digital forensics: bridging the gap in legislation, investigation, and prosecution of cybercrime in Nigeria. Int J Cybersecur Intell Cybercrime 2(1):56–63
56. Mohay, G. (2005, November). Technical challenges and directions for digital forensics. In First International Workshop on Systematic Approaches to Digital Forensic Engineering (SADFE'05) (pp. 155–161). IEEE
57. National Institute of Justice (2020) Digital evidence policies and procedures manual. https://nij.ojp.gov/library/publications/digital-evidence-policies-and-procedures-manual
58. Ngobeni S, Venter H, Burke I (2010) A forensic readiness model for wireless networks. In: Chow K-P, Shenoi S (eds) Advances in digital forensics, vol VI
59. Nwafor IE (2022) Cybercrime and the law: issues and developments in Nigeria
60. Obamanu G (2023) Legal issues and challenges in the admissibility of digital forensic evidence in courts in Nigeria. AJIEEL 8(01):96–109
61. Obideyi OM (2022) Cybercrime and digital evidence: the Nigeria Police Force in perspective. In: The 178th international training course on criminal justice—cybercrime and digital evidence. www.unafei.or.jp/publications/pdf/RS_No114/No114_23_PART_THREE_Participants_Papers_02.pdf
62. Olayemi OJ (2014) A socio-technological analysis of cybercrime and cyber security in Nigeria. Int J Sociol Anthropol 6(3):116–125

63. Oraegbunam IK (2015) The Nigerian police and problems of cybercrime investigation: need for adequate training. Niger Law J 18(1):1–28
64. Overill RE, Silomon JA (2010) Digital meta-forensics: quantifying the investigation. In: Proceedings of 4th international conference on cybercrime forensics education & training (CFET 2010), Canterbury, UK, Sept 2010
65. Pangalos G, Katos V (2010) Information assurance and forensic readiness. In: Next generation society. Technological and legal issues: third international conference, e-democracy 2009, Athens, Greece, 23–25 Sept 2009. Revised selected papers 3. Springer Berlin Heidelberg, pp 181–188
66. Pollitt M (1995) Computer forensics: an approach to evidence in cyberspace. In: Proceedings of the national information systems security conference, vol 2, pp 487–491
67. Pooe A, Labuschagne L (2012) A conceptual model for digital forensic readiness. In: 2012 information security for South Africa, Aug 2012. IEEE, pp 1–8
68. Pooe A, Labuschagne L (2013) Cognitive approaches for digital forensic readiness planning. In: Advances in digital forensics IX: 9th IFIP WG 11.9 international conference on digital forensics, Orlando, FL, 28–30 Jan 2013. Revised selected papers 9. Springer Berlin Heidelberg, pp 53–66
69. Reith M, Carr C, Gunsch G (2002) An examination of digital forensic models. Int J Digit Evid 1(3):1–12. https://www.just.edu.jo/~Tawalbeh/nyit/incs712/digital_forensic.pdf
70. Reyes A, Wiles J (2007) Developing an enterprise digital investigative/electronic discovery capability. In: The best damn cybercrime and digital forensics book period. Syngress, pp 83–114
71. Rowlingson R (2004) A ten step process for forensic readiness. Int J Digit Evid 2(3):1–28
72. Ryan DJ, Shpantzer G (2002) Legal aspects of digital forensics. In: Proceedings: forensics workshop, Sept 2002
73. Shedden Piya, Atif Ahmad, Ruighaver A B (2010) Organisational learning and incident response: promoting effective learning through the incident response process
74. Sommer P (2004) The future for the policing of cybercrime. Comput Fraud Secur 2004(1):8–12
75. Symantec Corporation and African Union (2016) Cybercrime & cybersecurity trends in Africa. www.thehaguesecuritydelta.com/media/com_hsd/report/135/document/Cyber-security-trends-report-Africa-en.pdf
76. Tahiri S (2016) Digital forensic models. https://resources.infosecinstitute.com/topic/digital-forensics-models/
77. Tan J (2001) Forensic readiness. @ Stake, Cambridge, MA, pp 1–23
78. Tan T, Ruighaver AB, Ahmad A (2003, November) Incident Handling: where the need for planning is often not recognised. In 1st Australian computer, network & information forensics conference (pp. 1–10).
79. Tonye WS (2018) Cyber forensic and data collection challenges in Nigeria. Glob J Comput Sci Technol 18(3)
80. United States Computer Emergency Response Team (2008) Computer forensics. https://us-cert.cisa.gov/sites/default/files/publications/forensics.pdf
81. United States Department of Justice (2004) Forensic examination of digital evidence: guide for law enforcement. https://nij.ojp.gov/library/publications/forensic-examination-digital-evidence-guide-law-enforcement
82. Valjarevic A, Venter HS (2012) Harmonized digital forensic investigation process model. In: 2012 information security for South Africa, Aug 2012, pp 1–10
83. Yasinsac A, Manzano Y (2001) Policies to enhance computer and network forensics. In: Proceedings of the 2001 IEEE workshop on information assurance and security, June 2001, pp 289–295
84. Yusoff Y, Ismail R, Hassan Z (2011) Common phases of computer forensics investigation models. Int J Comput Sci Inf Technol 3(3):17–31

Chapter 4
Methodology

Abstract This chapter presents the methodology for this research. The chapter begins with the research statement, purpose of study, research objectives, and research questions. The study has two primary research questions and 9 research subquestions. This study was structured as a qualitative case study, relying on semi-structured interviews, review of reports, official documents, and archival records. The research population was the Economic and Financial Crimes Commission (EFCC) and the Nigeria Police Force. The research sample consisted of 18 cybercrime investigators, prosecutors, and digital forensic examiners. This chapter ends by presenting the processing and analysis methods. The qualitative analysis tool, NVivo, was used to analyse the interview transcript.

Keywords Cybercrime · EFCC · Economic and Financial Crimes Commission · Nigeria Police · Digital forensic resources · Digital forensic readiness · Cybercrime caseloads · Qualitative case study

4.1 Introduction

In Chaps. 1 and 2, the study outlined key literature on cybercrime, digital forensics, and law enforcement in Nigeria. These two chapters provide the research foundations on the nature of the cybercrime challenge in Nigeria. Despite the rich reviews from literature, the study exposed gaps. First, despite the fact that all literature reviewed highlighted the rising caseloads, there were no studies that drilled deeper to specifics of this rise. For instance, how many convictions were made over the last 5 years? What are the frequent cybercrime types in Nigeria? How sophisticated are cybercriminals in Nigeria? What are the trends and dynamics fueling the surge in cybercrime caseloads? And many other questions that will be critical to solving the cybercrime problem in Nigeria.

R. T. Sibe and C. Kaunert, *Cybercrime, Digital Forensic Readiness, and Financial Crime Investigation in Nigeria*, Advanced Sciences and Technologies for Security Applications, https://doi.org/10.1007/978-3-031-54089-9_4

The findings from the reviews done in Chaps. 1 and 2 also pointed to lack of forensic resources among the cybercrime agencies in Nigeria. While this was agreed by several researchers, there were gaps in specificity. The opinions on this appear anecdotal, and it was important to investigate this in a structured manner. With these gaps found in the literature, this research was structured to investigate the extent of the lack of forensic resources in the cybercrime law enforcement agencies in Nigeria and how this has affected the fight against cybercrimes. This chapter presents the methodology for this study.

4.2 Statement of the Problem

Nigeria is one of the cybercrime hotbeds in the world. This increased cybercrime activity has led to very high caseloads, making it increasingly difficult for law enforcement to efficiently investigate and prosecute perpetrators [9]. While several articles did point to the overwhelming caseloads, there are no studies that interrogated the numbers and the dynamics of the cybercrime caseloads in Nigeria. This research seeks to look at the specifics of what constitutes these numbers—the specific number of cybercrime convictions, cybercrime taxonomy, reasons fueling the case loads, trends and patterns, and other dynamics.

Also, existing studies highlight Nigeria's law enforcement agencies' deficiencies as a significant impediment to the fight against cybercrime. For instance, Olayemi [35], Oraegbunam [37], and Bello and Griffiths [4] all pointed to this lack of forensic capabilities of the law enforcement agencies. However, none of these studies drilled into the specifics of the lack of technology, human resources, technical capabilities, and others. Little is known of the parameters and magnitude of this lack. It is essential to get a proper resource inventory of the agencies' forensic capabilities to confront the growing threat of financial crimes successfully. The lack of such clear information makes it challenging to develop a roadmap for digital forensic readiness and capability maturity for the law enforcement agencies in Nigeria.

4.3 Purpose of Study

The purpose of this qualitative multiple case study is to understand the dynamics and complexity of cybercrime investigation in Nigeria and to identify the extent of the lack of digital forensic resources amongst law enforcement agencies in Nigeria and how this affects the cybercrime caseloads and prosecution. Law enforcement agencies in Nigeria continue to struggle with the cybercrime caseloads [9]. While this apparent lack of forensic resources is evident from the outside, this study, a qualitative case study, identified the extent of the lack of digital forensic resources, both from the insider's perspective and from available literature and documents. Good knowledge of the dynamics and complexity of the cybercrime scourge and the scale and scope of the lack of digital forensic resources will be an essential first step to developing a digital forensic readiness roadmap or digital forensic capability maturity model.

4.4 Research Objectives

Most of the research on the cybercrime caseloads in Nigeria end with generalized findings, pointing to a high caseload. There are no studies that drill into the specifics of what constitutes the numbers—the actual figures, the number of convictions, the cybercrime taxonomy, and any other trend or dynamics behind the surge.

Also, a key objective of this study is to examine the lack of digital forensic resources at the law enforcement agencies in Nigeria. The study identified the gaps in digital forensics skillset and technological capabilities and how this has affected Nigeria's fight against internet fraud and financial crimes. This research is a case study, with the research population consisting of the two major agencies in Nigeria responsible for law enforcement and prosecution of internet fraud and financial crimes. The two agencies considered in this research are Nigeria Police Force (NPF) and the Economic and Financial Crimes Commission (EFCC). The outcome of this study could help shape policy formulation and serve as a basis for developing a roadmap for upgrading forensic capability and bridging the technological gaps in the agencies.

4.5 Research Questions

The study has two primary research questions. The first primary research question has seven research subquestions and the second primary research question has two research subquestion listed below:

Primary Research Question 1: What is the assessment of digital forensic resources and capabilities of law enforcement agencies in Nigeria?

Research Subquestion 1: What challenges prevent law enforcement agencies in Nigeria from having adequate forensic capabilities and being forensically ready?
Research Subquestion 2: What is the extent of digital forensic tools adoption by Nigerian law enforcement agents?
Research Subquestion 3: How has the lack of digital forensic resources affected the law enforcement agencies in Nigeria, and by extension, their efficiency in the fight to stop cybercrime?
Research Subquestion 4: What are the areas of digital forensic skills deficiency needing an upgrade?
Research Subquestion 5: What is the specific digital forensic training needed by law enforcement agents in Nigeria?

Research Subquestion 6: What specific digital forensic tools are in short supply or with expired licenses needing an upgrade?
Research Subquestion 7: What are the daily cybercrime caseload and available digital forensics resources?

Primary Research Question 2: What is the composition and complexity of the cybercrime cases in Nigeria?

Research Subquestion 1: What are the frequent cybercrimes committed in Nigeria?
Research Subquestion 2: How many persons are convicted of cybercrime in Nigeria?

4.6 Research Paradigm

This study examined the lack of forensic resources and the digital forensic readiness of law enforcement agencies in Nigeria. This research used the qualitative case study method to investigate the lack of digital forensic resources amongst Nigeria's two primary cybercrime and financial crime prevention and prosecution agencies. A qualitative study is suitable when investigating a relatively unknown phenomenon or subject of interest, and the resources available will allow for interviews and reviews of related documents [17]. It is exploratory, and therefore more suitable in the context of this study.

Specifically, the research adopted the case study approach, which is a type of qualitative paradigm. Yin [50] gives four scenarios suitable for qualitative case studies. These includes:

1. When answers to the "how" and "why" questions are critical to research;
2. When it is impossible to manipulate research participants;
3. When the contextual conditions are relevant to study; and
4. When there is an unclear boundary between the phenomenon of interest and the prevailing contexts.

This research fits the four conditions specified by Yin [50], which informed the choice of a qualitative case study. Qualitative case studies are structured for a phenomenon to be explored within its context to understand complex issues. Case studies allow several data sources to provide a multidimensional view of the phenomenon under review [2, 52]. Case studies explore details from the lenses of participants from multiple sources. Such a broad perspective is good for in-depth investigation, such as this research. By structuring this as a case study, the lack of forensic resources amongst law enforcement agencies in Nigeria can be analyzed in-depth, from different sources, including serving officers, documents, publications, and other stakeholders, where necessary. Also, a case study review of casefiles, reports, and official documents will reveal the exact specifics and dynamics of the cybercrime caseloads in Nigeria, beyond the often generalized reports and newspaper headlines on the issue.

4.7 Research Design

This research used the steps outlined by Baxter and Jack [2]. An essential first step in a case study is the determination of the case. Miles and Huberman [28] define a "case" as a phenomenon occurring in a bounded context. It is the unit of analysis. This research established the lack of digital forensic resources in Nigeria's financial crimes agencies as the case. The definition of the boundary followed once the "case" was determined [43, 50]. Defining the boundaries will keep the research focused. This research is limited to the law enforcement agencies in Nigeria responsible for combatting financial crimes—EFCC and the Nigeria Police Force.

4.7.1 Rigor and Quality

From a historical perspective, critics noted that qualitative research lacked rigor, due primarily to what critics thought were subjective and anecdotal dispositions [26]. This perception has changed over time, as qualitative research is now widely accepted as an established research paradigm like quantitative [49]. One thing that is common to both paradigms is the need for rigor and quality. While quantitative research addresses criteria such as reliability and validity [24], Lincoln and Guba [22] posit that qualitative research should ensure trustworthiness by addressing four criteria: credibility, transferability, dependability, and confirmability.

Credibility. The concept of credibility is basically how congruent research findings are concerning reality [27]. This research adopted the following methods to ensure credibility:

1. ***Prolonged engagement***. This research ensured prolonged engagement of the researchers and participants for the researchers to have ample time to understand the research environment and participants [12, 27]. The researchers gave participants sufficient time to answer questions and follow-up questions. Designing the research for prolonged engagement to better understand the research participants—in this case, the law enforcement agencies in Nigeria—addressed the issue of credibility.
2. ***Persistent observation***. This study was structured to adopt persistent observation to provide depth in research findings [22]. Such prolonged interaction with participants gave room for this study to understand the research environment and participants better. The researchers noted all observations and engaged participants on any observations of interest to the study.

3. ***Triangulation***. Triangulation involves using multiple data sources to understand better what is being studied [27]. Themes derived from numerous sources can be more easily justified than those derived from just a handful [7]. This research used data from different sources, such as interviews, official documents, websites, case files and court judgement, and news articles. The paper also compared findings with recent peer-reviewed publications. Themes were created from the various submissions by the participants to ensure validity.
4. ***Rich and thick description***. The use of detailed and thick descriptions to describe research findings. Describing findings in great detail adds to the credibility of the research [22]. This research adopted this approach to ensure depth. The researchers presented the research findings in great detail.
5. ***Member checks***. This process ensures that information recorded for each participant is what was intended by the participant [22]. In this study, interviewees had a chance to request their transcripts to ensure that recording accurately represented the participant's intended response. Interviews were structured to allow time to review answers across participant(s) before a follow-up interview.
6. ***Peer debriefing and external audit process to avoid researcher's bias***. This method enhances the credibility of qualitative research [22]. This method is beneficial in ensuring that the investigation is not influenced or shaped by the researchers' biases. In this research, the researchers field-tested the primary interview questions by getting the reviews of four different researchers. The qualifications of the field test participants include a Ph.D. holder in Artificial and Computational Intelligence, with over two decades of research and industry experience, two Ph.D. candidates of Information Technology (Digital Forensics Specialty); and a Ph.D. Candidate in Engineering Management, all with over a decade of professional experience. All four participants agreed with the structure, language, and suitability of the questions concerning the research questions and the problem statement.
7. ***Negative cases***. One way to enhance qualitative research credibility is by reporting emerging responses that contradict the research expectations [5]. This research reported all findings, including emerging findings that do not necessarily corroborate research expectations. An analysis of the negative cases was done and documented. This level of transparency adds to the credibility of a qualitative study.

Transferability. This research allowed findings to be transferred to other settings or groups to ensure rigor. This criterion for qualitative studies is known as transferability [18]. That is, generalizing research findings in another environment outside of the scope of this study. This research adopted detailed and thick descriptions to add more details, clarity, and insight [6]. When the researcher gives sufficient information and all assumptions clearly stated, it clarifies the applicability of the research method and outcome in another setting.

Dependability. This criterion has to do with data stability over time [15]. This research allowed layers of review to ensure dependability and reliability [46]. The study also went through at least two institutional scrutiny and quality review process.

Also, to ensure dependability, all processes in this research were recorded in detail so that another researcher could easily understand and repeat the process [42].

Confirmability. This criterion for establishing trustworthiness has to do with data accuracy and neutrality [46]. The qualitative researchers ought to show that the outcome reflects data gotten from participants and not induced from his personal experiences and biases [6]. The researchers recorded all interview sessions with a Sony digital recorder. The recorded sessions were played many times and compared with the transcripts. This research had layers of supervision and reviews to establish confirmability. Also, the study used triangulation to ensure confirmability [21]. Using data from many sources added to the confirmability of this qualitative research.

4.7.2 Population

A research population is a demography that is studied. Members have shared characteristics that are of interest to the research. Organizational, spatial, or demographical factors determine the research population [11]. This study investigated the specifics of what constitutes the cybercrime caseloads in Nigeria—the actual figures, the number of convictions, the cybercrime taxonomy, and any other trend or dynamics behind the surge. The study also investigated the lack of forensic resources amongst financial crimes agencies in Nigeria. In Nigeria, according to the enactment of the EFCC Act 2004, the Economic and Financial Crimes Commission (EFCC) was set up with the sole purpose of investigating and prosecuting financial crimes [32, 47]. Also, the Nigerian Police Force has a Fraud Investigating Unit dedicated to investigating fraud and financial crimes. They also have a dedicated cybercrime unit with a mandate to crack down on cybercrime [31, 48]. In 2022, the Inspector General of Police announced a merger of all cybercrime related departments, under the newly formed Nigeria Police Force National Cyber-crime Centre, currently under the Force Criminal Investigations Department, Force Headquarters, Abuja [41]. This was to give way for focused unit for better efficiency in investigating and prosecuting cybercrime.

Also, in exercise of its responsibilities as contained in the Cybercrime (Prohibition, Prevention, etc.) Act 2015, the Office of the National Security Adviser coordinates stakeholder input and release the National Cybersecurity Strategy and Policy, on behalf of the President of the Federal Republic of Nigeria. Two editions have since been released; one in 2014 and a review in 2021. The last edition which was released in 2021 also outlined structural measures in line with the extant provisions. For instance, the National Computer Emergency Response Team, also known as the Nigeria Computer Emergency Response Team (ngCERT), the focal point of the nation's cyber incident response management is now domiciled under the National Cybersecurity Coordination Centre (NCCC).

Also, to be domiciled under the NCCC is the National Digital Forensic Laboratory (NDFL), to provide the requisite tools and facilities for investigation and intelligence gathering of cyber related issues. Also, in reflection of the growing call for the amendment of the Cybercrime (Prohibition, Prevention, etc.) Act 2015, the Cybersecurity Advisory Council (CAC) is charged with the responsibility of driving the process for the amendment [33]. However, despite playing such a key role in the nation's corporate response to cybercrime, the Office of the National Security Adviser is not a frontline prosecutorial agency like the Nigeria Police Force or the Economic and Financial Crimes Commission.

Beyond this, the Independent Corrupt Practices and Other Related Offences Commission (ICPC) also investigates cybercrime related offences. Although the establishment act predates the cybercrime act 2017, and did not specifically mention cybercrime, however, specific sections of the Establishment Act, such as sections 15 and 43 did make reference to investigating computer related crimes. Therefore, while the commission is focused on investigating corruption, they also investigate the intersection of computers and digital technology used for perpetrating crime—and this falls within the context of cybercrime. For instance, in 2022, the ICPC busted a cybercrime syndicate in connection to a N30.4 million fraud [20]. To boost their investigative capacity, the commission had in 2012 set up a digital forensic laboratory [19].

In this study, the population consisted of the Economic and Financial Crimes Commission (EFCC) and the Nigerian Police Force, the two leading agencies responsible for financial crimes investigation. These two organizations have staff with access to digital forensic resources, and they formed the core of this qualitative case study. The two organisations principally investigate cybercrime in Nigeria, hence their choice as the research population.

4.7.3 Sample

While it could perhaps look interesting to study the entire population, this is not always practical or ethical. The challenge was to determine what should constitute an appropriate sample size. Marshall [25] suggested that the correct sample size should sufficiently answer the research question. Certain factors may affect the estimate for the number of participants in a study. These include scope, data quality, nature of the research topic, and the valuable information from each participant [30]. This study was structured to focus on the law enforcement agencies principally responsible for financial crimes prosecution.

The primary investigating agency for Internet fraud and financial crimes in Nigeria is the Economic and Financial Crimes Commission (EFCC). Set up by the Economic and Financial Crimes Commission (EFCC) Act 2004, the commission's mandate extends beyond Internet fraud to other financial crimes [32, 47]. From 2010 to 2015, the commission investigated 15,124 petitions, securing only 568 convictions between 2010 and 2015 [36].

In 2022, the commission secured a total of 3785 convictions across all it's command, representing an improvement of 70.5% and a success rate of 98.93%

in convictions (losing only 41 cases—representing 1.07%). Following the previous trends, the zones with the top three convictions are Lagos (765), Ibadan Command (573 convictions) and Port Harcourt Command (567 convictions) [10]. Previous conviction statistics shows that majority of the convictions by EFCC are cybercrime related. For instance, in 2021, 80% of the convictions by EFCC were cybercrime related [14].

However, other agencies often play overlapping roles in this regard. For instance, the Nigerian Police Force has a dedicated cybercrime unit with a mandate to crack down on cybercrime [31]. This unit investigates and prosecutes Internet fraud [48]. Also, the Office of the National Security Adviser plays a central role in cybercrime investigation, as host to Nigeria's Computer Emergency Response Team [44]. They coordinate the nation's corporate response to cyber attacks.

This research focused on the two leading agencies to maintain a focused and detailed study. The two agencies are EFCC and the Nigeria Police Force. The researchers conducted interviews with select officers of the EFCC and the Nigeria Police Force. The EFCC Digital Forensic Unit at the Agency's head office has only has about eight staff, but with units at the regional offices [34]. In reflection of this, the researchers interviewed eighteen investigating officers with digital forensic capabilities and exposure. This number consisted of officers of both the EFCC and the Nigeria Police Force. This sample size ensured focused research to understand the extent of the lack of forensic resources.

4.7.4 Materials/Instruments

This study is a qualitative case study, and the researchers are the primary research instruments in a qualitative case study [13]. This role as the primary research instrument puts specific responsibilities and expectations on the researchers. For instance, as the primary research instrument for data collection in qualitative research, the researchers are expected to spend considerable time in the research environment [17]. Also, in a qualitative study, the researchers as the primary instrument are expected to be very knowledgeable in the subject or topic studied [39]. This way, the human instrument is expected to process, analyze and summarize data intelligently and seek clarifications where necessary [22]. The literature review of this study provided rich context and baseline knowledge that guided the research.

Beyond the human instrument, interviews were the primary data collection method. In this context, interviews provide a vital and natural means of investigating participants' truths, facts, and experiences [45]. The researchers used interviews to get participants to discuss the lack of digital forensic resources from their unique perspectives. Questions were structured for participants to discuss in detail the forensic readiness of the organization, in line with the conceptual framework of the studies. Questions followed the themes identified—people, technology, processes, policy, and data.

4.7.5 Sampling Procedures

Yin [51] listed the six possible sources of data collection in a case study: documentation, archival records, interviews, direct observation, and physical artifacts. In this study, the primary sources for data collection were interviews, documentation, and archival records. Documents could come in different forms. For instance, Internet sources could prove very useful [17]. This study, therefore, considered data from various documents, including those sourced from reliable Internet sources. The study relied greatly on official press releases, reports, and case files.

This research used interviews as the primary data collection method. Interviews could be structured, semi-structured, and unstructured. This study adopted semi-structured interviews to allow for more flexibility and give room to understand participants' unique perspectives. This way, interview responses could prompt further evolving questions, providing opportunities to dig deeper into views [3, 8]. The researchers used one-on-one interview sessions. Participants nominated locations comfortable for them for the interviews. The researchers carefully crafted interview questions along the themes identified in the conceptual framework. In this research, all participants were comfortable with the interview sessions, and none declined or elected to use questionnaire instead.

This research focused on the two leading agencies prosecuting financial crimes and Internet fraud, to maintain a focused and detailed study. The Researchers had interview sessions with select officers of the EFCC and the Nigeria Police Force. The researchers adopted two main selection criteria. First, interviewees had to be officers tasked with investigating financial crimes (cybercrime, internet fraud, and advance fee fraud); and secondly, they had to be officers with digital forensic capabilities or in need of digital forensic capabilities. The EFCC Digital Forensic Unit at the Agency's head office only has about eight staff, with a limited presence at the regional offices (Okolorie 2020). In reflecting this situation, this study had 18 interviews, subject to the condition that it did not reach saturation. A case study reaches saturation when the data collected cannot produce new themes [16].

4.7.6 *Primary Interview Questions*

While semi-structured interviews were used for this study, guiding questions ensured a focused and organized discussion. The five critical components of the Digital Forensic Readiness model identified by Pooe and Labuschagne [40] shaped the interview questions. These five components are People, Process, Policy, Technology, and Data. The researchers grouped the primary interview questions under the components identified by Pooe and Labuschagne [40]. This grouping helped to keep things focused and organized. The researchers also created a general theme for generic questions.

People

Question 1: Please comment on the availability of digital forensic training for the staff of your unit and organization.
Question 2: What is your opinion on the staff adequacy; regarding the ratio of the number of investigating officers to the digital forensic capability to the financial crimes caseload?
Question 3: How does the digital forensic unit currently cope with the current high caseloads?
Question 4: In your opinion, what are the areas of digital forensic skills deficiency you need further training? (List in the order of importance).

Processes

Question 5: What role do the current processes play in reducing or increasing the caseloads?
Question 6: How often does your organization review its policies as it concerns the digital forensic investigation process?

Policy

Question 7: What is your opinion on the availability or not of a robust policy framework to guide digital forensic investigation?
Question 8: Please share your perspectives on the availability or not of a forensic readiness roadmap for your organization.
Questions 9: Please share policy suggestions that you think can help the efficiency of the investigative process.

Technology

Question 10: Please share your perspectives on the availability or lack of digital forensic investigation technology in your organization.
Question 11: How does your organization cope with digital forensic investigations in our fast-paced world of emerging technologies?
Question 12: Please share specific digital forensic technologies (hardware or software) you think your organization lacks.

Question 13: How does your organization cope with the expensive tenured licenses of forensic software and the high cost of their renewal?
Question 14: Please share your perspectives on funding adequacy (or the lack of it) of digital forensic technologies in your organizations.
Question 15: What is your assessment of the adoption of digital forensic tools by Nigerian law enforcement agencies?

Data

Question 16: How does your organization cope with increasing data controls and policies on information governance?
Question 17: Data is ubiquitous, and digital forensic investigations often leave investigators flooded with data. How does your organization cope with this big data challenge—processing capability and the storage dilemma?

General

Question 18: What are your perspectives on the lack of forensic resources in your organization?
Question 19: What are the top three reasons for the high caseloads of Internet fraud and financial crimes in your agency?
Question 20: What are the challenges preventing law enforcement agencies in Nigeria from being forensically ready?
Question 21: How has the lack of digital forensic resources affected the law enforcement agencies in Nigeria, and by extension, their efficiency in the fight to stop cybercrime?

4.7.7 Field Test

The researchers used a field test to ensure the quality and suitability of the interview questions. The researchers used four qualified persons for field-testing. The participants were carefully selected to reflect the study area. The qualifications of the participants include a Ph.D. holder in Artificial and Computational Intelligence, with over two decades of research and industry experience; two Ph.D. candidates of Information Technology (Digital Forensics Specialty); and a Ph.D. Candidate in Engineering Management, all with over a decade of professional experience. All four participants agreed with the structure, language, and suitability of the questions concerning the research questions and the problem statement. They all stated that the primary interview questions sufficiently reflect and address the research questions and problem statement.

4.7.8 *Data Collection Sources*

4.7.8.1 Ethical Assurances

Research involving human subjects requires ethical assurances. This requirement is even more so for qualitative studies involving face-to-face interviews involving vulnerable populations [1]. While this study did not involve vulnerable people, the study design reflected established ethical considerations. The study's research population had law enforcement agents. Therefore, the study protected participants and guaranteed their anonymity and confidentiality. Participants were not required to disclose their names, and the interview environment was such that it reflected the need for privacy and confidentiality.

This research is in strict compliance with the ethical principles in the Belmont Report. These principles include respect for persons, beneficence, and justice [29]. Before embarking on any field data collection exercise, the University of the Cumberland Institutional Review Board (IRB) approved the methodology. The research obtained informed consent and voluntary participation of all participants before interviewing them. Arifin [1] suggested participants should have sufficient knowledge and understanding of interview questions, and participants should be competent to consent. All participants were practitioners with knowledge and depth of the subject, and consented to the interview.

4.7.9 *Assumptions*

This study assumed that the financial crime agencies' lack of digital forensic resources was a significant factor behind the slow pace of prosecution and the high caseloads of financial crimes and Internet fraud in Nigeria. Following the theoretical framework of Routine Activity Theory and particularly capable guardianship, digital forensic readiness of law enforcement plays a role in the volume of caseloads. That is, a lack of digital forensic resources is assumed to be a motivation for Internet fraud. While most studies involving law enforcement, participants are usually conservative with their answers, the researchers noted that participants spoke freely and sincerely during the interviews. The researchers informed participants of the potential role the study's outcome could play in both institutions to get their buy-in. Understanding the extent of the lack of forensic resources and the impact on the caseloads could be crucial to developing a roadmap towards building forensic capability and readiness for the agencies.

4.7.10 *Limitations*

While the two agencies chosen as the population for this study are principally responsible for prosecuting financial crimes in Nigeria, in reality, there are also overlapping roles by other related agencies. For instance, the Office of the National Security Adviser plays a central role in cybercrime investigation, as host to Nigeria's Computer Emergency Response Team [44]. They coordinate the nation's corporate response to cyberattacks and therefore play a role in the fight against Internet fraud. However, this study did not capture them because they are not frontline agencies in financial crime investigation.

Beyond this, the law enforcement agencies' lack of forensic resources also impacts other critical stakeholders. For instance, the justice system is a crucial stakeholder affected by this lack. This study did not capture their perspective on this. Cybercrime incidents happen at a blistering pace, in contrast to the slow wheel of justice. Most of the investigations of financial crimes end up in court. Where there is a technological gap, either within the financial crimes agencies, the justice system, or between both, this presents a challenge. This study is limited to the extent that it did not consider the lack of digital forensic resources from the perspectives of the justice system.

4.7.11 *Delimitations*

This study was limited to the EFCC and the Nigeria Police Force. The research was delimited to sample the staff of the digital forensics unit of the EFCC and the Cybercrime Unit of the Nigeria Police Force. Expectedly, these are elite units of small teams. For instance, the EFCC digital forensics unit at the agency's head office has an eight-man team (Okolorie 2020). Extending the sample far beyond this might affect the focus of the study. The sample size for the Police is also limited to staff of the unit at the Force Headquarters. It is noteworthy to mention that the 36 states in Nigeria all have fraud units of the Nigeria Police Force. Therefore, limiting the study to just the force headquarters may not accurately represent the opinion of the rank and file of the Police Force in the country. Further studies could benefit from the outcome of this study to extend the research to all the 36 states and beyond just the cybercrime unit.

4.8 Processing and Analysis

The researchers used Sony digital audio recorder for the interviews, with the consent of the participants. The researchers used the qualitative software NVivo to analyze the transcription of recorded interviews. This tool codified themes from the interview transcripts. This study used inductive thematic analysis for the categorization of interview data. A thematic analysis could come in three forms: inductive analysis, theoretical analysis, and that which comes with constant comparison [38]. This research adopted the theoretical analysis method. This method allowed some predetermined themes were generated from existing literature and research questions while also being flexible to creating new ones inductively from patterns observed in the interview transcripts. Data collected was analyzed to look out for repeating patterns and themes. The study was structured to follow the analytic procedure recommended by Marshall and Rossman [23]. This procedure adopted in this research is summarized below as:

1. Interview transcripts were studied, organized, and loaded into NVivo.
2. Interview transcripts were further analyzed, read, and re-read.
3. The researchers generated categories and themes using NVivo.
4. The researchers used NVivo to code data.
5. The research interpreted data analyzed by NVivo.
6. Searched for alternative understandings.
7. The researchers presented research findings.

4.9 Summary

This study investigated the specifics and dynamics of the cybercrime caseloads in Nigeria. The study also investigated lack of digital forensic resources of the cybercrimes agencies in Nigeria, and how this affected the caseloads. The research is a case study, with the research population as the EFCC and the Nigeria Police Force. This chapter presented the study methodology and design. This chapter also considered the population, sample, data collection, processing and analysis, and ethical considerations. In this study, the primary sources for data collection are interviews, documentation, and archival records. This chapter also included data from different documents, including those sourced from reliable Internet sources. The paper also compared findings with recent peer-reviewed publications. The study used NVivo for processing transcripts and codifying themes.

References

1. Arifin SRM (2018) Ethical considerations in qualitative study. Int J Care Scholars 1(2):30–33
2. Baxter P, Jack S (2008) Qualitative case study methodology: study design and implementation for novice researchers. Qual Rep 13(4):544–559
3. Baškarada S (2014) Qualitative case study guidelines. Qual Rep 19(40):1–25
4. Bello M, Griffiths M (2021) Routine activity theory and cybercrime investigation in Nigeria: how capable are law enforcement agencies? In: Rethinking cybercrime. Palgrave Macmillan, Cham, pp 213–235
5. Bitsch V (2005) Qualitative research: a grounded theory example and evaluation criteria. J Agribus 23(1):75–91

6. Cope DG (2014) Methods and meanings: credibility and trustworthiness of qualitative research. Oncol Nurs Forum 41(1):89–91
7. Creswell JW, Creswell JD (2018) Research design: qualitative, quantitative, and mixed methods approaches. Sage
8. Daymon C, Holloway I (2010) Qualitative research methods in public relations and marketing communications. Routledge
9. Eboibi FE (2017) A review of the legal and regulatory frameworks of Nigerian Cybercrimes Act 2015. Comput Law Secur Rev 33(5):700–717
10. Economic and Financial Crimes Commission (2023) Poverty, unemployment no excuses for cybercrimes-bawa. https://www.efcc.gov.ng/efcc/news-and-information/news-release/9246-poverty-unemployment-no-excuses-for-cybercrimes-bawa
11. Edgar TW, Manz DO (2017) Research methods for cyber security. Syngress
12. Erlandson DA, Harris EL, Skipper BL, Allen SD (1993) Doing naturalistic inquiry: a guide to methods. Sage
13. Frankel R, Devers K (2000) Qualitative research: a consumer's guide. Educ Health 13(1):113–123
14. Guardian Newspaper (2021) 80% of EFCC's 978 convictions cybercrime related. https://guardian.ng/news/80-of-efccs-978-convictions-cybercrime-related/
15. Guba EG, Lincoln YS (1989) Fourth generation evaluation. Sage
16. Guest G, Bunce A, Johnson L (2006) How many interviews are enough? An experiment with data saturation and variability. Field Methods 18(1):59–82
17. Hancock DR, Algozzine B (2017) Doing case study research: a practical guide for beginning researchers. Teachers College Press
18. Houghton C, Casey D, Shaw D, Murphy K (2013) Rigour in qualitative case-study research. Nurs Res 20(4)
19. ICPC (2012) ICPC establishes forensic laboratory. https://icpc.gov.ng/2012/09/07/icpc-establishes-forensic-laboratory/
20. ICPC (2022) ICPC arraigns impersonator of ex-primate of anglican communion, others over N30.4m fraud. https://icpc.gov.ng/2022/04/10/cpc-arraigns-impersonator-of-ex-primate-of-anglican-communion-others-over-n30-4mfraud/
21. Krefting L (1991) Rigor in qualitative research: the assessment of trustworthiness. Am J Occup Ther 45(3):214–222
22. Lincoln YS, Guba EG (1985) Naturalistic inquiry. Sage, Beverly Hills, CA
23. Marshall C, Rossman GB (2014) Designing qualitative research. Sage
24. Marshall C, Rossman GB (2014) Designing qualitative research. Sage publications
25. Marshall MN (1996) Sampling for qualitative research. Family Practice 13(6):522–526
26. Mays N, Pope C (1995) Qualitative research: rigour and qualitative research. BMJ 311(6997):109–112
27. Merriam SB (1995) What can you tell from an n of 1?: issues of validity and reliability in qualitative research. PAACE J Lifelong Learn 4:51–60
28. Miles MB, Huberman AM (1994) Qualitative data analysis: an expanded sourcebook. Sage
29. Miracle VA (2016) The Belmont Report: the triple crown of research ethics. Dimens Crit Care Nurs 35(4):223–228
30. Morse JM (2000) Determining sample size. Qual Health Res 10(1)
31. News Agency of Nigeria (2016) Police to create special unit to tackle cybercrime. Guardian Newspaper. https://guardian.ng/news/police-to-create-special-unit-to-tackle-cybercrime/
32. Obuah E (2010) Combatting corruption in Nigeria: the Nigerian economic and financial crimes (EFCC). Afr Stud Q 12(1)
33. Office of the National Security Adviser (2021) National cybersecurity policy and strategy. https://cert.gov.ng/ngcert/resources/NATIONAL_CYBERSECURITY_POLICY_AND_STRATEGY_2021.pdf
34. Okolorie GR (2020, December 22) Uncovering patterns in complex investigations is no match for Nigeria's Economic and Financial Crimes Commission (EFCC) [Interview]. Cellebrite. https://www.cellebrite.com/en/uncovering-patterns-in-complex-investigations-is-no-match-for-nigerias-economic-and-financial-crimes-commission-efcc/

35. Olayemi OJ (2014) A socio-technological analysis of cybercrime and cyber security in Nigeria. Int J Sociol Anthropol 6(3):116–125
36. Onyema E, Roy P, Oredola H, Ayinla S (2018) The EFCC and the politics of (in)effective implementation of Nigeria's anti-corruption policy. https://eprints.soas.ac.uk/31283/1/ACE-WorkingPaper007-EFCC-Nigeria.pdf
37. Oraegbunam IK (2015) The Nigerian police and problems of cybercrime investigation: need for adequate training. Niger Law J 18(1):1–28
38. Percy WH, Kostere K, Kostere S (2015) Generic qualitative research in psychology. Qual Rep 20(2):76–85
39. Peredaryenko MS, Krauss SE (2013) Calibrating the human instrument: understanding the interviewing experience of novice qualitative researchers. Qual Rep 18(43):1
40. Pooe A, Labuschagne L (2012) A conceptual model for digital forensic readiness. In: 2012 information security for South Africa, Aug 2012. IEEE, pp 1–8
41. Punch Newspaper (2022) IGP shakes up cybercrime unit. https://punchng.com/igp-shakes-up-cybercrime-unit/
42. Shenton AK (2004) Strategies for ensuring trustworthiness in qualitative research projects. Educ Inf 22(2):63–75
43. Stake RE (1995) The art of case study research. Sage
44. Symantec Corporation and African Union (2016) Cybercrime cybersecurity trends in Africa. https://www.thehaguesecuritydelta.com/media/com_hsd/report/135/document/Cyber-security-trends-report-Africa-en.pdf
45. Talmy S (2010) Qualitative interviews in applied linguistics: from research instrument to social practice. Annu Rev Appl Linguist 30:128
46. Tobin GA, Begley CM (2004) Methodological rigour within a qualitative framework. J Adv Nurs 48(4):388–396
47. Umar I, Samsudin RS, Mohamed M (2016) Understanding the successes and challenges of Anti-Corruption Agency (ACA) in Nigeria: a case of Economic and Financial Crimes Commission (EFCC). Asian J Multidiscip Stud 4(5):27–33
48. Vanguard Newspaper (2020) Nigeria police, interpol arrest three suspects over cybercrime. Vanguard Newspaper. https://www.vanguardngr.com/2020/07/nigeria-police-interpol-arrest-3-suspects-over-cybercrime/
49. Vishnevsky T, Beanlands H (2004) Qualitative research. Nephrol Nurs J 31(2):234
50. Yin RK (2003) Case study research: design and methods, 3rd edn. Sage, Thousand Oaks, CA
51. Yin RK (2009) Case study research: design and methods, 4th edn. Sage, Thousand Oaks, CA
52. Zainal Z (2007) Case study as a research method. J Kemanusiaan 5(1)

Chapter 5
Research Findings—The State of Digital Forensic Readiness of Nigeria's Cybercrime Agencies

Abstract This chapter presents the findings of the study, structured to investigate the digital forensic readiness of Nigerian cybercrime agencies. The findings were presented within the context of themes and emergent themes. The chapter presents the perspectives of cybercrime investigators and digital forensic examiners from the Economic and Financial Crimes Commission and the Nigeria Police Force. The chapter presented specifics of the lack of forensic resources in both agencies, such as lack of competent personnel, digital forensic tools, structured training programmes, and others. The chapter ended by presenting the top three reasons behind the rising caseloads of cybercrime, as well as other supplementary findings relating to policy.

Keywords Cybercrime · Internet fraud · EFCC · Economic and Financial Crimes Commission · Nigeria police · Digital forensic resources · Digital forensic readiness · Cybercrime caseloads

5.1 Introduction

Nigeria continues to struggle with the caseloads of cybercrime. The scale and magnitude have been quite disturbing, not just to Nigeria but also to the international community, given the limitless boundaries of cybercrime [4, 12]. Nigeria loses a lot to cybercrime annually. The Nigeria Communications Commission (NCC) puts total annual loss to cybercrime at $500 million. That is, cybercrime contributes to about 0.08% loss in GDP [6]. The victims cut across the financial sector to other institutions and even individuals across different jurisdictions. Nigeria's primary Internet fraud investigating agency is the Economic and Financial Crimes Commission [7, 9, 16]. However, other agencies appear to have overlapping functions. For instance, the Nigerian Police Force set up a dedicated cybercrime unit [8]. Recently, the Nigeria Police Cybercrime Unit, in a joint operation with the Interpol National Central Bureau (NCB), made arrests of Internet fraud suspects [17]. Also, the Office of the National Security Adviser plays a central role in cybercrime investigation. The Office of the National Security Adviser hosts Nigeria's Computer Emergency Response Team,

R. T. Sibe and C. Kaunert, *Cybercrime, Digital Forensic Readiness, and Financial Crime Investigation in Nigeria*, Advanced Sciences and Technologies for Security Applications, https://doi.org/10.1007/978-3-031-54089-9_5

created by the Cyberbercrime (Prevention, Prohibition, etc.) Act 2015 [15]. Despite these overlapping roles, there is a noticeable lack of available literature examining these overlapping and sometimes duplicitous functions, potentially creating a chaotic cybercrime investigation landscape.

Over the years, Nigeria has implemented several reforms to stem the surge in cybercrime numbers. Despite the various institutional and structural reforms embarked upon, this has not been sufficient to meet one of the highest cybercrime caseloads in the world. While there are many other reasons for this failure to stem the surging incidents of cybercrime in the country, one primary reason is the lack of technical capability and forensic resources [5]. The current system has a noticeable gap in digital forensic infrastructure and resources. Apart from the lack of forensic technology, there is also a shortage of investigators with forensic capabilities [11, 13]. For instance, Okolorie [10] noted that the EFCC digital forensics unit at the agency's head office has an eight-man team. With caseloads averaging about two per day—each case with a possibility of multiple devices—it is challenging to cope with the surge.

A few studies have been conducted, highlighting the deficiencies in the law enforcement agencies as a significant impediment to the fight against cybercrime. For instance, Olayemi [11], Oraegbunam [13], and Bello and Griffiths [1] all pointed to this lack of forensic capabilities of the law enforcement agencies. However, previous studies did not drill into the specifics of this lack of technology, human resources, technical capabilities, and others. For the Nigerian law enforcement agencies to successfully confront the growing threat of financial crimes, it has to ascertain the capabilities of these agencies. The absence of such clear information on their capabilities makes it challenging to develop a roadmap for digital forensic readiness and capability maturity for the law enforcement agencies in Nigeria. This book addresses this, which is an important step in building the forensic readiness of Nigeria's cybercrime agencies.

This study is structured to investigate this challenge of clarity of the state of forensic readiness of both institutions. Chapters 1–3 established the need for and the basis of this study. While Chap. 1 introduced the topic, theoretical framework, and research questions, Chap. 2 was structured to review relevant literature on cybercrime in Nigeria. Chapter 3 presented the concept of Digital Evidence, Digital Forensics, and Digital Forensic Readiness, to give the technical and foundational insight to conduct the study on digital forensic readiness of cybercrime investigating agencies in Nigeria. Chapter 4 presented the methodology for this study. This study was structured as a qualitative case study, utilizing semi-structured interviews to understand the subject. The research population consists of personnel from the Nigerian Police Force and the Economic and Financial Crimes Commission (EFCC). The participants were carefully selected from related departments to ensure a deep understanding of the subject. The participants from the Nigerian Police Force consisted of personnel from the Cybercrime and Cryptography unit, and the participants from the EFCC consisted of the following related departments: Digital Forensic Department, Cybercrime Unit, Advance Fee Fraud (AFF) department, and Legal (Cybercrime prosecution). Chapter 5 presents the results of the field data collection process, in relation to the research questions.

5.2 Participants and Research Setting

5.2.1 Description of Research Sample

This study was structured to investigate the dynamics and complexity of the cybercrime caseloads in Nigeria, as well as investigate the lack of digital forensic resources in the financial crimes agencies in Nigeria. To this end, the research sample consisted of officers of the two principal agencies responsible for fighting financial crimes and internet fraud. They are the Economic and Financial Crimes, set up by the EFCC Act 2004, and the Nigerian Police Force [9, 16]. The sample consisted of personnel from only departments directly involved or impacted by the use of or the lack of digital forensic technology in financial crimes prosecution, to keep this study focused. The sample consisted of five persons from the Cybercrime department of the Nigerian Police and 13 officers of the EFCC, drawn from four different related (forensic-dependent) departments within the organization—Digital Forensic department, Cybercrime Department, Advance Fee Fraud Department, and Legal (Cybercrime Prosecution) Department. This diversity was necessary to ensure broad perspectives. Participants had varying years of experience, ranging from four to over 20 years. Participants had the requisite work experience to discuss the subject, with 14 out of the 18 participants with more than ten years of experience. Table 5.1 summarizes the participants' information.

The researchers only conducted the interviews after approvals by the institutional Review Board. The interviews lasted for about a month, with the first on August 7th, 2021, and the last on September 3rd, 2021. The study adopted a face-to-face interview method at comfortable locations chosen by each participant. The researchers ensured the anonymity of participants by assigning corresponding codes of P01–P18 to participants 1–18, respectively. Also, the two organizations were coded as organizations A and B, respectively, to ensure participants' anonymity. Table 5.2 shows a summary of interview settings. The researchers used a Sony digital voice recorder for recording each session.

5.2.2 Research Methodology Applied for Data Analysis

This research used semi-structured interviews administered orally and recorded using a Sony Voice Recorder. Interview transcripts were done manually and saved in Microsoft Word documents with a uniform naming convention. Transcripts were original and with no attempt to make grammatical corrections. The researchers edited all personal identifiers, such as names, to ensure the anonymity of all participants. For data analysis, this research utilized the QSR NVivo Mac (Release 1.5). The researchers chose NVivo for several reasons: rich text capabilities, character-based

Table 5.1 Participant demographics

S/N	Participants	Department
1	P01	Cybercrime
2	P02	Cybercrime
3	P03	Cybercrime
4	P04	Cybercrime
5	P05	Cybercrime
6	P07	Digital forensics
7	P08	Digital forensics
8	P09	Digital forensics
9	P10	Digital forensics
10	P11	Legal (Cybercrime)
11	P12	Legal (Cybercrime)
12	P13	Legal (Cybercrime)
13	P14	Digital forensics
14	P15	Advance fee fraud
15	P16	Advance fee fraud
16	P17	Advance fee fraud
17	P18	Cybercrime
18	P19	Cybercrime

Note This table summarizes the participants, departments, and date of the interview

Table 5.2 Summary of interview setting

S/N	Variables	Description
1	Number of participants	18
2	Location of interviews	Abuja, Nigeria. Participants chose interview locations where they were comfortable
3	Mode of interview	Face-to-face
4	Recording device	Sony digital recorder
5	Documents presented to participants permission	Invitation to participate Informed consent

Note This table summarizes the interview settings for the participants

coding, visualization features, and broad applicability in several research designs [18]. The researchers imported transcripts of all 18 participants to NVivo for analysis.

This study utilized thematic analysis in analyzing data. It involved searching through the interview transcript to find patterns [2]. While thematic analysis could be inductive, theoretical analysis, or thematic analysis with constant comparison [14], this research adopted the theoretical analysis method. This method allowed some pre-determined themes were generated from existing literature and research questions while also being flexible to creating new ones inductively from patterns observed in the interview transcripts. The researchers adopted the six-step recommendation by Braun and Clark [2].

Step 1 involved familiarizing with the data set. This process began with the transcription of the recorded interview. After the transcription process, the transcripts were read and re-read. The analysis processes of transcription, reading and re-reading the transcript allowed the researchers to get immersed in and become familiar with the data. After this process, step 2 involved coding interesting features noticed during the data familiarization process. The researchers used NVivo software for the coding process, with nodes and sub-nodes created for codes. Step 3 involved the searching and grouping of similar codes into themes. Step 4 involved going through and reviewing the themes to ascertain if the codes fit into assigned themes. Step 5 involved Analyzing and refining themes, with each theme named and defined. The last phase is the presentation of the result. Figure 5.1 shows a word cloud, showing the most frequently used words by participants.

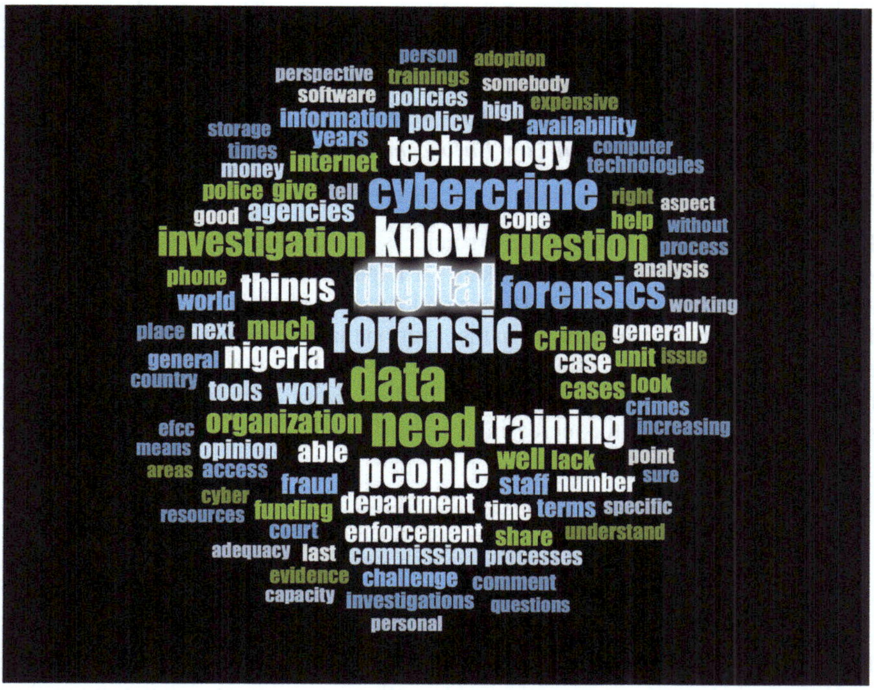

Fig. 5.1 Word cloud generated from interview files. *Note* This figure shows frequently used words by participants as generated by NVivo

5.3 Analyses of Research Questions

Six themes and twenty-five subthemes emerged from the analysis. The main themes are personnel, digital forensic technology, digital forensic training, processes, policy, and challenges. The personnel theme had subthemes for personnel adequacy and personnel capability. The digital forensic technology theme had the following subthemes: tool availability, tool licensing challenge, tools needed, digital forensic adoption, and the impact of lack of digital forensic technology. The digital forensic training theme had the following subthemes: structured training and training need. The process theme had the following subthemes: defined processes, structured process reviews, and process challenges.

The policy theme had four subthemes: policy framework, policy challenges, and the roadmap for digital forensic readiness. The challenges theme had the following subthemes: collaboration, jurisdictional, emerging technologies, funding, the pace of Cybercrime, rising caseloads, top 3 reasons, information governance, big data challenge, and the roadmap for digital forensic readiness. The themes reveal the perspectives shared by participants drawn from the two agencies. The researchers analyzed the research questions within the context of these themes. Table 5.3 summarizes the themes and codes in NVivo.

Primary Research Question 1: What Is the Assessment of Digital Forensic Resources and Capabilities of Law Enforcement Agencies in Nigeria?

Six themes emerged from participants' responses. Table 5.4 shows the six themes.

Theme 1.1 Personnel adequacy. Personnel is an essential resource in any organization; therefore, the interviewer asked participants to share their perspectives on the adequacy of personnel. All 18 respondents shared their views on this theme. There was an apparent agreement on the position that the current staff strength is not enough. Participants P01, P02, P03, P04, P05, P06, P07, P08, P09, P12, P13, P14, P15, P16, P17, and P18 all stated clearly in their interview that the staff strength is poor when compared to the increasing caseload.

P17 stated:

> In the cybercrime department and all the departments I've worked in the past ten years, the manpower is low. Embarrassingly low because with each cybercriminal you catch, 5 to 10 more pop up in his place, and as they're increasing, we have limited staff strength and digital strength, let me use that word…manpower is low, training is low, but the zeal to fight it is what is sustaining us till now.

Theme 1.2: Personnel capability. There were mixed responses on staff capability. While some indicated presence of capable staff, others suggested they were in short supply. Direct quotes from select participants are shared in Appendix at the end of the Chapter.

Table 5.3 Themes from interview

S/N	Themes	Description
1	Personnel	Staff availability and capability
1.1	Personnel adequacy	Adequacy of staff to increasing caseloads
1.2	Personnel capability	Staff digital forensic skill capability
2	Digital forensic technology	Issues around availability of digital forensic tools
2.1	Tool availability	Availability of digital forensic tools
2.2	Tool licensing challenge	Issues around maintaining tools licenses
2.3	Tools needed	Tools needed
2.4	Digital forensic adoption	Digital forensic technology adoption
2.5	Impact of lack of digital forensic technology	The impact of the lack of digital forensic technology in financial crimes prosecution
3	Digital forensic training	Digital forensic training for staff
3.1	Structured training	Availability of structured training in digital forensics
3.2	Training need	Training needed by participants
4	Processes	Availability of documented processes
4.1	Defined processes	Clearly defined and documented processes
4.2	Structured process reviews	Structured process review mechanism
4.3	Process challenges	Challenges associated with current processes
5	Policy	Digital forensic policy framework
5.1	Policy framework	Policy framework shaping the digital forensic practice
5.2	Policy challenges	Challenges associated with current policy
5.3	Roadmap for digital forensic readiness	Roadmap for digital forensic readiness
6	Challenges	Challenges faced by cybercrime investigators
6.1	Collaboration	Inter-agency collaboration
6.2	Jurisdictional	Challenges of cross-border crime investigation
6.3	Emerging technologies	Complexities of investigating emerging technologies
6.4	Funding	Funding challenges
6.5	Pace of cybercrime	Challenges of investigating fast-paced cybercrime
6.6	Rising caseloads	Rising caseloads of internet fraud and financial crimes
6.7	Top 3 reasons	Top 3 reasons for rising caseloads
6.8	Information governance	Challenges with information governance
6.9	Big data challenge	The big data challenge to forensic investigation
6.10	Roadmap for digital forensic readiness	Roadmap for digital forensic readiness

Note This table summarizes the themes from the interview

Table 5.4 Themes from primary research question

S/N	Themes	Themes
1	Theme 1.1	Personnel adequacy
2	Theme 1.2	Personnel capability
3	Theme 2.1	Tool availability
4	Theme 4.1	Clearly defined and documented processes
5	Theme 4.2	Structured process review mechanism
6	Theme 5.1	Policy framework shaping the digital forensic practice

Note This table summarizes themes from the primary research question

P12 responded that:

> Yeah, I want to suggest that in that aspect, we have staff that are not really trained to man the forensic lab. I know the person in charge right now is actually vast in areas of forensic examination; he's an expert in that, but I can really say only him or a few, so we'll need well-trained staff to man such. So, that would be my suggestion.

P08 also shared a similar view, noting that: "I think we lack in that capacity; we lack the tools, we lack the trained people, and then yeah, the human capacity in that regard".

One way to build personnel capability is through structured training. Participants had divided opinions on the availability of a structured training program. Participants P01, P10, P11, P13, P04, P06, P07, P08, and P09 all suggested having been beneficiaries of such structured training. Participants P12, P15, P16, P17, P18, P02, P03, and P05 all submitted no structured training program existed in both organizations. This study presented more on this perspective in the training theme.

Despite the unanimous submission on staff capacity and adequacy, P06 was optimistic, suggesting that staff had certifications. The participant (P06) said "with the coming of this present administration, I am proud to beat my chest and tell you all our licenses are active, and we are working towards getting retrained because we've already had the certifications".

Theme 2.1: Tools availability. Digital Forensic investigation is a specialist discipline requiring the use of specialist tools. No matter the level of expertise a forensic examiner may have, without access to the right tool, he/she is not able to do much. Therefore, this research asked participants questions on digital forensic tool availability. The majority of the participants (cutting across both organizations) submitted that they lack or have limited access to the right digital forensic technology. Participants P01, P11, P12, P15, P02, P04, P05, P08, and P09 all stated that they lack digital forensic tools to effectively combat internet fraud and financial crimes.

P05 stated that:

> So, the only thing we have regarding forensics that we have access to is this mobile extraction using Cellebrite. Even that one is not done here fully. Send an investigative activity letter to them, they do the work, they send it back to us, and we get it back, and we work on it. Sometimes it takes time, two weeks or more…I will say on a scale of 1-10, I will say we are, maybe we only have about 2.

Theme 4.1: Defined and Documented Processes. The interviewer asked participants to share their perspectives on the availability of documented processes and Standard Operating Process (SOP). There were mixed responses from the participants. An analysis of the responses shows that eleven participants stated or inferred that they had defined and documented processes at both organizations. However, not all in this category were categorical about documented processes. Participants P01, P03, P06, P07, P08, P09, P10, P11, P12, P14, and P15 fall in this category.

P06 said:

> We use this principle of the Association of Chief of Police, that's the APO principles, and that is what we use. Apart from that, we're trying to get our accreditation with ISO 17025, so based on that, everything we do is documented. You don't do things because you feel you want to do it, there is always a guideline you have to follow, and I think we are doing the best we can do there.
>
> P10 is one of the participants who did not clearly state the organization had documented processes but suggested it existed.

P10 said:

> The process is to the extent that each person knows his area of competence and professionalism. Those in the forensic department know their protocols. They know what they have to do, and we know what we are looking for in the legal department. When they are done with their investigation, and they bring it to legal, we do an analysis; we do a review; we study the case file. If there is something that is not properly done, we do not take it to court without those evidence being properly positioned to be admitted in court, so there is this in and out flow and discussion that goes on. It's fluid between us; if there is something they need clarification on, they clear, they write, they come to us, they don't need to come to us.

Some participants referred to legislation and laws as processes. P04 and P14 are in this category. P14 said:

> Yes, we do. We're guided by the law, and there are enabling Acts that govern our activities. Whatever we do, we work within the ambit of the law, and there are provisions of the law in Evidence Act, Administration of criminal justice Act, and most of the other laws governing our activities. So, whenever we carry out our duties, we always put that at the back of our mind to guide our work.

Only one participant (P05) stated that there were no documented processes available.

P05 stated that, "generally, no. but the three of us; we are IT people, we are very conversant with the forensic guidelines". One participant, P18, did not know whether processes existed or not.

P18 noted:

> Ok, statutorily, I can't tell. I've not seen any procedure on conducting cybercrime investigation domiciled in "Organisation B", but, however, based on training and self-development, we've been able to set standards, for instance, the type that the likes of Interpol adopt on cybercrime investigation, we try to implement that ourselves; formerly I've not seen any.

Theme 4.2: Structured Process Review Mechanism. The cybercrime and technological landscape is always evolving. Therefore, it is expected that processes and policies are regularly reviewed to reflect emerging dynamics. To address this, the researchers asked participants on the presence of structured process review mechanism. Two participants made mixed submissions on the presence of a structured review process for the processes. While P01 said there was a structured process review mechanism, P02 submitted there was none. Both P01 and P02 are from the same department in the same organization. P01 said that:

> We review policies, systems, procedures, and the approach at which we go about our investigations; and that is why at this point, we are in need of getting the equipment and facilities that we really need because we know that the usual system is no longer working and can no longer serve us.

> Perspectives of P02 are in Appendix under the theme heading.

Theme 5.1: Policy Framework. The researchers asked participants to share their perspectives on the policy framework guiding or shaping their activities. Only four participants responded to this, and all four pointed to the Cybercrime Act 2015 as the guiding framework.

Participant 17 said:

> In the cybercrimes department, we use the cybercrimes act [3], that was enacted into law in 2015. It guides us…crimes that are committed under the cybercrimes act and the penalties for them. And also tells us how we can liaise with government agencies, and some financial agencies, and telecommunication agencies to get what we want.

Research Subquestion 1: What challenges prevent law enforcement agencies in Nigeria from having adequate forensic capabilities and being forensically ready? Table 5.5 summarizes the nine themes that emerged from participants' responses.

Theme 2.2: Tool Licensing Challenge. The challenge of maintaining the recurrent licenses appeared to be a recurring challenge faced by the law enforcement agencies in Nigeria. This challenge cuts across both organizations, as reflected in the responses. Participants P01, P11, P16, P02, P03, P04, P05, P06, and P08 alluded to the challenges of renewing digital forensic tool licenses.

P11 said:

> There were instances where I forwarded devices of suspects, and we were told their software have expired, and they need renewal of license. That was prior to this time. I don't know If there's an update on that. So, it makes your work slow-paced and then leaves you at log jam, getting results of what you want and of course, over time, evidence can be tampered with,

Table 5.5 Themes from research subquestion 1

S/N	Themes	Themes
1	Theme 2.2	Tool licensing challenge
2	Theme 3.1	Lack of structured training program
3	Theme 5.2	Policy challenges
4	Theme 5.3	Roadmap for digital forensic readiness
5	Theme 6.1	Collaboration
6	Theme 6.2	Jurisdictional
7	Theme 6.3	Emerging technologies
8	Theme 6.4	Funding
9	Theme 6.5	Pace of cybercrime

Note This table summarizes themes that emerged from research subquestion 1

Theme 3.1: Lack of Structured Training. The interviewer asked participants to share their perspectives on the availability of a structured training program in their organization. Participants had a split position on this, with 50% submitting they had a structured training program and the other 50% stating they do not have one. Participants P04, P06, P07, P08, P09, P10, P11, P12, and P13 all said they have a structured training program.

P11 said:

> I will speak for myself. I have been exposed to a couple of training presently. I have just been notified that I have just been nominated to attend a training, relating to cybercrime. It's a training organized by the FBI. The training is coming up sometime this month. I am also aware some of my colleagues are also attending diverse training. These trainings come intermittently.

Further analysis of participants' responses shows the decisions appeared shaped by the participant's organisation and/or departments. All but one (P04) that exuded such positivity and optimism regarding training are from Organization B. Particularly noticeable is that all five participants from the Digital Forensic Department from Organization B all stated their satisfaction with the training program they currently have. The other participants from other investigative departments of the same Organization B did not express the same level of satisfaction. Participants P14, P15, P16, P17, and P18, all from the same organization, stated the lack of a structured training program.

P17 said:

> Training as a whole for law enforcement is poor, and in the cybercrime department, it's really poor because these boys move at the speed of light, and we are moving at a slow pace. For every ten yards they make, we just make one step forward. So most of us sometimes resort to personal training using our self-help. We have to train ourselves to better the work just because of the love we have for the job, but if it's to comment on training in the cybercrimes unit, it is very, very poor.

Four out of five participants from Organization A (P01, P02, P03, and P05) all stated that there was no structured training program, and this impacted their performance.

P03 stated:

> The truth of the issue is, outside "Organisation A", there are a lot of training for digital forensics, but it's the cost implication, as we all know. But for us here in this department, I don't think we've had such intense training. I don't think we've had such training. We'll like to, but we have not.

Theme 5.2: Policy challenges. The researchers asked participants to share their perspectives on the policy challenges faced. Five participants shared several challenges, such as lack of efficient framework for inter-agency information sharing (P01 and P04), jurisdictional roadblocks (P17), poor implementation (P02), and legal roadblocks (P04).

P17 said:

> In the cybercrimes department, we use the cybercrimes act 2015 that was enacted into law at 2015. It guides us and also tells us how we can liaise with government agencies and some financial agencies and telecommunication agencies to get what we want. But at the place we have the logjam is when we are dealing with foreign agencies. They expect us to answer them informally, but when we need information from them, they come up with a brick wall and ask us to jump through the ropes to get what we want, but because we are eager to please them, we accede to all kind of cost in whatever form it might come from them.

This study presented select participant views on this in Appendix.

Theme 5.3: Roadmap for Digital Forensic Readiness. As reviewed in this book, there are several studies pointing to the lack of forensic readiness by the law enforcement agencies. Therefore, the researchers sought to find out from participants if there are any documented roadmap for forensic readiness. To this end, the researchers asked participants to share their perspectives on the availability of a documented roadmap for the digital forensic readiness of their organizations. A total of 12 participants responded to this. The researchers classified these responses under three groupings: those who said there was a roadmap in place or in the process of developing one; those who said there was none; and those who could not say if there was a roadmap or not. Participants P01, P02, P03, P06, P09, P11, P12, P13, P18 all said there was a roadmap—either already in place or under development. Participants P04, P05, and P17 said there was none. Participant P07 did not know if there was a roadmap for digital forensic readiness or not. Follow-up questions did not produce any definite response to confirm if such a document is available to participants.

P11 said:

> Yeah, there is a road map. The "establishment A" is doing a lot in the area of training for officers that are assigned to the forensic department. Anything linking to forensic investigations, the cost implications are so high, and of course, there are other needs of the agency, but a lot still needs to be done to help have access to this software that we need to move with time.

Theme 6.1: Collaborations. An analysis of participants' responses shows an existing collaboration between the agencies, both locally and internationally. P06 submitted that the digital forensic laboratory of Organization B services requests from other law enforcement agencies. P07 said organization B routinely trains the staff of other law enforcement agencies. P07 also pointed to the support gotten from the government of the United Kingdom. P11 mentioned a training by the United States Federal Bureau of Investigation (FBI). P06 also pointed to a recent training program organized by the South Korean Police. These submissions point to the existing collaborative handshakes between the agencies. Interestingly, participants in this category are all from the digital forensic unit of Organization B.

P09 said:

> What we do is that, when we find an incident that now becomes a trend, we begin to develop our capabilities, and we have got some international partners, some agencies that partner with the commission. So, they have been able to support us in terms of training, in terms of daily capacity, both training and material needs. They help us a lot. They have been helping us.

Participants P04, P05, P09, P10, P15, P18 (cutting across both organizations) pointed to the lack of effective collaboration as a challenge and the need to create a framework for collaboration.

P15 said:

> Yes, there should be - the relationship should be improved between the three departments I have just mentioned: the operation, the forensic and the legal department, so as to achieve our collective objective and aim of ridding Nigeria of the economic and financial crime, particularly, cybercrime and other related offense.

Theme 6.2: Jurisdictional challenges. Participants highlighted the international dimension of cybercrime and the jurisdictional challenges this poses. Participants P07, P11, and P06 highlighted existing collaboration with agencies from other nations. Participants P17 and P18, however, highlighted some of the challenges of dealing with jurisdictional roadblocks.

P17 said:

> Yes, there is more. Like those days, it used to be the cult in the universities, but now they have evolved into cyber criminality. Right now, rather than go into a cult and kill themselves, they've now formed a group of people that just sit down and have a structure. They come together to do cybercrime in school. If they get to graduate without being caught, then they now get to scatter themselves all over the world. Somebody goes to Malaysia; somebody goes to America; somebody stays in Nigeria here. So, those that are in America do the stuff, and they send the monies to Nigeria directly or they send it to Malaysia. Nigeria doesn't have any joint bilateral agreement with Malaysia or Turkey, so when the people send the money to Turkey or Malaysia, then they now launder the money and send it back to Nigeria. Those that are in Nigeria here will now use the money…to start real estate on behalf of those that are in America and Malaysia.

Theme 6.3: Emerging Technologies. Participants highlighted the challenges of coping with emerging technologies. Participants P01, P02, P10, P11, P12, P13, P14, P17, and P18 (cutting across both organizations) all pointed to the existence of this challenge.

P12 noted that:

> I can say that's why we need to be trained. You mentioned bitcoin; bitcoin is one that is giving us headaches, if I can say that. It"s something that a lot of these criminals use to launder money, and from my experience and even research and then reports from even the Investigators, it seems to be something that just disappears; it's something you can't really lay your hands on. I think we really, really need to be trained in that aspect for us to be able to do adequate investigation and prosecution.

Theme 6.4: Funding Challenges. Funding is an issue that kept reoccurring in the interviews by all participants. Participants P01, P02, P03, P04, P05, P06, P07, P08, P09, P10, P11, P12, P13, P14, P15, P16, P17, and P18 all said funding was a significant challenge. P16 said:

> I think government should really fund our digital forensics department because, you see, sometimes for a long time, their license has expired, they could not renew, and most of the devices are there; they could not do anything. It's little they can do if their license is expired. So I think maybe in our budget, government should give priority to that aspect because it really helps our work.

Theme 6.5: Speed of cybercrime. Participants shared the challenges they faced coping with the fast pace of cybercrime to their investigative pace. Participants P01, P08, P09, P11, P15, P17, and P18 alluded to this challenge. P17 stated that "these boys move at the speed of light, and we are moving at a slow pace. For every ten yards they make, we just make one step forward. So most of us sometimes resort to personal training using self-help".

Theme 6.8: Information Governance. Globally, there have been increased awareness on privacy, data protection and the responsible use of data. Therefore, as a digital forensic investigator, it is important to practice with these emerging responsibilities of information governance in consideration. The researchers asked participants to share their perspectives on information governance and the challenges faced during a digital forensic investigation. Participants P01, P03, P06, P09, P17, and P18 stated that information governance considerations affect their cybercrime investigation and digital forensics. Participants P02, P05, P07, P10, P12, P15, and P16 think information governance demands do not affect financial crimes investigation. Participants in both groups are from both organizations.

P09 said:

> It may be interesting to mention the fact that, because of the nature of work we do, we have access to people's privacy. Ok so, one of the things we emphasize is that confidentiality. I mean, I have seen people's credit cards in plain text; okay, credit card. Real-life credit card with huge sums. I have seen people's email and passwords. I have seen people's information that you will consider private. I have seen them in plain text. Sometimes you go issue report on them. Our data is classified. Data from the accused person will generate a report which is incident on the request. So, our data is classified to make sure that we don't invade or divulge personal information that are quite sensitive. So, this mechanism is all in place.

P10 submitted that Nigeria does not have a data protection law. The participant's (P10) submission is in Appendix.

Theme 6.9: Big Data Challenge. The last decade has witnessed an explosion of data. There is so much data available, and this makes digital forensic examination even more complicated. This research sought to find out how this affected forensic investigation. The interviewer asked participants to share their perspectives on the big data challenge in digital forensic investigation. Most participants stated that the big data challenge affected their analysis, processing capability, and storage. Participants P01, P03, P05, and P09 all submitted that this was a challenge affecting their efficiency. Three participants out of four in this group are from Organization A, with only P09 from Organization B. Participants P02, P06, P07, P08, P10, P13, P15, and P18 all admitted to the challenge but gave different perspectives on possible solutions. All but one (P02) are from Organization B. P02, P06, and P18 all said they adopted focused investigation to overcome this challenge. P07, P08, and P13 noted that their organization has recently set up a large data center to alleviate the storage dilemma.

P09 said:

> Talking about a big data challenge, it is quite a challenge. The way we are trying to manage them is to develop a server infrastructure. So, we have a backup in our server, so we extract data, download data, put them onto our server, access them at a convenient time to do our examination. That's the way we are managing it. Even though sometimes we have downtime, we have challenges accessing the data on the server. Basically, that's the way we have been able to manage it. Again, we are scaling up our forensic workstation so as to bridge the gap of huge data, because again, it takes a long time for some of them to run through, sometimes the ram is very minimal, then it takes more time.

Research Subquestion 2: What is the extent of digital forensic tools adoption by Nigerian law enforcement agents? One theme emerged from this. Table 5.6 captured the emerged theme.

Theme 2.4: Digital Forensic Adoption. The researchers asked participants to assess the level of digital forensic adoption in their agencies. The majority of the respondents viewed this from a user acceptance point of view and claimed an appreciable level of acceptance of digital forensic technology. Thirteen out of the seventeen participants cutting across both organizations that responded to this question believed that the level of adoption (user acceptance) is good. The participants in this category include P01, P02, P03, P04, P05, P06, P07, P08, P11, P12, P15, P17, and P18. P07 said:

> In Nigeria, digital forensics is a new thing, and I've been able to go outside to work with private investigators, and I schooled here too. As of last two years, and what I'm seeing here now, you see they are coming up with getting acquainted with the technology, embracing it and opening up to making use of it, so I think they're coming on….even other agencies we've been able to train our sister agencies

Table 5.6 Theme for research subquestion 2

S/N	Themes	Themes
1	Theme 2.4	Digital forensic adoption

Note This table summarizes the theme from research subquestion 2

Table 5.7 Themes for research subquestion 3

S/N	Themes	Themes
1	Theme 2.5	Impact of lack of digital forensic technology

Note This table summarizes themes for research subquestion 3

Participants P13, P14, P16, and P09 think there is a low adoption and user acceptance. P09 said:

> Based on my perception, I think that a lot of people, for obvious reasons, are not very open to embrace new technology, and the reason is they get so conversant with a particular tool that they think this tool is capable of giving them what they want, and they have got a lot of jobs. This psychology is always there. I have got a lot of jobs. I don't even have the time to go and learn this new tool so, let me stick to what I am comfortable with because it is giving me what I want. Okay, this is one of psychology.

Appendix shows perspectives from other participants.

Research Subquestion 3: How has the lack of digital forensic resources affected the law enforcement agencies in Nigeria, and by extension, their efficiency in the fight to stop cybercrime? An analysis of the participants' responses produced one theme. Table 5.7 captures the emerging theme.

Theme 2.5: Impact of lack of digital forensic technology. The researchers asked the participants to share their perspectives on how the lack of digital forensic technology has impacted efficient investigation of financial crimes and internet fraud. All 10 participants gave different accounts of the impact. Participants P01, P02, P03, P04, P05, P12, P15, P16, P17, and P18, cutting across both organizations, all said it impacted their operations adversely.

P17 said:

> It's impacting on us a great deal because, like I said, these boys have money at their disposal so they can do whatever they want to do. Get whatever, software, hardware they want to get, but we have been constrained, and you know, like having a dog on a leash and expecting him to guard your perimeter. It's not possible. All we can do is bark while these boys stroll around in the compound. All we can do is bark because we are tied to a leash…we can't do anything. For those who are scared of our bark, they take precautionary measures, but for those that know that we are on a leash, they do their nefarious activities without any care.

Research Subquestion 4: What are the areas of digital forensic skills deficiency needing an upgrade? One theme emerged from this research question. Table 5.8 captures the emergent theme.

Table 5.8 Theme for research subquestion 4

S/N	Themes	Themes
1	Theme 3.2	Digital forensic skills needed

Note This table summarizes the theme for research subquestion 4

Theme 3.2: Skills deficiency. The interviewer asked participants to share their perspectives on the areas of skills deficiency they would like to have more training. Participants identified a total of seventeen different skill areas they needed further training. The broad classification, digital forensic examination, had the most nominations by participants. Participants P12, P14, P16, P03, and P04 (cutting across both organizations) said they needed digital forensic examination training. This generalized response may have reflected an overwhelming need for digital forensic investigation training, generally. Computer forensics (with nominations from P01, P17, P07, and P08—consisting of participants from both organizations), network forensics (with nominations from P01, P13, P02, and P08—consisting of participants from both organizations), and Cryptocurrency investigation (with nominations from P11, P12, P17, and P05—also reflecting both organizations), received the second-highest nomination from four participants, respectively. Mobile forensic training (with nominations from P01, P02, and P07, reflecting both organizations), cloud forensic training (with nominations from P07, P08, and P09—all from organization B), and JTAG/Chip-off/Phone repairs (with nominations from P06, P09, and P13—all from organization B) had the joint-third highest nomination from three participants each.

A closer look at this showed participants from organization B tend to be more desirous of advanced forensic skills such as cloud technology investigation, JTAG, and chip-off forensics. This different training interest may be reflective of their respective digital forensic capability maturity. Table 5.9 summarizes the various training program suggested by the participants and the participants that nominated them.

P01 nominated "Ethical Hacking First, Computer Forensic second, Mobile Device third, then Network Forensics'. P09 said:

> I think the training that I would recommend training around cloud forensic investigation, because again, a lot people now store their data in digital devices and cloud data application. A lot of people now store their data on the cloud. So, I recommend that here. That is quite minimal around in this part of the world. JTAG is also another thing, chip-off another aspect of it; network forensics is another thing that I think is quite lacking that we will be happy to build capacity.

Research Subquestion 5: What is the specific digital forensic training needed by law enforcement agents in Nigeria? An analysis of Research Subquestion 4 and Research Subquestion 5 produced one theme, as shown in Table 5.8. This theme was discussed above and further discussed with the context of research subquestion 5. Based on an analysis of user submissions, Table 5.9 summarizes the training nominations by participants.

P12 said:

> I can say that's why we need to be trained. You mentioned bitcoin; bitcoin is one that is giving us headaches, if I can say that. It's something that a lot of these criminals use to launder money, and from my experience and even research, and then reports from even the Investigators, it seems to be something that just disappear. It's something you can't really lay your hands on. I think we really, really need to be trained in that aspect for us to be able to do adequate investigation and prosecution.

Table 5.9 Training courses recommended by participants

S/N	Training desired	Participants	Nominations
1	Digital forensic investigation	P12, P14, P16, P03, P04	5
2	Computer forensics	P01, P07, P08, P17	4
3	Network forensics	P01, P13, P02, P08	4
4	Cryptocurrency investigation	P05, P11, P12, P17	4
5	Mobile forensics	P01, P02, P07	3
6	Cloud forensics	P07, P08, P09	3
7	Chip-off/JTAG/Phone repairs	P06, P09, P13	3
8	Malware analysis	P13, P08	2
9	Cybercrime investigation	P15, P03	2
10	Ethical hacking	P01	1
11	Digital evidence	P10	1
12	Social media investigation	P17	1
13	Web forensics	P05	1
14	Application forensics	P09	1
15	Credit card analysis	P07	1
16	Geolocation analysis	P07	1
17	Document examination	P02	1

Note This table summarizes courses nominated or suggested by participants

Research Subquestion 6: What specific digital forensic tools are in short supply or with expired licenses needing an upgrade? This analysis produced one theme, as shown in Table 5.10.

Theme 2.3: Digital forensic tools needed. The researchers asked participants to list tools they do not have which they would like to have. The responses to this varied between participants, but there were common areas of interest. Also, the areas of specialization of each participant seem to shape their recommendations. Mobile forensic tools were the most frequently mentioned category of tools needed. Participants P01, P17, P02, P05, P09, P03, P04, P17, and P18 (cutting across both organizations) all stated that they needed mobile forensic tools. P09 said: "I think we still need capabilities more for mobile phone forensics…We would like to scale up our capabilities for mobile phones".

Table 5.10 Theme for research for subquestion 6

S/N	Themes	Themes
1	Theme 2.3	Digital forensic tools needed

Note This table summarizes the theme for research subquestion 6

The second most frequently mentioned tool category needed was Cryptocurrency Investigating tools. Participants P01, P18, P02, and P08 (cutting across both organizations) all stated that they needed tools that could assist them in investigating cryptocurrency transactions.

P01 stated that:

> And considering now that everybody is into virtual currency, what they call cryptocurrency, and in years to come now, let me say 80% of the world will move to it. So now, there is a need to have a platform that could actually investigate crimes perpetuated in that space. To have a blockchain analysis...Blockchain analysis is actually used to investigate and check crypto movement in the crypto world.

P04 stated that:

> We can only go as far as what we can do because we lack most of the tools we need. Recently, we made a proposal about seven different tools CDR, qualitative analysis tool, chainanalysis for scripting crypto, about seven CDR, about seven tools, and they are going to cost us about 3 billion So, we don't know if "Organisation A" will be able to approve it and fund it. I'm not sure, but if that will be done, I think we will be on top of the matter.

The third most mentioned tool needed was a tracker. Participants P01, P02, and P16 all stated that they needed trackers. All three participants in this category are cybercrime investigators, and they are from both organizations.

P16 said:

> We need a tracker; yes, we need a tracker. We need a jammer because sometimes when we go, we are just using...we don't have a jammer. So when we go there we have to have access to their phone to see whether he's into it or not before we confiscate the phone, but when we have something like this, I think it will help our work and the tracker mostly when you've arrested some people, you see that there are other people involved or maybe when we go for arrest some people will run, we'll just have their devices, but when we get their numbers, we'll be able to track them and arrest them. I think we need jammer and this thing is very important.

There are several other tools mentioned by other respondents. P18 submitted that there is a need to have Call Details Record (CDR) analyzer. P05 stated they need to have social media monitoring tools, pentesting tools, Access Data Forensic Toolkit (FTK), and Cellebrite. Participants P08 and P09 submitted that there is a need to have network forensic and cloud forensic tools. Participant P13 stated the need to have a Chip-Off forensic tool. P17 stated the need for a mobile cybercrime laboratory to allow for on-field extraction and analysis where necessary. P07 made a generalized submission without being specific on any tool. P13 noted the need for more hardware without being specific on any type or category. Table 5.11 and Fig. 1 summarize the top six tool recommendations by the participants.

Research Subquestion 7: What are the daily cybercrime caseload and available digital forensics resources? Two themes emerged from this analysis, as captured in Table 5.12.

Table 5.11 Top 6 tools needed by participants

S/N	Tool type/category	Participants
1	Mobile forensics tools	P01, P02, P03, P04, P05, P09, P17, P18
2	Cryptocurrency investigating tools	P01, P18, P02, P08
3	Trackers/Jammers	P01, P02, P16
4	Cloud forensics	P08, P09
5	Network forensics	P08, P08
6	Call data records (CDR) analyzer	P05, P18

Note This table summarizes the top 6 tools needed at both organizations

Table 5.12 Themes for research subquestion 7

S/N	Themes	Themes
1	Theme 6.6	Rising caseloads
2	Theme 6.7	Top three reasons for rising caseloads

Note This table summarizes themes for research subquestion 7

Theme 6.6: Rising of cybercrime. Participants shared their perspectives on the rising caseloads of cybercrime. Of the 18 participants interviewed, 17 Participants (P01, P02, P03, P05, P06, P07, P08, P09, P11, P12, P13, P14, P15, P16, P17, and P18) cutting across both organizations all pointed to the rising caseload as a significant challenge. Only participant P10 questioned the premise for the claims of a high caseload. Participant P10's perspective is in Appendix. P14 said that "what I can tell you is we have a lot of cases that overwhelm us. Because if you just do the math, we are less than ten thousand against cases covering the whole country".

P12 said that:

> It's quite much. In a day we can get up to a hundred. Yes, it has increased, and even the courts…are saddled with such cases now. So, it has really increased and like I said in my organization can get up to hundred in a day.

P17 stated that:

> It's really massive. Cybercrimes in the headquarters here was started in 2019 or barely two years, and we have over 500 cases. In barely two years, we have had 500 cases, and each year, we are expected to deliver on the 500 cases, at least 500 cases. So, for a department to have over 500 cases in just two years - and that is minus the ones we've sent to court - and I can guarantee you before the end of this year, it's going to get to 700. And the team in the whole department, we are 10 in the whole department. So, you can imagine in the whole department dealing with 500 cases and growing.

P18 said:

> Although no data to back it up, but I can tell you out of 10 young boys in Lagos about three will be into computer-related fraud, one way or the other, directly or indirectly, investment scam, non-delivery scam, phishing scam, just name it…even nowadays, we caught somebody

> who just finished secondary school because of that, so it's rampant, because out of 10 persons in Nigeria, at least 7:3, and if we are not mindful in the next few years you will just discover that 70% of Nigerian youths are ex-convicts, sorry to say.

P04 also seemed in close agreement with P18. P04 said:

> I'll say these, 4 to 10 young boys are in cybercrime in Nigeria. Let me give you Lagos for instance; South-East, South-South they are now much in it. In South-West, 5 to 10 of young boys are into it because they see it's a passion; he's my friend he just made money let me make that money too.

P08 said:

> Most times, we receive up to 50, 20... Most times it's more than that. You know most times they go for a raid, and you know what they will pack is, you can't even count, and you know we also have cases from sister agencies that come in. There was a time we had over a hundred laptops, we don't even know where to start from. So, the cases are actually absolutely overwhelming. Absolutely!

P09 said:

> So, on a daily basis, we have enormous request for digital forensic investigation because "Organisation A" is engaged in raiding cyber-café based on intelligence. People are arrested and brought, and we have to look at their devices, and they have to be screened out... So, averagely in a day, I can say we receive like 3-5 phones every day, averagely I will just say. So, if you do that calculation, then you will know what we get in a week and in a month and a year and will account for the backlogs we have in a department.

Theme 6.7: Top 3 reasons for rising caseloads. The interviewer asked participants to share their perspectives on the rising caseloads. Participants shared several reasons ranging from economic, social, cultural, peer pressure, and others. Unemployment topped the reasons, with 11 participants submitting that unemployment is a significant reason for the high caseload of cybercrime. Participants P01, P03, P05, P06, P07, P08, P09, P10, P14, P15, and P18 (from both organizations) said poverty was a significant reason. Table 5.13 summarizes the various reasons given by each participant.

Poverty was the second most frequently mentioned reason, with participants P02, P04, P05, P06, P08, and P16 (from both organizations) all submitting that poverty was a significant reason behind the rising caseloads. The next factor was peer pressure and greed, respectively. Participants P03, P08, P09, P14, and P16 (from both organizations) submitted that peer pressure is one of the key factors behind the rising numbers. Participants P11, P15, P16, P17, and P18 (all from organization B) stated that greed is behind the increase. Participants P01, P10, and P15 (from both organizations) submitted that the relative ease of cybercrime compared to other traditional crimes like robbery is one reason for the high figures. Participants P04, P14, and P17 (from both organizations) stated that poor parenting is a significant reason youths turn to cybercrime.

Table 5.13 Top three reasons for high caseloads

S/N	Participants	Top reasons
1	P01	Unemployment, ease of cybercrime, and corruption
2	P02	Poverty
3	P03	Unemployment, peer pressure, and weak penalties
4	P04	Bad parenting, poverty
5	P05	Unemployment, poor education, and poverty
6	P06	Poverty, unemployment, and get-rich-quick syndrome
7	P07	Unemployment
8	P08	Unemployment, poverty, and peer pressure
9	P09	Unemployment, peer pressure, and moral decadence
10	P10	Unemployment, ease of cybercrime, and corruption
11	P11	Poor orientation, greed
12	P12	The increasing popularity of internet crime
13	P13	Access to internet,
14	P14	Unemployment, peer pressure, bad parental upbringing
15	P15	Greed, ease of cybercrime, and unemployment
16	P16	Greed, peer group, and poverty
17	P17	Greed, parental pressure
18	P18	Greed, unemployment, lack of self-perception

Note This table summarizes the top three reasons given by participants for the high caseloads of cybercrime in Nigeria

P14 said:

> The major reason is unemployment. They're all social problems triggering this unabated or progress the skill at which the internet fraud is being committed. It outweighs what was obtainable in the past. It keeps growing. It keeps growing because a lot of our youths who are majorly the culprits in this regard are unemployed. They do not have job security; hence, they turn to crime. When you interview some of them, you'll hear this thing; they'll say if they have a choice. Some are even graduates; that's the painful part in all these things. People who have gone through the four walls of the university and after seeking employment they turn to crime. There's no excuse for that anyway, but it's the reality we just have to face. It's growing, and the more we deny the obvious, the more it keeps escalating.

5.4 Supplementary Findings

5.4.1 Policy Suggestions

The researchers asked participants to make policy recommendations or suggestions. Six participants—P04, P05, P09, P10, P15, P18 (from both organizations)—suggested that a policy should be in place to promote better collaboration between agencies and departments (both technical and non-technical) within the agencies. Participants P07, P12, P17, P18 (from both organizations) said a policy should encourage training and re-training of digital forensic examiners and cybercrime prosecutors. Participants P03, P09, and P10 (from both organizations) pointed to the need to review the Cybercrime Act 2015. Participants P02 and P14 (reflecting both organizations) suggested a policy that promotes decentralized forensic laboratories (the need for digital forensic laboratories to be set up in other states and zones).

Participants gave many other suggestions apart from the ones stated earlier. For instance, P01 suggested a framework for access to citizen databases and encouraging big-tech companies to have offices in Nigeria to help smoothen out some of the jurisdictional roadblocks during investigations involving their platforms. P11 suggested fusing lawyers into the forensic department to ensure synergy in the investigative and prosecutive processes. P13 suggested the need for a better chain of custody. P14 advocated for more funding. P16 emphasized the need for orientation and public enlightenment. P03 suggested the need for adopting global best practices. P06 suggested the need to invest in research and development to encourage indigenous innovations in digital forensics. P03 suggested the need for an autonomous funding structure for the digital forensic unit and the need for a review of the existing laws to ensure stiffer punishment. P09 suggested the need for incentives and protection of the mental health of digital forensic practitioners given the exposures in the course of work. Selected participant views on this are in Appendix.

5.5 Summary

This Chapter captured the perspectives of officers of Nigeria's financial crimes investigative agencies—the Economic and Financial Crimes Commission (EFCC) and the Nigerian Police Force. The chapter presented the findings of this study. The researchers interviewed eighteen participants and analyzed the transcripts with NVivo. Six themes emerged from this analysis. Theme one presented perspectives on personnel capability and adequacy. Theme two presented perspectives on the availability of digital forensic tools. Theme three presented perspectives on training. Theme four presented perspectives on processes. Theme five presented perspectives on policy. Theme six highlighted the challenges. Challenges identified include lack of an efficient framework for collaboration, jurisdictional challenges, emerging technologies funding, the pace of cybercrime, big data challenge, and the lack of a roadmap for digital forensic readiness.

This chapter made other essential findings. For instance, the perspectives of the participants showed that the financial crimes agencies lacked digital forensic resources. A deeper probe into this lack showed the agencies lacked competent personnel, structured training programs, digital forensic resources, funding, and many more. The chapter's findings confirmed that the cybercrime caseload was increasing, overwhelming the law enforcement agencies. The chapter also showed that the speed of cybercrime was a key challenge, given the lack of forensic resources.

The findings of this chapter showed the top three reasons for rising caseloads of cybercrime in Nigeria as unemployment, poverty, and peer pressure. The chapter also made an essential finding of identifying the top three tools needed by cybercrime investigators in Nigeria—Mobile Forensics tools, Cryptocurrency investigating tools, and Trackers/Jammers. An important finding from this chapter was identifying the top training courses needed by the participants as Digital forensic investigation, Computer forensics, Network forensics, Cryptocurrency investigation, Mobile forensics, Cloud forensics, Chip-off/JTAG/Phone repairs, and many others. The chapter also made significant findings on digital forensic adoption and many other findings.

References

1. Bello M, Griffiths M (2021) Routine activity theory and cybercrime investigation in Nigeria: how capable are law enforcement agencies? In: Rethinking cybercrime. Palgrave Macmillan, Cham, pp 213–235
2. Braun V, Clarke V (2006) Using thematic analysis in psychology. Qual Res Psychol 3(2):77–101
3. Cybercrimes (Prohibition, Prevention, etc) Act (2015) https://cert.gov.ng/ngcert/resources/CyberCrime__Prohibition_Prevention_etc__Act__2015.pdf
4. Eboibi FE (2017) A review of the legal and regulatory frameworks of Nigerian Cybercrimes Act 2015. Comput Law Secur Rev 33(5):700–717
5. Ehimen OR, Bola A (2010) Cybercrime in Nigeria. Bus Intell J 3(1):93–98
6. Guardian Newspaper (2022) NCC puts cybercrime losses in Nigeria at $500m, sets to implement DMS. https://guardian.ng/news/ncc-puts-cybercrime-losses-in-nigeria-at-500m-sets-to-implement-dms/
7. Mohammed KH, Mohammed YD, Solanke AA (2019) Cybercrime and digital forensics: bridging the gap in legislation, investigation, and prosecution of cybercrime in Nigeria. Int J Cybersecur Intell Cybercrime 2(1):56–53
8. News Agency of Nigeria (2016) Police to create special unit to tackle cybercrime. Guardian Newspaper. https://guardian.ng/news/police-to-create-special-unit-to-tackle-cybercrime/
9. Obuah E (2010) Combatting corruption in Nigeria: the Nigerian economic and financial crimes (EFCC). Afr Stud Q 12(1)
10. Okolorie GR (2020, December 22) Uncovering patterns in complex investigations is no match for Nigeria's Economic and Financial Crimes Commission (EFCC) [Interview]. Cellebrite. https://www.cellebrite.com/en/uncovering-patterns-in-complex-investigations-is-no-match-for-nigerias-economic-and-financial-crimes-commission-efcc/
11. Olayemi OJ (2014) A socio-technological analysis of cybercrime and cyber security in Nigeria. Int J Sociol Anthropol 6(3):116–125
12. Omodunbi BA, Odiase PO, Olaniyan OM, Esan AO (2016) Cybercrimes in Nigeria: analysis, detection, and prevention. J Eng Technol 1(1):37–42
13. Oraegbunam IK (2015) The Nigerian police and problems of cybercrime investigation: need for adequate training. Niger Law J 18(1):1–28
14. Percy WH, Kostere K, Kostere S (2015) Generic qualitative research in psychology. Qualitative Rep 20(2):76–85
15. Symantec Corporation and African Union (2016) Cybercrime & cybersecurity trends in Africa. www.thehaguesecuritydelta.com/media/com_hsd/report/135/document/Cyber-security-trends-report-Africa-en.pdf
16. Umar I, Samsudin RS, Mohamed M (2016) Understanding the successes and challenges of Anti-Corruption Agency (ACA) in Nigeria: a case of Economic and Financial Crimes Commission (EFCC). Asian J Multidisc Stud 4(5):27–33

17. Vanguard Newspaper (2020) Nigeria police, interpol arrest three suspects over cybercrime. Vanguard Newspaper. https://www.vanguardngr.com/2020/07/nigeria-police-interpol-arrest-3-suspects-over-cybercrime/
18. Zamawe FC (2015) The implication of using NVivo software in qualitative data analysis: evidence-based reflections. Malawi Med J 27(1):13–15

Chapter 6
Research Findings—Cybercrime Composition, Frequency, and Complexity in Nigeria (From a Law Enforcement Perspective)

Abstract This chapter aims to present the findings of this study, investigating the cybercrime dynamics (composition, frequency, and complexity) in Nigeria. The study is a qualitative case study, structured to rely on semi-structured interviews of 18 cybercrime investigators, prosecutors, and digital forensic examiners, triangulating the findings with official documents, reports, and archival records. This chapter presented key findings, such as prosecution and conviction records of cybercrime (by taxonomy) in Nigeria since 2015, and others. This chapter also presented a synthesis of the analysis of official press releases as well as cybercrime case files, identifying trends and patterns in the process. The chapter ended with a comparative analysis of cybercrime investigation and prosecution in other jurisdictions, with the United States of America as case study.

Keywords Cybercrime · Internet fraud · EFCC · Economic and Financial Crimes Commission · Nigeria police · Digital forensic readiness · Cybercrime caseloads · Cybercrime taxonomy

6.1 Introduction

Nigeria have recorded a disturbing wave of rising caseloads of cybercrime. Several authors have report pointed to these increasing incidents of cybercrime in Nigeria. For instance, Eboibi [6] highlighted Nigeria as one of the hotbeds of cybercrime, globally. Omodunbi et al. [20] noted the increased cybercrime activities in Nigeria, and the associated devastating impact on the economy. The Nigeria Communications Commission (NCC) puts total annual loss to cybercrime in Nigeria at $500 million. The implication of this is that cybercrime contributes to about 0.08% loss in GDP [10]. Even more disturbing is that the rising caseloads of cybercrime is fueled by a growing number of youths taking to the crime. In a study by Suleiman [21], 55% of youths sampled were involved in Internet fraud; 30% aged between 23 and 45 years were also involved. This was further corroborated in studies by Abdulkadir and Abdulkadir [1], noting that while cybercrime cuts across different age strata, majority

R. T. Sibe and C. Kaunert, *Cybercrime, Digital Forensic Readiness, and Financial Crime Investigation in Nigeria*, Advanced Sciences and Technologies for Security Applications, https://doi.org/10.1007/978-3-031-54089-9_6

of perpetrators in Nigeria are the youths. The victims cut across the financial sector to other institutions and even individuals across different jurisdictions, and is a concern to both Nigeria and the international community.

With the rapidly evolving technological landscape, internet fraudsters have taken advantage of new toolkits and technology to launch more sophisticated attacks. This has also been the case in Nigeria, where Nigerian Internet fraudsters have increased in sophistication over the years. The internet fraudsters have progressed from poorly written bulk emails to spear-phishing attacks and sophisticated Business Email Compromise (BEC) schemes. For instance, Nigerian cybercriminals reportedly caused a breach involving confidential health records of over 750,000 persons in Los Angeles [3, 4]. They now use sophisticated malware tools such as Zeus, Darknet, Predator pain, ISpySoftware, and other malware families [11]. This increased sophistication have become an incentive for more attacks and perhaps explains the numbers. Such high prevalence is of significant concern to the country.

A major driving force behind the use of complex and sophisticated tools, specialist hacking tools and powerful malware is the increasing availability of these dangerous tools on the internet. These tools are readily available on the cyberspace for less expensive amounts. Thus, people with less sophisticated skills can now procure these tools and deploy same to vulnerable and unsuspecting people. This model is increasingly sophisticated and have evolved to Cybercrime-as-a-service or crimeware as a Service [17, 18]. The proliferation of cybercrime-as-a-service is a major driving force behind the increase in cybercrime, opening the cybercrime space to both the experienced and inexperienced. Today, a rookie cybercriminal can easily procure dangerous tools for as little as $20 dollars, with full instruction on how to deploy it, and in some cases money-back guarantee.

To be able to tackle the cybercrime scourge in Nigeria, it is important to first understand the complexity, dynamics, and frequency of the attacks in Nigeria. Unfortunately, while several authors point to the high caseloads, there is no dedicated study that investigated this beyond anecdotal accounts and newspaper highlights, particularly, from a law enforcement perspective. The law enforcement agencies are at the fore front of combatting the cybercrime scourge and they have first-hand experience given the arrests and number of cases prosecuted. Also, for the law enforcement agencies to lead the war against internet fraud effectively, a good knowledge of the dynamics and complexity is needed to build the forensic readiness of the institutions.

This research relied on official statistics and documents from the Economic and Financial crimes commission. The EFCC is the major agency in Nigeria saddled with the responsibility for prosecuting cybercrime. Over the last few years, the commission has recorded remarkable success in terms of prosecution numbers. For instance, in 2020, the commission recorded 976 convictions. Out of this number, 345 are listed as cybercrime and 4 listed as computer related fraud. In 2021, the number of convictions increased to 2220. Out of this number, 394 are listed as cybercrime and 13 listed as computer related fraud [7]. In 2022, the number of convictions rose to 3785. This number represents a 98.93% prosecution success rate, which underscores their effective and diligent prosecution. Out of this number, 747 are listed as cybercrime and 83 listed as computer related fraud [8].

This chapter presents the results, in relation to the research findings. The chapter also reviewed two high profile cybercrime cases of Nigerians prosecuted in other jurisdictions.

Primary Research Question 2: What is composition and complexity of the cybercrime cases in Nigeria?

Research Subquestion 1: What are the frequent cybercrimes committed in Nigeria?
Research Subquestion 2: How many persons are convicted of cybercrime in Nigeria?

To answer Primary Research Question 2, this research further Triangulated Supporting Information for Cybercrime Caseloads, Taxonomy, Dynamics, Complexity, and frequency of cybercrime incidents and conviction in Nigeria. This research further analysed data from three sources (1) Official conviction record of the EFCC (2) Analysis of official press release of the EFCC from their website (3) detailed conviction records of last 3 years, and (4) court judgments and charge sheets for cybercrime prosecution.

6.2 Official Statistics of Cybercrime Investigation and Prosecutions by the EFCC Over the Last 8 Years

To better understand the magnitude, dynamics, frequency, and taxonomy of cybercrimes in Nigeria, the researchers reached out to the Economic and Financial Crimes Commission for conviction statistics. This was graciously shared by the commission, through the research and development unit, and is directly reproduced below (also see table note as supplied by the EFCC) (Tables 6.1 and 6.2).

6.3 Analysis of Official Press Release of the EFCC in Relation to Cybercrime

A press release by the Economic and Financial Crimes Commission [8] show that in 2022, a total of 3785 convictions were secured across all commands. This conviction statistic for 2022, shows an improvement of 70.5% year-on-year. In terms of success rate of prosecution, the commission recorded 98.93%, having lost only 41 cases out of 3785 cases in all. In terms of spread, the Lagos Command had the highest convictions, with a total of 765 convictions. This was followed by Ibadan command with 573 convictions and the Port Harcourt Zonal Command with 567 convictions. From a historical point of view, the conviction statistics in 2022 is the highest ever in Nigeria since the inception of EFCC. The figures have showed an annual increment in the last decade (except the year 2020 due to the COVID-19 lock down). A breakdown

Table 6.1 Breakdown of cybercrime investigations by EFCC

Offences	2015	2016	2017	2018	2019	2020	2021	2022
Email hacking (BEC)	24	46	12	21	13	147	90	49
Internet fraud* (Computer related fraud)	33	112	56	120	26	302	–	–
Cybercrime (Other forms of cybercrimes)			2	18	916	923	433	74
Internet banking fraud	12	25	59	1		5	–	–
Identity theft							1057	865
Electronic signature theft							944	729
Credit card fraud							31	18
Theft of electronic device							133	
Fraudulent issuance of e-instruction							200	6

Source EFCC

Note Breakdown of Cybercrime Investigations by EFCC, from 2015 to 2022

*The Commission conducted a review of its system for classification of offences in 2020. Internet Fraud was initially a classification of Cybercrime offence where commission of crime was with the use of a computer device with or without internet access. Then, generalised classification of cybercrime offences as internet fraud/scam was prevalent. However, these groups of offences are now identified in other forms such as Identity theft, Credit Card Fraud, etc. The same case applies to internet banking

Table 6.2 Breakdown of cybercrime convictions by EFCC

Convictions	2015	2016	2017	2018	2019	2020	2021	2022
Internet fraud	2	0	3	7	344	309	N/A	–
Computer related fraud	–	–	–	–	1	0	N/A	–
Business email compromise	–	–	–	–	2	2	N/A	746
Cybercrime								20
Identity theft								24
Electronic signature theft								84

Source EFCC

Note Breakdown of cybercrime convictions by EFCC, from 2015 to 2022

of this shows that in 2015, the EFCC recorded a total of 103 convictions. In 2018, this increased to 312; increased to 1280 in 2019; reduced slightly to 976 convictions in 2020 (largely due to the COVID-19 pandemic, with the lockdown of courts); increased to 2220 in 2021; and now 3785 in 2022. This is an increment of 3574.8% over a 7-year period.

It is noteworthy that not all the convictions were for cybercrime. However, majority of these were cybercrime related. For instance, the Economic and Financial Crimes Commission (EFCC) disclosed that as at September 2021, 80% of its 978 convictions were connected to cybercrime and cybercrime related offences [10].

To zero in to the specifics, official Press Releases of the Economic and Financial Crimes Commission were analyzed for February 2023, to get further insight into the caseload of cybercrime in Nigeria. A total of 13 Press Releases reviewed from the official EFCC website (www.efccnigeria.org), showed a total of 16 convictions. Within the period under review. Rivers State command of the EFCC recorded 7 convictions in the month, followed by Abuja with 5 convictions, and Makurdi with 1 conviction. A closer look at the excerpts of the charge shows that the convictions where mostly internet fraud, romance scam, and fraudulent impersonation. The highest sentence given was two years, but all (except one) had options of fines not more than N200,000. All convictions followed a guilty plea. The press releases have been distilled and paraphrased below:

February 2020

- The EFCC, Port Harcourt, Rivers State Command secured the conviction of an internet fraudster to two years imprisonment on a one count charge for impersonation, contrary to Section 22(2) (b)(i) of the Cybercrimes (Prohibition and Prevention Etc) Act, 2015. Excerpts of the charge reads: "That you, <name redacted> on or about 1st June, 2022 in Port Harcourt, Rivers within the jurisdiction of this Honourable Court, fraudulently represented yourself in your Telegram links on YouTube as Thomas Alex, and many others, with intent to gain advantage for yourself and thereby committed an offence contrary to Section 22(2) (b)(i) of the Cybercrimes (Prohibition and Prevention Etc.) Act, 2015 and punishable under Same Section". The suspect pleaded guilty to the charge and was convicted and sentenced to two years in the Correctional Service with Three Hundred Thousand Naira (N300,000.00) payable into the Consolidated Revenue Account of the Federal Republic of Nigeria, as option of fine. The judge also ordered the forfeiture of the convict's Samsung Galaxy A305 used in committing the offence.
- The Kaduna zonal command of the Economic and Financial Crimes Commission, secured the conviction of a student at the Kaduna State High Court on a one count charge bordering on internet fraud. "The defendant fraudulently impersonated one Major Michael Scales of the United States of America Army, by creating a Facebook account with the name Michael Scales and had correspondences with unsuspecting women. The defendant pleaded guilty to the charge and was sentenced to 5-years imprisonment with an option N 150,000 fine. He is also to forfeit to the Federal Government all gadgets used to perpetrate the crime, including one HP Laptop and an Infinity S5".
- The Kaduna Zonal Command of the EFCC secured the conviction of a "Yahoo Boy" (a name used for internet fraudsters in Nigeria) at the Kaduna State High Court on a one count charge of impersonation. The defendant pleaded guilty for dishonestly inducing his victim on Instagram to deliver the sum of Twenty Seven Thousand, Nine Hundred Pakistani Rupees (27,900). Defendant was sentenced to 5 years imprisonment or a fine of N 100,000 to be paid to the Kaduna State Government.
- Three "Yahoo Boys" sentenced to community service in Abuja. All three were brought before the FCT High Court Gwagwalada Abuja on one-count charge each, bordering on internet fraud. The first defendant allegedly pretended to be a marine engineer named Zhang Li and obtained N150,000 (One Hundred and

Fifty Thousand Naira Only) from his victim, a Chinese citizen, while second defendant also posed as a Bryan Alex on various social media apps and obtained N1,500,000 (One Million Five Hundred Thousand Naira Only) from his victims. The third defendant impersonated one John Alpha, an American engineer and defrauded his victim, a United States of America citizen of $170 (One hundred and seventy US Dollars). All three defendants pleaded guilty to the charges and were convicted and sentenced to community service. The first defendant "is to clean the court premise for seven days and pay a fine of N50,000 (Fifty Thousand Naira Only), while the third who had restituted $100 (One Hundred Dollars) from the $170 (One Hundred and Seventy Dollars) he benefited from the scam, is to cut the grass in the court premises and refund the balance of $70 (Seventy Dollars) to the Federal Government. His phone is to be sold and proceeds also paid to the Federal Government". The second defendant "is to fill up every container in the court with water. In addition, he is to pay a fine of N200, 000 (Two Hundred Thousand Naira Only) while his phones are to be sold and proceeds paid into the account of the Federal Government".

- The Federal High Court in Port Harcourt, Rivers State convicted and sentenced two internet fraudsters to various jail terms for Impersonation, contrary to Section 22(2) (b)(ii) of the Cybercrimes (Prohibition, Prevention, etc.) Act, 2015. They pleaded guilty to the charges preferred against them by the prosecution. The first defendant was convicted and sentenced to one year imprisonment with One Hundred Thousand Naira as option of fine. The second defendant was convicted and sentenced to three years in prison with Two Hundred Thousand Naira as option of fine. "The Judges also ordered that one iPhone 7 and Infinix S4 phones belonging to the convicts be forfeited to the Federal Republic of Nigeria. It shall be sold via public auction by the EFCC and the proceeds deposited into the EFCC Recovery Account domiciled in the Central Bank of Nigeria, CBN".
- The Federal High Court sitting in Port Harcourt, Rivers State, convicted and sentenced two internet fraudsters to various jail terms for Impersonation, contrary to Section 22(2) (b) of the Cybercrimes (Prohibition, Prevention, etc.) Act, 2015. The charges bothers on fraudulent impersonation on Telegram, thereby committing an offence contrary to Section 22(2) (b)(i) of the Cybercrimes (Prohibition, Prevention, etc.) Act, 2015 and punishable under Section 22(2) (iv) of the same Act". Both pleaded "guilty" to the charges preferred against them by the prosecution. The court convicted and sentenced the first defendant to one year in prison with an option of fine of Two Hundred Thousand Naira (N200,000.00) fine; while the second defendant was sentenced to two years with Three Hundred Thousand Naira (N300,000.00) fine. The Judge also ordered that, one Apple iPhone, ash colour iPhone 6S, one black itel phone, one black Asus laptop and one iPhone 7 recovered from the convicts be forfeited to the Federal Republic of Nigeria.
- The Kaduna Zonal Command of the EFCC secured the conviction of one suspect at the Kaduna State High Court on a one count charge bordering on cybercrime. The defendant was accused for impersonation and dishonestly inducing the suspect on social media (Instagram) to deliver the sum of 400 USD (Four Hundred U.S Dollars) committing an offence contrary to Section 308 of the Kaduna State Penal

Code Law, 2017 and punishable under Section 309 of the Same Law. The court convicted and sentenced the defendant to 5 years imprisonment or pay a fine of One Hundred Thousand Naira. In addition, the suspect is to forfeit his Infinix Zero X cell phone, which was used to commit the crime, to the Federal Government Nigeria.

- The Abuja Zonal Command of the EFCC secured the conviction of one cyber criminal at the FCT High Court Gwagwalada. The suspect who pleaded guilty of the crime was accused of fraudulent impersonation on Facebook to defraud a Thailand citizen and a telecom technician based in Madison, New Jersey, USA, committing an offence contrary to Section 95 of the Penal Code Laws of the Federation of Nigeria (Abuja) 1990 and punishable under Section 322 of the same Laws. The court convicted and sentenced the defendant to one year imprisonment with the option of fine of N100,000 (One Hundred Thousand Naira). He is also to forfeit his HP laptop to the Federal Government.
- The Abuja Zonal Command of the EFCC arraigned one suspect before the FCT High Court, Kuje on one count charge bordering on impersonation. The charge reads that the suspect, "(aka Natasha) sometime in 2022 at Abuja within the jurisdiction of this Honourable Court, through a platform called Reddit cheats by pretending to be a porn star named Natasha, in that regard you pose as female to trick your victims, which delivered to you the sum of $300 (Three Hundred Dollars) and you thereby committed an offence contrary to and punishable under Sections 321 and 322 of the Penal Code Act, Laws of the Federation (Abuja) 1990". The defendant pleaded not guilty to the charge.
- An internet fraudster was convicted and sentenced to one year in prison by the Federal High Court sitting in Port Harcourt, Rivers State for impersonation contrary to Section 22(2) (b)(i) of Cybercrimes (Prohibition, Prevention, etc.) Act, 2015. The suspect defrauded his victims through romance scam. The suspect was jailed after pleading "guilty" to a one count charge preferred against him by the Economic and Financial Crimes Commission, EFCC, Port Harcourt Command, on Wednesday February 15, 2023. Convicted and sentenced the suspect to one year imprisonment with an option of fine of Fifty Thousand Naira (N50,000.00) payable into the Consolidated Revenue Account of the Federation. In addition, the Court ordered that one black Tecno Pop 3 and one Tecno mobile phone recovered from the convict be forfeited ot he Federal Government of Nigeria.
- The EFCC Makurdi Zonal Command on February 15, 2023 secured the conviction of a suspect on one count charge of fraud before Justice James Kolawole Omotosho of the Federal High Court Maitama, Abuja. The count reads: The male suspect "fraudulently frank electronic message by which you represented yourself to be one NOAL HILLS, a Military Doctor from United State of America on Instagram and obtained from one Miss. PETRA BONACOVA, a Czech Republic National, the sum of $104 USD (One Hundred and Four Dollars) worth of Bitcoin, which you converted and transferred to your Zenith Bank Account No. 2264654328 and thereby committed an offence contrary to Section 14(3) of the Cybercrime (Prohibition, Prevention, etc.) Act, 2015 and punishable under the same Section of the Act". The court convicted and sentenced the suspect to one year imprisonment

or a fine of N50,000 (Fifty Thousand Naira). Also, suspect is to forfeit his INFINIX HOT 8 phone and the amount in his Zenith bank account to Federal Government of Nigeria, while the account will be closed forthwith.

- On February 21, 2023, at the Federal High Court Port Harcourt, after pleading guilty to a one count charge, internet fraud suspect was convicted and sentenced to two years imprisonment for impersonation contrary to Section 22 (2) (b) (ii) of the Cyber Crime (Prohibition, Prevention Etc) Act, 2015. The suspect "fraudulently impersonated one Kerry James, an American citizen in your Gmail and Telegram accounts with intent to gain advantage for yourself and thereby committed an offence contrary to Section 22 (2) (b) (ii) of the Cyber Crime (Prohibition, Prevention, Etc) Act, 2015, and punishable under Section 22 (2) (b) (iv) of the same Act". The suspect was convicted and sentenced two years with One Hundred Thousand Naira (N100,000.00) as an option of fine payable into the Consolidated Revenu Account of the Federal Republic of Nigeria. The judge also ordered that one white iPhone X Max, one iPhone 13 Pro Max and one Redmi note 9 recovered from the convict be forfeited to the Federal Republic of Nigeria.
- On 21st February 2023, the Abuja zonal command of EFCC at the High Court of the Federal Capital Territory, Kwali, secured the conviction of a suspect on a one count charge bordering on internet fraud. Excerpt of the charge reads, "that you, <name redacted> 'M' 23 years old sometime in 2022 at Abuja within the jurisdiction of the High Court of the Federal Capital Territory did cheat by impersonation when you presented yourself to the Chinese women using the profile names 'Chen', 'Chengi' and 'Ziang' on WECHAT and INSTAGRAM online apps and obtained the sums of 8,000 and 50,000 Yauns, where you benefited the sum of Six Hundred Thousand Naira (N600,000) which was paid into your <bank name redacted> Bank account number <account number redacted>, a fact you know to be false and you thereby committed an offence contrary to Section 321 of the Penal Code Act, Laws of the Federation (Abuja), 1990 and punishable under Section 324 of the same Law". The defendant after pleading guilty to the charge was convicted and sentenced by the judge to 6 months in prison without an option of fine. He is also to forfeit his phone and the financial proceeds of his crime (N600,000) to he Federal Government.

6.4 Detailed Conviction Records for Last Three Years—Patterns and Trends

To further triangulate the findings of this study with other available data, the researchers downloaded the conviction summary on the Economic and Financial Crimes Commission [9] website for 2020, 2021, 2022. The 2020 conviction summary shows 976 convictions by the EFCC. It is noteworthy that while cybercrime and cybercrime related offences constitute the majority of this, there were also other offences such as economic sabotage, OBT (Obtaining by tricks), money laundering, currency trafficking, Abuse of office, diversion, and many others.

2020

Downloaded data from the Economic and Financial Crimes Economic and Financial Crimes [9] shows that in 2020, the EFCC successfully secured 976 convictions, according to the 107-page report. This research made a few observations of the trends and patterns. For instance, like the other years, the **convictions were dominated by cybercrime and cybercrime related cases**. The summary of convictions did not have detailed breakdown of the specifics or taxonomy of the cybercrime convictions. It was also observed that majority of the cases were decided by guilty pleas or plea bargain.

Another trend observed was that in terms of volume, most of the cases convicted were relatively small amounts ranging from as low as $25 to a few instances of high amounts such as as $30,000 and N12,104,753.93, respectively. For instance, in the case of Itiowe Kelvin, with charge number FHC/IB/118C/2020 at the Federal High Court Ibadan, the sum involved $25 only. The suspect was found guilty of cybercrime and sentenced to 3 months imprisonment. In the case of Adeyemi Habib, with charge number FHC/ABJ/CR/161/19, with the dollar amount involved put as $30,000, the suspect was found guilty for cybercrime. This was the highest amount (dollar) in the conviction list for cybercrime for 2020, as seen on the list. It is noteworthy that as seen in the published report, there were cases were "NIL" was entered in the column for "Amount involved" in some of the cybercrime cases. This research could not ascertain the exact meaning or implication of the "NIL" entries.

Also, another trend observed was that in almost all the cases, there were **forfeitures and restitutions**. For instance, in the case of Itiowe Kelvin cited above, the judge sentenced the suspect to 3 months imprisonment, as well as restitute $25 (amount involved) to the victim. Also, the judge ruled for the forfeiture of an iPhone 11 and MIQI phone to the Federal Government. In the case of Osanyintoba Temitope Dare with charge number FHC/OS/42/2019 at the Federal High Court, Osogbo, the suspect was ordered to restitute the sum of $1000 to the victim. Also, the judge ruled for the forfeiture of the following items: 1 Nokia phone, 1 Apple Macbook Laptop, 1 HP Laptop, and 1 Lexus ES 350 car to the federal government. In the case of Oginni Femi Rufus with charge number I/13EFCC/2020, who was convicted at the federal high court Ibadan, and sentenced to 6 months imprisonment, the judge ordered the defendant to restitute his victim the sum of ₦12,104,753.93. The judge also ordered the forfeiture of a Toyota Venza, 2 Apple Macbook Laptops, 1 Apple iPad, and several other devices.

2021

Downloaded data from the Economic and Financial Crimes Commission [9] website shows that in 2021, the EFCC successfully secured 2220 convictions, according to the 174-page report. This research made a few observations of the trends and patterns. For instance, like the other years, the **convictions were equally dominated by cybercrime and cybercrime related cases**. However, unlike the report for the year 2020, the year 2021 report showing summary of convictions did have new taxonomies, other than the general "cyber crime" classification. For instance, this research observed the following cybercrime conviction classification such as “cybercrime, internet fraud”, “OBT and Computer Related Fraud”, “Impersonation”, “Internet Fraud”, “Identity Theft and Impersonation”, and “Interference with Device”.

As noted above, there were new cybercrime related offences noticed in 2021. For instance, in the case of Wada Godday Ojodomo with charge number FHC/ABJ/CR/84/2021, the suspect was convicted for “interference with Device” and sentenced to 6 months imprisonment or payment of fine of N500,000. Similarly, in the case of Adamu Safiyan with charge number K/EFCC87/2021 at HCT No. 21 Kano was convicted of “OBT and Computer Related Fraud” and sentenced to 1 year imprisonment or an option of a fine of ₦10,000. However, there were no specific breakdown of the offence. For instance, no mention if it was Business Email Compromise, Romance Scam, etc.

Also noticeable was that the 2021 report did not have a column for amount involved, unlike that of 2020. However, going from the 2020 report, the restitution in each case may be indicative or suggestive of the amount involved. In 2021, the restitution amount range from as little as $50 to a few thousand dollars. For instance, in the case of Wasiu Taiwo Opeyemi with charge number FHC/AB/4C/2021 at the Federal High Court Ibadan, the suspect was convicted of “cyber crime, fraud” and sentenced to 5 months imprisonment. The judge ordered the suspect to restitute $500, as well as forfeit Samsung Phone to the federal government.

The forfeiture trend continued in 2021, as almost all the convictions had an order of forfeiture, ranging from the electronic devices used in the perpetration of the crime, to other assets such as cars. For instance, in the case of Yusuf Suleiman with charge number KTH/29C/2021 at the HCT No 1 Katsina, the suspect was convicted for “cyber crime, fraud” and sentenced to 3 months imprisonment or an option of a fine of ₦50,000. The judge also ordered the forfeiture of his phones to the federal government. Also, in the case of Kolawole Abiodun Henry, with charge number FHC/AB/57C/2021 at the Federal High Court Abeokuta, the defendant was convicted and sentenced to 3 months imprisonment. The court ordered the restitution of $50 and forfeiture of 1 Infinix Note 7 phone. In the case of Uthman Dolapo Muhammed with charge number FHC/AB/76C/2021, the suspect was convicted of “cyber crime, fraud”, the judge ordered the forfeiture of the following items: 1 Apple Macbook Pro, 1 iPhone 6, 1 iPhone 8 Plus, 1 iPhone X Max, 1 iPad, 1 Samsung A71, 1 Infinix S4 Mobile Phone, 1 Lenovo Idea pad, and 1 Toyota Corolla to the federal government.

Another trend observed was that while cybercrime and related offences dominated the conviction record for 2021, in terms of amount involved, other crimes were relatively more. For instance, in the case of Temitope Oluwasanmi and Augustine Olayinka with charge number ID/6518C/2017, the suspects were convicted for “stealing, fraudulent false accounting and conspiracy to commit felony”. The judge sentenced the 1st defendant to 10 years imprisonment while the 2nd defendant was sentenced to 2 years imprisonment. The judge also ordered the 1st defendant to restitute ₦116,000,000. This is comparatively a lot higher than any other amount for a cybercrime case in the report for the year 2021. Also, the sentencing was more stringent for other crimes than for cybercrime.

2022

The year 2022 showed similar trend as 2021 and 2022. Downloaded data from the Economic and Financial Crimes Commission [9] showed that in 2022, the EFCC successfully secured 3785 convictions, according to the 605-page report. This research made a few observations of the trends and patterns. For instance, like the other years, the convictions were equally dominated by cybercrime and cybercrime related cases. The 2022 report showed similar cybercrime taxonomy, just like that of 2022. The observations in terms victim restitution and asset forfeiture also followed similar pattern.

In terms of the trends for convictions, there are a few patterns of note. A good number of the cybercrime or related cases ended up as "non-custodian" sentences and plea bargain. A count of the non-custodian sentences show about 305 cases. For instance, in the case of Theophilus Ademola Bukola, with charge number I/231EFCC/2022, the defendant was convicted for impersonation and was sentenced to "six months community service with consequential orders to forfeit the sum of $1,500 only and also forfeit one iphone 13 phone to the federal government of Nigeria".

Expectedly, in quite a good number of cases, the convicts chose the fine options, instead of serving prison terms. A count shows about 97 cybercrime or cybercrime related cases ended up paying fines instead of serving prison terms. For instance, in the case of Abubakar Kabir, with charge number KDH/KAD/EFCC/51/22, the defendant was convicted of cybercrime, and sentenced to 3 months imprisonment or an option of fine of ₦100,000. The Economic and Financial Crimes [9] conviction report shows that the convict has already paid the fine. While this research was not structured to evaluate the impact of the fine options in place of the prison sentences, however, it is important to report this as a possible factor.

It is noteworthy that there were others convicted of cybercrime or related offences that were sentenced with prison terms with option of fine, yet ended up in correctional facilities. For instance, in the case of Ndubuisi Emeka N. with charge number PHC/EN/CR/61/2020, the suspect was convicted of "Cyber crime and AFF Related Offences", after pleading guilty. The Judge sentenced him to 1-year imprisonment with option of a fine of ₦1,000,000, as well as forfeiture of phone used to commit crime. Despite the option of fine, the EFCC conviction report shows that the suspect was still at the Enugu correctional facility.

Also, quite a lot of the cases ended with a plea bargain. A count for the key phrase "plea bargain" returned about 64 cases of cyber crime convictions with plea bargains. For instance, in the case of Teddy Agbam Agum, with the charge number FHC/ABJ/243/2021, the suspect was convicted of cyber crime (in contravention of Cybercrime Act Section 32(2)(B)(iii)) and sentenced to 6 months imprisonment with an option of a fine of ₦500,0000. The EFCC conviction report for 2022 showed that this case was a plea bargain and the fine has already been paid.

Finally, an important observation was that in one of the cases listed in the EFCC 2022 conviction report, the offence was listed as "MLAT" (an acronym for "Mutual Legal Assistance Treaty"). Specifically, in the case of Adesina Surajudeen Lasis, with charge number FHC/ABJ/CS/126/2022, the offence was listed as "MLAT". The EFCC report shows that this case ended with the defendant being extradited to the United States of America. It is noteworthy that the EFCC Conviction Report did not provide specific details or context of the conviction. To get more information, this research did a google search, and it returned a news on this, by one of Nigeria's major newspaper dailies. The news report states that Adesina Surajudeen Lasis was "charged with sundry offences including conspiracy to commit wire and mail fraud, actual commission of mail and wire fraud, money laundering, among others" [10].

As was presented in Chapters one and two of this book, cybercrime is of international dimension, and this poses several challenges. This borderless nature of cybercrime presents complex jurisdictional roadblocks to law enforcement agencies during investigation and prosecution. To arrest and prosecute a suspect in another country requires a lot of complex international diplomacies, collaborations, and sometimes frustrating extradition processes, which are mostly slower compared to the fast pace of cybercrime (International Telecommunication [12], [13]). The case of Adesina above, is one of the few successful cases were there was a successful extradition. In fact, in the three years reviewed—2020, 2021, and 2022—this was the only reported case of success, as showed in the EFCC conviction report.

6.5 Review of Court Judgments and Charge Sheets for Cybercrime Prosecution

To drill more into the dynamics and complexity of the prosecuted cybercrime cases, this research reviewed selected case files (charge sheets, affidavits, plea bargain agreement, and judgements) of the convictions. A total of 20 cases from the Federal High Court, Port Harcourt were reviewed to look out for trends, patterns, and complexities. A review of the case files showed similar trends and patterns showed in the EFCC conviction reports. The similar trends include sentencing, plea bargains, restitutions, fine options, and amount involved.

Almost all the cases reviewed ended in plea bargains. For instance, in the case with charge number FHC/PH/645C/2022, the defendant and the prosecutor entered a plea bargain agreement, with the defendant pleading guilty. Also, in the case with charge number FHC/PH/C/2022, the defendant entered a plea bargain agreement. The terms of the plea bargain are showed below:

1. Plead guilty for committing cybercrime impersonation as charged.
2. That the sentence shall be either 2 years imprisonment or a fine of ₦400,000, payable to the consolidated revenue account of the federation in lieu of imprisonment.
3. Forfeiture of Apple XS Max phone, used in commission of crime.
4. Restitute the sum of $2500 recovered from him to the victim, based in the United States of America. The amount is to be forwarded to the victim through the EFCC,

and where they are unable to trace the victim within 12 months, the amount will be forfeited to the federal government.
5. The defendant to depose to an affidavit of good behaviour.

All case files reviewed were mostly for fraudulent impersonation using email and/or social media accounts. For instance, in the case with charge number FHC/PH/1033C/2022, the defendant was accused of impersonation using Gmail and Telegram social media accounts, thereby committing an offence contrary to Section 22(3)(a) of the Cybercrimes (Prohibition, Prevention, etc.) Act 2015 and punishable under Section 22(4) of the same Act. Also, in the case with charge number FHC/PH/276C/2023, the defendant was charged for fraudulent impersonation through email, Telegram account, Twitter account, and Facebook account, contrary to Section 22(2)(b)(i) of the Cybercrimes (Prohibition, Prevention, etc.) Act 2015 and punishable under Section 22(2) of the same Act.

Also, this review looked out for the amount involved in the cases reviewed. As reflected in the EFCC conviction records, the amount involved ranged from as little as $100 to a few thousands. None of the cases reviewed had an amount that is up to $10,000. For instance, in the case with charge number FHC/PH/09C/2020, the defendant was accused of fraudulently obtaining the sum of $5868.91 and $1767.48, respectively, from the victim. Also, in the case with charge number FHC/PH/85C/2022, the defendant was accused of impersonation and fraudulently obtaining $2500 from the victim, thereby committing an offence contrary to Section 22(2)(b)(ii) of the Cybercrimes (Prohibition, Prevention, etc.) Act 2015, and punishable under Section 22(2)(b)(iv) of the same Act.

Also of note was that the review exercise did not reveal the complexity and technical capability of the cybercriminals. That is, there was no in-depth description of the technical complexity and sophistication of the cybercriminals. Specifically, the charge sheet, affidavit, plea bargain agreements, and the court judgements did not present sufficient details that reveal the technological capability and skillset of the cybercriminals. The documents only contain first level description of the nature of crime committed, without revealing further technical details. Therefore, this exercise could not answer the question of the level of technical sophistication of the Nigerian cybercriminals.

Similarly, the reviewed court documents did not present technical information suggesting the technological capability and digital forensic readiness of the cybercrime prosecution agency. For instance, in all the cases reviewed, only one of the charge sheets alluded to their use of technology in the investigation. Specifically, in the case with charge number FHC/PH/C/2022, the Plea Bargain agreement shows that the seized exhibits (Gold Apple XS Max Phone) was forensically examined, and produced vital evidence that shows the defendant was into internet fraud. Several incriminating documents were forensically extracted, printed, and confirmed by the defendant. This research compared these case files with what is obtainable in other jurisdictions. Specifically, the research reviewed two celebrated cases involving Nigerian cybercriminals in the USA, presented in next section.

6.6 Cybercrime Prosecution in Other Jurisdictions: A Case Study of Two Nigerian Cybercriminals Prosecuted in the United States of America

To understand how other jurisdictions tackle their cybercrime challenge from a law enforcement point of view, this research investigated the prosecution and conviction of two high profile Nigerian Cybercriminal by the United States of America. The two cases under review are that of Obinwanne Okeke (aka Invictus Obi) and Ramon Olorunwa Abbas (aka Huspuppi). These two cases captures all of the key aspects and complexities of cybercrime prosecution: arrests and seizures, jurisdictional complexities of extradition, digital forensic readiness and capability maturity, emerging issues such as crimeware-as-a-service, plea bargains, sentencing, information governance, etc.

6.6.1 Ramon Olorunwa Abbas aka "Ray Hushpuppi" (Case no: 2:20-mj-02992)

Ramon Olorunwa Abbas aka "Ray Hushpuppi", a Nigerian citizen based largely in Dubai is a well-known social media influencer. With millions of followers on Social Media, including an active followership of over 2.5 million on Instagram, he is known for flaunting extravagant and flambouyant lifestyle. In June 2020, the Dubai Police Department swooped in on him at his residence and arrested him. He was subsequently handed over to the Federal Bureau of Investigation (FBI) and flown to Chicago, USA in July 2nd 2020 [14]. To understand the dynamics of the case, this research reviewed relevant court documentations such as affidavit, plea bargain agreement, etc.

A review of the affidavit filed by Andrew John Innocenti, a special agent with the FBI, shows that the defendant, Hushpuppi, was accused of conspiring to launder funds fraudulently obtained from a law firm in violation of 18 U.S.C. § 1956(h). The affidavit also affirmed that the defendant was a Nigerian living in the United Arab Emirate. The suspect was clearly identified, correlating several digital artifacts and unique identifiers from evidential items. His social media handles with millions of followership frequently show him with expensive designer clothing, cars, private jets, houses, wrist watchers, etc. The FBI, through the affidavit accused the defendant of financing his expensive and luxurious lifestyle through crime. He was alleged to be one of the leaders of a sophisticated network that facilitates internet fraud and money laundering, designed to steal millions of dollars [25].

The details presented in the affidavit is indicative of a painstaking forensic investigative process, linking the accused in connivance with others to commission of the following crimes:

1. Business Email Compromise (BEC) scheme that defrauded the victim, a United States citizen, of approximately $922,857.76, including $396,050 laundered by one of the coconspirators.
2. Conspired with others to launder funds intended to be stolen through fraudulent wire transfers, totaling approximately €13 million (proceeds of a cyber-heist from a financial institution). The defendant was specifically accused of providing two bank accounts in Europe (Romania and Bulgaria) [24], where €5 million of the fraudulently obtained funds was meant to be sent to.
3. Conspired with others to "launder tens, and at times hundreds, of millions of dollars that were proceeds of other fraudulent schemes and computer intrusions, including a fraudulent scheme to steal £100 million from an English Premier League Football Club."

The nature of the findings presented in the affidavit suggested valuable evidential artifacts gotten through mobile forensics, computer forensics, social media investigations, Open Source Intelligence (OSINT), email forensics, and others. The FBI also relied on records provided by Snap Inc and Apple to correlate and establish connection between chat histories, email addresses, and phone contacts [19].

Digital forensics is a very procedural, methodical, and detailed discipline [5] and this affidavit reflects the painstaking investigative process. From reviewing the complaints, proceeding with preliminary investigation, securing arrest warrants, lawful arrests and device seizures, international collaborations, extraditions, digital evidence preservation, extraction, and analysis, follow up interviews and triangulating other possible sources of evidence, and reporting. The affidavit showed vital evidence, including conversations of evidential value, pictures, documents, and others, linking suspect to crime.

The suspect pleaded guilty to the allegations in April 2021, following a plea bargain reached [16]. This research reviewed the plea bargain agreement, wherein the defendant pleaded guilty to the following [26]:

a. That beginning from June 9th, 2020, the defendant conspired with multiple persons to conduct financial transaction, into, within, and outside the United States of America, involving property, and representing proceeds of wire fraud.
b. That the coconspirators "targeted multiple victims and laundered or attempted to launder funds fraudulently obtained, through bank cyber-heists, Business Email Compromise (BEC) frauds, and other fraud schemes". The victims of the schemes include a financial institution (a bank in Malta), the victim's law firm in New York, and two companies in the United Kingdom.
c. Knowingly conspired to defraud victims. Also, admitted to knowing about the fraudulent schemes and willfully participating.
d. Admitted that around December 2019, defendant conspired with coconspirator to defraud a business person who was seeking for a lender to invest $15 million to build an international school. The defendant and coconspirators induced victim to make payments of approximately $330,000 to fund the opening of an account, to facilitating the "fraudulent" loan of $15 million. The victim ended up paying $230,000 and $100,000 to the account number provided by the defendant. The

funds were used by the defendant to fund his luxury lifestyle. $230,000 was used to purchase a luxury Richard Mille RM11-03 watch. The $100,000 was to be withdrawn and converted to Naira by coconspirators and paid as instructed. It is noteworthy that one of the coconspirators was based in Nigeria.

In summary, in terms of losses, the defendant admits to the following audacious loss amounts, done with a sophisticated ring of coconspirators [26]:

1. Foreign Financial Institution (Maltese Bank): approximately $14,700,000.00 (€13,000,000);
2. Victim Companies in the U.K.: approximately $7,740,000.00
3. Victim Law Firm: $922,857.76; and
4. Victim Businessperson and Qatari Victim Company: $809,983.58.

The defendant, Ramon Olorunwa Abbas aka "Ray Hushpuppi", was sentenced to over 11 years in a federal prison, following the plea bargain agreement. In the sentencing, Judge Wright, ordered Abbas to restitute $922,857 and $809,983 to the victim's law firm and businessperson in Qatar, respectively [24]. This case highlighted the intricate details of cybercrime investigation, trans-national network and global dimension, scale, and sophisticated network of the modern cybercriminals.

6.6.2 Obinwanne Okeke aka Invictus Obi

In August 2019, many Nigerians were shocked by the news of the arrest of Obinwanne Okeke aka "Invictus Obi". With the suspect who was believed to be an educated and refined business man, his arrest for cybercrime related offence came as a surprise to many. Invictus Obi operates a group of companies known as Invictus Group. He has a respected following and has spoken at top events such as London School of Economics African Summit. He even got a special mention by the BBC, describing him as a "rising star". He even made it to the Forbes 30-under-30 list [19]. He has a degree in International Studies and Forensic Criminology and a Masters of International Relations and Counter-Terrorism from Monash University in Australia [23]. What a profile such as this, his arrest was a surprise to many.

This research reviewed several documents in relation to this case. The affidavit deposed by Marshall Ward, a special agent of the Federal Bureau of Investigation (FBI), shows that Obinwanne Okeke, was accused of conspiracy to commit computer fraud, in violation of 18 U.S.C. § 1030, and conspiracy to commit wire fraud in violation of 18 U.S.C. § 1349. The affidavit shows that Unatrack, the UK export sales office for Caterpillar heavy industrial and farm equipment, contacted the FBI to complain of a Busineess Email Compromise (BEC) attack.

The affidavit captures details of how Unatrack's Chief Financial Officer's (CFO) email was compromised through a phishing attack, and his login credentials harvested via a spoofed page he thought to be Microsoft Office 365 login page. With the stolen credentials, the attackers were able to remotely access the CFO's email. The affidavit alleged that the attackers logged into the CFO's email at least 464 times, with

IP address originating from Nigeria. With access to the CFO's email and other associated digital artifacts such as documents, invoices, logo, etc., the intruders crafted fraudulent emails with fake invoices and sent from an external email to the CFO's email. They remotely accessed the CFO's email and forwarded same fraudulent email with the attached invoice to the finance team. The finance staff believing same to be a proper invoice processed the payment. In all, about 15 fraudulent invoices were processed between April 11–19, 2019 to foreign accounts. These funds, totaling approximately $11 million, were transferred to fraudulent accounts provided by the fraudsters.

The affidavit detailed several complex investigation steps taken by the FBI. Some of the investigative steps include open source queries, correlation with official records from Google, in relation to the suspects Gmail account (a federal search warrant was obtained for this), and this produced valuable artifacts of evidential value, including links to collaborators and coconspirators. Spooled chats show conspiratorial conversations between the suspect and his partners, such as design of fraudulent websites, among others. Analysed evidential artifacts from this process and open source queries eventually linked email to the accused. The affidavit suggested investigators deployed highly analytical open source tools, in addition to search warrants producing further evidential artifacts from Google and Instagram, which linked suspect to crime.

In June 2020, following a plea bargain agreement, Obinwanne Okeke pleaded guilty to the crime of computer based intrusion fraud scheme, resulting in losses of about $11 million to the victim. In February 2021, Mr Okeke was sentenced by the Chief District Judge, Rebecca Smith to 10 years in prison for committing wire fraud [2]. To underscore the international dimension of cybercrime, while Invictus Obi was standing trial in the USA, a federal high court in Lagos ordered the final forfeiture to the federal government, the sum of N280.5 million belonging to two companies allegedly owned by the defendant. The case was filed by the EFCC, to prevent the coconspirators of the defendant from dissipating same [27].

6.7 Summary

This chapter presented the results of the findings of this research. For Nigeria to stem the surge in cybercrime figures, it is important to first understand the complexity, dynamics, and frequency of the cybercrime. Unfortunately, beyond the anecdotal accounts and newspaper highlights on the caseloads, very little was known of the specifics of cybercrime in Nigeria; particularly, from a law enforcement perspective. This chapter presented the findings of this study, which addresses this gap in literature. The chapter presented important EFCC investigation and conviction statistics that showed the taxonomy, frequency, and dynamics of cybercrime caseloads in Nigeria. The investigation statistics by EFCC shows that Identity theft, Electronic signature theft, and Credit card fraud are the three most investigated cybercrime taxonomy in Nigeria. In terms of conviction, in 2022, Business Email Compromise had the highest figure of 746 in 2022.

The chapter also presented results of the review of press releases on the subject, by the EFCC. The findings corroborated the earlier statistics graciously shared by the commission and underscores the rising caseloads of cybercrime in Nigeria. The chapter also presented a review of casefiles of cybercrime in Nigeria. The study showed a noticeable trend of plea bargains, where the cybercriminals opt for the fine options. The study also showed that the successfully prosecuted cybercrime cases in Nigeria involved relatively small amounts, when compared to other jurisdictions, such as the United States of America.

Findings from this research also suggests the lack of digital forensic resources. A review of the casefiles did not reflect the digital forensic processes involved. In contrast, the affidavits in the casefiles of cybercrime cases in select jurisdictions had more technical and procedural details, suggesting the forensic and investigative processes. Specifically, the two high profile Nigerian cybercriminal cases (Ramon Olorunwa Abbas aka "Hushpuppi" and Obinwanne Okeke aka "Invictus Obi") prosecuted in the United States of America captured the technical, technological, and procedural details reflecting their level of digital forensic readiness. These two cases captures of the key aspects and complexities of cybercrime prosecution: arrests and seizures, jurisdictional complexities of extradition, digital forensic readiness and capability maturity, emerging issues such as crimeware-as-a-service, plea bargains, sentencing, information governance, etc.

Finally, this chapter also highlighted the cross-boarder nature of cybercrime and the complex investigative processes involving law enforcement from different countries. Most of the cases analysed involved offshore victims. The reviewed casefiles from the EFCC show that most of the cybercrime cases are dollar-denominated (for context, Nigeria uses the Naira). Also, the case files of Invictus Obi and Hushpuppi involved victims from several jurisdictions.

References

1. Abdulkadir AB, Abdulkadir AO (2019) Cybercrimes Act in Nigeria: experimenting compliance with internationally recognized human rights provisions. J Int Stud 15:117–132
2. Akinkuotu E (2021) US court sentences Invictus to 10 years in prison for $11m fraud. https://punchng.com/us-court-sentences-invictus-to-10-years-in-prison-for-11m-fraud/
3. Associated Press (2016) Nigerian man charged with hacking Los Angeles county emails. Guardian newspaper. https://www.theguardian.com/us-news/2016/dec/18/los-angeles-county-email-hack-kelvin-onaghinor
4. Barboza T (2016) L.A. County targeted in phishing cyberattack; Private information of 750,000 people compromised. Los Angeles times. https://www.latimes.com/local/lanow/la-me-ln-county-cyberattack-20161217-story.html
5. Casey E (2011) Digital evidence and computer crime: forensic science, computers, and the internet. Academic
6. Eboibi FE (2017) A review of the legal and regulatory frameworks of Nigerian Cybercrimes Act 2015. Comput Law Secur Rev 33(5):700–717
7. Economic and Financial Crimes Commission (2021) EFCC operational statistics. https://www.efcc.gov.ng/efcc/efcc-operational-statistics

8. Economic and Financial Crimes Commission (2023a) EFCC secures 3785 convictions in 2023. https://www.efcc.gov.ng/efcc/news-and-information/news-release/8781-efcc-secures-3785-convictions-in-2022
9. Economic and Financial Crimes Commission (2023b) Convictions. https://www.efcc.gov.ng/efcc/public-notices-3
10. Guardian Newspaper (2022) NCC puts cybercrime losses in Nigeria at $500m, sets to implement DMS. https://guardian.ng/news/ncc-puts-cybercrime-losses-in-nigeria-at-500m-sets-to-implement-dms/
11. Hinchliffe A (2017) Nigerian princes to kings of malware: the next evolution in Nigerian cybercrime. Comput Fraud Secur 2017(5):5–9
12. International Telecommunication Union (2012) Understanding cybercrime: phenomena, challenges and legal response. http://www.itu.int/ITU-D/cyb/cybersecurity/docs/Cybercrime%20legislation%20EV6.pdf
13. Interpol (2017) Global cybercrime strategy. https://www.interpol.int/en/Crimes/Cybercrime
14. Karimi F (2020) He flaunted private jets and luxury cars on Instagram. Feds used his posts to link him to alleged cyber crimes. CNN. https://edition.cnn.com/2020/07/12/us/ray-hushpuppi-alleged-money-laundering-trnd
15. Karimi F, Madowo L (2020) A man who flaunted private jets and luxury cars on Instagram gets 11 years in prison for money laundering. https://edition.cnn.com/2022/11/08/us/instagram-star-ray-hushpuppi-sentenced-cec/index.html
16. Karimi F, Madowo L (2022) A man who flaunted private jets and luxury cars on Instagram gets 11 years in prison for money laundering. https://edition.cnn.com/2022/11/08/us/instagram-star-ray-hushpuppi-sentenced-cec/index.html
17. Manky D (2013) Cybercrime as a service very modern business. Comput Fraud Secur 2013(6):9–13
18. Mihai IC, Pruna Ş, Petrica G (2017) A comprehensive analysis on cyber-threats against elearning systems. ELearn Softw Educ 3:344–351. https://doi.org/10.12753/2066-026X-17-225
19. Nwoye CI (2020) How the FBI used Instagram and Snapchat to track down an alleged conman in Dubai. https://qz.com/africa/1879261/fbi-use-instagram-to-get-dubai-nigerian-fraudster-hushpuppi
20. Omodunbi BA, Odiase PO, Olaniyan OM, Esan AO (2016) Cybercrimes in Nigeria: analysis, detection, and prevention. J Eng Technol 1(1):37–42
21. Suleiman AO (2019) The Impulsive upsurge of yahoo-yahoo in the 21st century in Nigeria: Islamic perspective. Afr J of Criminol Justice Stud 12(1)
22. The Nation Newspaper (2022) Alleged fraud: court okays extradition of Lagos businessman Surajudeen Lasisi. https://thenationonlineng.net/alleged-fraud-court-okays-extradition-of-lagos-businessman-surajudeen-lasisi/
23. TVC News (2021) Obinwanne Okeke 'Invictus Obi' sentenced to 10-year jail term in US for $11m fraud. https://www.tvcnews.tv/2021/02/obinwanne-okeke-invictus-obi-sentenced-to-10-year-jail-term-in-us-for-11m-fraud/
24. United State's Attorney's Office (2021) Nigerian man sentenced to over 11 years in federal prison for conspiring to launder tens of millions of dollars from online scams. https://www.justice.gov/usao-cdca/pr/nigerian-man-sentenced-over-11-years-federal-prison-conspiring-launder-tens-millions
25. United States District Court (2020) Criminal complaint by telephone or other reliable electronic means. https://www.justice.gov/usao-cdca/press-release/file/1292066/download
26. United States District Court (2021) Plea agreement for defendant Ramon Olorunwa Abbas. https://saharareporters.com/sites/default/files/gov.uscourts.cacd_.790162.46.0-4.pdf
27. Vanguard News (2019) Court orders permanent forfeiture of N280.5m linked to Invictus Obi. https://vanguardngr.com/2019/11/court-orders-permanent-forfeiture-of-n280-5m-linked-to-invictus-obi/

Chapter 7
Implications for Financial Crime in Nigeria

Abstract This chapter aims to present the implications of the findings of this study on financial crime in Nigeria. The chapter begins with a practical assessment of the findings of this study, within the context of the research questions. The chapter presented a thematic analysis of the findings, and the implications on financial crimes in Nigeria. Some of the key findings presented include the lack of forensic resources, the training gaps, specific tools needed by the cybercrime agencies interviewed. This chapter also presented vital cybercrime prosecution and conviction statistics since 2015, identifying trends and patterns. The chapter ended with a synthesis of EFCC press releases reviewed, as well as a summary of all the findings and the associated implications for financial crime in Nigeria.

Keywords Cybercrime · Internet fraud · Financial crimes · EFCC · Economic and Financial Crimes Commission · Nigeria Police · Digital forensic readiness · Cybercrime caseloads · Cybercrime taxonomy

7.1 Introduction

Cybercrime caseloads continue to rise in Nigeria, despite key reforms over the years. While law enforcement agents continue to work tirelessly to stem the tide, the caseloads continue to be on the rise [35]. There are several challenges preventing cybercrime agencies in Nigeria from putting up an effective fight against cybercrime. One of this is the lack of forensic resources, which has now been established by this study, in Chaps. 5 and 6. The study also investigated the specifics, dynamics, and complexity of cybercrime cases in Nigeria. This study was structured as a qualitative study, with the Economic and financial Crimes Commission (EFCC) and the Nigeria Police Force as case studies. The study triangulated findings with official documents from the commission's website, case files, and reputable websites online.

Chapter 5 presented findings of the qualitative interviews involving both EFCC and Nigeria Police Force cybercrime investigators. Chapter 6 presented important EFCC investigation and conviction statistics that showed the taxonomy, frequency,

R. T. Sibe and C. Kaunert, *Cybercrime, Digital Forensic Readiness, and Financial Crime Investigation in Nigeria*, Advanced Sciences and Technologies for Security Applications, https://doi.org/10.1007/978-3-031-54089-9_7

and dynamics of cybercrime caseloads in Nigeria. Chapter 6 also presented results of the review of press releases on the subject by the EFCC, as well as reviews of casefiles such as charge sheets, affidavits, plea bargain agreement, and court judgments. The chapter also looked at cybercrime cases in other jurisdictions, with two celebrated cases of *Ramon Olorunwa Abbas aka "Ray Hushpuppi"* and *Obinwanne Okeke aka Invictus Obi* (both Nigerians), respectively, reviewed as case studies. This chapter will look at a practical assessment of the research questions, as well as the implications for financial crime in Nigeria.

7.2 Practical Assessment of Research Questions

Research Questions

The study has two primary research questions and nine research subquestions listed below:

Primary Research Question 1: What is the assessment of digital forensic resources and capabilities of law enforcement agencies in Nigeria?

Research Subquestion 1: What challenges prevent law enforcement agencies in Nigeria from having adequate forensic capabilities and being forensically ready?
Research Subquestion 2: What is the extent of digital forensic tools adoption by Nigerian law enforcement agents?
Research Subquestion 3: How has the lack of digital forensic resources affected the law enforcement agencies in Nigeria, and by extension, their efficiency in the fight to stop cybercrime?
Research Subquestion 4: What are the areas of digital forensic skills deficiency needing an upgrade?
Research Subquestion 5: What is the specific digital forensic training needed by law enforcement agents in Nigeria?
Research Subquestion 6: What specific digital forensic tools are in short supply or with expired licenses needing an upgrade?
Research Subquestion 7: What are the daily cybercrime caseload and available digital ***forensics resources?***

Primary Research Question 2: What is composition and complexity of the cybercrime cases in Nigeria?

Research Subquestion 1: What are the frequent cybercrimes committed in Nigeria?
Research Subquestion 2: How many persons are convicted of cybercrime in Nigeria?

Primary Research Question 1: What Is the Assessment of Digital Forensic Resources and Capabilities of Law Enforcement Agencies in Nigeria?

Six themes emerged from participants' responses. The result was discussed by analyzing each theme against existing scholarly literature and emerging realities. The six themes are personnel adequacy, personnel capability, tools availability, defined processes, structured process review, and policy framework. The study investigated the lack of digital forensic resources in the financial crimes agencies using these themes in the digital forensic readiness framework. These themes fit into Pooe and Labuschagne's [38] five critical components of a Digital Forensic Readiness model of people, process, policy, technology, and data. Table 7.1 summarizes the six themes, findings, and corresponding scholarly literature.

The result of this study shows the financial crimes agencies lack digital forensic resources. The findings suggest they are not forensically ready and fall short of the expected capability maturity needed to perform efficiently and optimally in investigating financial crimes. This result is consistent with other scholarly works. Olayemi [33] submitted that the law enforcement agencies in Nigeria, particularly the Nigerian Police, lack computer forensic laboratories needed to investigate and analyze cybercrime effectively. Olayemi [33] further posited that beyond having enabling laws, the law enforcement agency needs to acquire more tools and more training for their personnel if they wish to be effective. Oraegbunam [37] also echoed this position by submitting that there was a need to upscale the digital forensic capabilities of law enforcement agencies across the various formations and not just restricted

Table 7.1 Themes and corresponding literature from research question 1

S/N	Themes	Research findings	Literature
1	Personnel adequacy	Agencies lacked personnel	Chigozie-Okwum et al. [10], Ebobi [13], Olayemi [33]
2	Personnel capability	Personnel of the agencies lacks forensic capabilities	Chigozie-Okwum et al. [10], Ehimen and Bola [16], Eboibi [13], Mohammed et al. [30], Olayemi [33]
3	Tools availability	Digital forensic tools were in short supply or outdated	Olayemi [33], Tonye [41], Bello and Griffiths [5]
4	Documented processes	No standard operating procedure is available	Abu et al. [1]
5	Structured process review	No structured process review	NA
6	Policy framework	Cybercrime Act 2015 is the guiding framework	Bello and Griffiths [5], Adesina [2], Nwankwo and Ukaoha [31], and Ajetunmobi et al. [4]

Note This table summarizes the themes and literature from the primary research question to an elite law enforcement squad. Ehimen and Bola [16] asserted that the Nigerian Police are not technologically savvy and lack the computer forensic skills needed for investigating cybercrimes. For Nigeria to be able to combat the rising caseloads of internet fraud successfully, the law enforcement agencies must be forensically ready.

7.2.1 Personnel Adequacy

The result of the study showed there was a lack of digital forensic personnel in Nigeria's financial crimes investigative agencies. This finding was emphatic as all 18 respondents stated unambiguously in their interviews that the staff strength was poor compared to the increasing caseload and the blistering pace of cybercrime. Participants gave different estimates for the rising caseloads. However, all pointed out that the institutions lacked the personnel to meet up with these demanding caseloads. This position is consistent with Olayemi [33], who submitted that trained personnel was inadequate. Chigozie-Okwum et al. [10] also supported this position by noting a shortage of law enforcement agents with digital forensic capabilities in Nigeria's law enforcement agencies. Eboibi [13] also supported this position by submitting that Nigeria lacks technologically savvy personnel and cyber forensic investigators.

7.2.2 Personnel Capability

This study investigated the lack of digital forensic resources amongst the financial crimes agencies in Nigeria. Looking at the three elements of Routine Activity Theory (RAT)—motivated offender, a suitable target, and the absence of a capable guardian [11]—this study situated the lack of forensic resources amongst law enforcement agencies within the context of the lack of a capable guardian. Tseloni et al. [43] define guardianship as the capability of the persons and objects to prevent the crime. The concept of capable guardianship has been used rather widely beyond traditional crime. Yar [45] suggested this could be the property owner, custodian, law enforcement, Computer Emergency Response Teams, banks, or any other, whose presence may discourage the occurrence of the crime in question. Although conceptualized initially for traditional crime, given the similarities between the terrestrial and the online world, it is applied to studying cybercrime [18, 26]. Bello and Griffiths [5] also used RAT in cybercrime investigations in Nigeria, submitting that the presence of a capable guardian demotivated the cybercriminal. Following this, the capability of law enforcement agents is an essential factor when studying the factors behind the rising caseloads of cybercrime.

This study shows there is a lack of forensic capability among personnel of the financial crimes investigative agencies. This finding is consistent with Chigozie-Okwum et al. [10], who stressed the lack of officers with technological skills as a significant concern and the root cause behind Nigeria's rising status as a haven for cybercriminals. Ehimen and Bola [16] also emphasized this with a definite verdict on the Nigerian Police as lacking internet policing capability and forensic training. This study's findings also reinforced the position of Eboibi [13], who submitted that the lack of capacity building has resulted in Nigeria having cybercrime investigators who are not technologically savvy and lack cyber forensic investigative skills. Mohammed et al. [30] also submitted that researchers generally accept Nigerian cybercrime investigators' lack of forensic capacity. This position was also consistent with Olayemi [33], who stated that the lack of training opportunities meant a shortage in the number of adequately trained personnel.

To further investigate this submission suggesting a gap in capability of personnel, this study went further to review case files of selected cybercrime cases and two case files of celebrated Nigerian Internet fraudsters prosecuted and convicted in another jurisdiction. A review of the case file of cases prosecuted in Nigeria did not leave any hint suggestive of the forensic readiness and capability maturity of the investigation process. In contrast, the affidavits in the casefiles of the two cybercrime cases in the United States, involving Nigerians, had more technical and procedural details, suggesting the forensic capability and mature investigative processes. Specifically, the affidavit deposed by the investigator captured the technical, technological, and procedural details reflecting their level of digital forensic readiness. A review of the EFCC website as well as the press releases on the subject did not produce any result suggestive of the level of forensic readiness. However, the researcher's physical visit to the EFCC Digital Forensic Laboratory at the headquarters, showed the commission has an impressive forensic laboratory.

7.2.3 Tool Availability

This study showed that financial crimes investigative agencies in Nigeria lack or have limited access to the right digital forensic technology. Tonye [41] also supports this position, noting that the lack of digital forensic tools was a common challenge affecting the efficiency of the investigative process. The findings of this study showed an ever-constant challenge of routinely renewing expensive tool licenses. Bello and Griffiths [5] also align with this position, stating that the agencies have expired licenses for the tool due to funding challenges. The study finds that of the two agencies, the Economic and Financial Crimes Commission had a working forensic laboratory at the headquarters and better access to forensic tools than the Nigerian Police, with minimal access. This finding reinforces Olayemi's [33] position that the Nigeria Police Force did not have a digital forensic laboratory.

Without access to the right tools, effective digital forensic investigation is impossible. Therefore, this is a major concern, particularly in the wake of growing economic challenges and a plunge in the value of the Naira in exchange to dollars. For context, Digital forensic tools are quite expensive, and dollar denominated. The Nigerian currency, Naira has lost value by about a 100% in one year. Therefore, this will make it increasingly difficult to keep up with the annual license renewal. This is an obvious challenge and will impact on Nigeria's ability to wage a formidable war against cybercrime.

7.2.4 Documented Processes

Criminal investigations and, by extension, digital forensic analysis is procedural, requiring well-documented procedures in line with best practice [19]. Also, following Pooe and Labuschagne's [38] identification of five critical components of a Digital Forensic Readiness model as People, Process, Policy, Technology, and Data, participants were asked to share their perspectives on the availability of documented processes in line with best practice. This study found that while most of the participants stated or inferred that there were processes in place that guide their operations, they were not categorical if these processes were documented or not. For a process to be effective, it needs to be documented, available, and mainstreamed. This study found there was no standard operating procedure (SOP) documents readily available to personnel. This finding is consistent with Abu et al. [1], who cited poor investigative procedures as challenging for law enforcement agencies.

Emerging details since this study corroborated the findings of this study that at the time of the field interviews for this study, there was no SOP. However, this is no longer the case as the Economic and Financial Crimes Commission unveiled their SOP in 2022 [15]. Also, as at the time of this study, the EFCC was in the process of having their laboratory certified by ISO (both ISO 90001 and ISO 17025). Standardised investigation processes are crucial to ensuring diligent prosecution, therefore, this is a positive development for the commission. As at the time of conclusion of this study, there is no available evidence that the Nigeria Police Force have any SOP that is properly mainstreamed.

7.2.5 Structured Process Review Mechanism

The researchers asked a follow-up question on the availability of a structured process review mechanism. Two participants made mixed submissions in response. This study finds no structured process review mechanism in both organizations since there are no SOPs in the first place. The researchers did not find any scholarly papers that support or refute this finding. It is commendable that the EFCC now has a Standard Operating Process, Policies, and Manuals [15]. However, in line with best practices, it is important that such should be periodically updated in line with best practices. There is no emerging details as at the time this book was finalized showing that there is a structured review mechanism.

7.2.6 Policy Framework

Policy is one of the five critical components of the Digital Forensic Readiness model identified by Pooe and Labuschagne [38]—the others being people, process, technology, and data. Therefore, the researchers asked participants to share their perspectives on the policy framework guiding or shaping their activities. The findings of this study show that the Cybercrime Act 2015 is the guiding framework that shapes policies of cybercrime investigation. Bello and Griffiths [2], Adesina [5], and Ajetunmobi et al. [4] all corroborated this finding. This study recommends the review of the Cybercrime Act 2015 given the rapidly evolving threat landscape and other emerging realities. This position aligns with Nwankwo and Ukaoha [31], who pointed out the need to review the legislation to address current challenges.

It is noteworthy that not all the cybercrime cases in Nigeria were prosecuted using the Cybercrime Act 2015. There were cases were other state laws were used for the prosecution. For instances, there are a few cases in the Kaduna zonal command, where the suspects were charged and convicted for cybercrime related activities (impersonation and dishonestly inducing the victim on social media), an offence contrary to Section 308 of the Kaduna State Penal Code Law, 2017 and punishable under Section 309 of the Same Law. A cursory look at the casefiles where this happened show a trend where the sentencing years in prison were longer for the Kaduna Penal Code Law, 2017 when compared to the cybercriminals convicted using the Cybercrime Act 2015.

Research Subquestion 1: What challenges prevent law enforcement agencies in Nigeria from having adequate forensic capabilities and being forensically ready?

In Nigeria, cybercrime investigative agencies face numerous challenges preventing them from being forensically ready [5, 13, 33, 37]. This study examined these challenges facing the agencies. Nine themes/subthemes emerged from participants' responses, summarized in Table 7.2.

7.2.7 Tool Licensing Challenge

Access to up-to-date tools is an essential success factor in cybercrime crime investigation [33]. Most digital forensic commercial tool licenses are tenured and expensive to maintain [24]. The findings of this research show that the challenge of timely renewal of the recurrent licenses was a recurring one faced by the law enforcement agencies in Nigeria and affects the efficiency of the investigative process. This challenge was particularly so given the expensive nature of the licenses and their annual renewal subscription. Bello and Griffiths [5] corroborated this finding, noting a funding challenge to provide the tools and other logistics needed for effective investigation. Situating this within the RAT framework, with the law enforcement agencies as the capable guardian, it follows that a capable guardian should be one with access

Table 7.2 Themes and corresponding literature from research subquestion 1

S/N	Themes	Research findings	Literature
1	Tool licensing challenge	The recurrent cost of forensic tools licenses is a significant challenge	Olayemi [33], James and Gladyshev [24], Bello and Griffiths [5], Cohen and Felson [11], Gabroski [18], Leukfeldt and Yar [26]
2	Lack of structured training program	The study established the lack of a structured training program	Olayemi [33], Oraegbunam [37], Chigozie-Okwum et al. [10], Abu et al. [1], and Eboibi [13]
3	Policy challenges	Lack of an efficient framework for inter-agency collaboration, jurisdictional roadblocks, other legal hurdles, and poor policy implementation mechanism	Pooe and Labuschagne [38], Chigozie-Okwum et al. [10], Eboibi [13], Bello and Griffiths [5], Mohammed et al. [30]
4	Roadmap for digital forensic readiness	No roadmap for digital forensic readiness	Tan [41], Carrier and Spafford [6], Elyas et al. [17], Grobler and Lowrens [19], Pooe and Labuschagne [38]
5	Collaboration	The study established the need for more effective collaboration	Bello and Griffiths [5], Mohammed et al. [30]
6	Jurisdictional challenges	The study established that the cross-border nature of cybercrime poses jurisdictional roadblocks	Bello and Griffiths [5], Weber (2003), Cassim [8], Cohen and Felson's [11]
7	Emerging technologies	The study concluded that emerging technologies were challenging to cybercrime investigators	Mihai et al. [29], Karie and Venter [25], Bello and Griffiths [5]
8	Funding	The study established that funding was a significant challenge	Leung et al. [27], Ahmed [3], Bello and Griffiths [5], Chigozie-Okwum et al. [10], and Olayemi [33]
9	Pace of cybercrime	The fast pace of cybercrime was a challenge to investigators	Li [28], Hadlington et al. [20], International Telecommunication Union [21]

Note This table summarizes themes and corresponding literature from research subquestion 1

to the right tools [5, 11, 18, 26]. Therefore, this study findings established this recurrent challenge of the annual subscription for tools licenses faced by Nigeria's law enforcement agencies. This is even more so give the current macroeconomic realities in the country.

7.2.8 *Lack of Structured Training*

This study found a gap in terms of the technical capability of the financial crimes investigators. The researchers asked participants to share their perspectives on the availability of a structured training program in their organization. This study found that aggregating the response by participants from both agencies, there was no structured training program that ensured investigators' sustainable training and capacity building. This finding is consistent with positions held by Olayemi [33], Oraegbunam [37], Chigozie-Okwum et al. [10], Abu et al. [1], and Eboibi [13]. Following closer analysis from the participants, the study findings show that the Digital Forensic department of the EFCC have a structured training program, as participants who gave positive responses were from that unit. There is no scholarly article supporting this position with regards to this specific information. This result, when dissected further, shows the Nigeria Police suffers the most lack in terms of digital forensic training. Digital forensics is an evolving discipline influenced by the rapidly changing technological landscape, therefore the cybercrime agencies should have a structured training programme to stay up to date with emerging technological realities.

7.2.9 *Policy Challenges*

Pooe and Labuschagne [38] identified policy as one of the critical components of the Digital Forensic Readiness model. The researchers asked participants to share their perspectives on the policy challenges faced. This study identified the following policy challenges: lack of an efficient framework for inter-agency collaboration, jurisdictional roadblocks, other legal hurdles, and poor policy implementation mechanisms. This finding is consistent with Chigozie-Okwum et al. [10], who held that the lack of proper feasibilities for policies before implementation was a significant reason why the policies fail. Eboibi [13] also corroborated this by citing the lack of implementation of the Cybercrime Act 2015. This position also aligns with Bello and Griffiths [5], who held that multiple laws and jurisdictions and a lack of collaboration were a significant challenge in cybercrime prosecution. Mohammed et al. [30] also stated a need to bridge existing gaps between stakeholders such as security professionals, law enforcement agents, and prosecutors.

7.2.10 *Roadmap for Digital Forensic Readiness*

Digital forensic readiness has two primary objectives: to maximize the usefulness of evidence collected; and minimize the cost of investigations [40]. Carrier and Spafford [6] further divided forensic readiness into operational readiness and infrastructural readiness, with the former being concerned with adequate training and equipment and the latter the efficient preservation of data. There are different perspectives to analyze digital forensic readiness, such as time, cost, training, and technology [17]. To be adequately empowered to investigate Nigeria's growing Internet fraud cases, the country's financial crime agencies will need to attain a considerable level of forensic readiness.

The absence of a roadmap to guide forensic readiness affects the capability of law enforcement agencies in investigating financial crimes. Grobler and Louwrens [19] support this position, noting that digital forensic readiness ensures streamlined processes and legal admissibility of digital evidence. This position aligns with Pooe and Labuschagne's [38] five critical components of a Digital Forensic Readiness model—People, Process, Policy, Technology, and Data. The researchers asked participants to share their perspectives on the availability of a documented roadmap for the digital forensic readiness of their organizations. The findings from this study show that while some participants said there was an ongoing process to develop one, at the time of this research, there was no well-articulated roadmap for digital forensic readiness that was available and mainstreamed in the organization. There are no research findings that support or refute the presence of a digital forensic readiness roadmap in Nigeria's financial crime investigative agencies. Available literature only points out elements of the readiness framework, like technology, training, and others. Given the established lack of forensic readiness by the agencies, the lack of a documented roadmap to build readiness and capability maturity is of great concern in the country's fight against cybercrime.

7.2.11 Collaborations

This study finds that while there are a few handshakes between the various agencies in Nigeria and beyond, the lack of an efficient framework for collaboration affected the efficiency of the respective agencies. It is noteworthy that since this study was completed, efforts have been made to correct this. For instance, the last edition of the National Cybersecurity Strategy and Policy 2021 released by the Office of the National Security Adviser [32] outlined structural measures in line with the extant provisions. For instance, the National Computer Emergency Response Team, also known as the Nigeria Computer Emergency Response Team (ngCERT), the focal point of the nation's cyber incident response management is now domiciled under the National Cybersecurity Coordination Centre (NCCC). Also to be domiciled under the NCCC is the National Digital Forensic Laboratory (NDFL), to provide the requisite tools and facilities for investigation and intelligence gathering of cyber related issues. While there is no available data showing if the NCCC is now fully operational and facilitating smooth collaborations between the agencies involved in cybercrime investigation, however, it is an encouraging step.

This study also finds a need to have a framework for improved cooperation between the law enforcement agencies in Nigeria and their counterparts in other countries. These findings align with the position of Bello and Griffiths [5], who held that multiple laws and jurisdictions, as well as lack of collaboration, were a significant challenge in cybercrime prosecution. Mohammed et al. [30] also supported this view, noting the need to bridge existing gaps between stakeholders such as security professionals, law enforcement agents, and prosecutors. Cybercriminals could potentially commit Internet fraud from a foreign country. This borderless reach of cybercrime presents complex jurisdictional roadblocks to law enforcement agencies. To overcome this requires closer cooperation [22]. To arrest and prosecute a suspect in another country requires a lot of international diplomacies, collaborations, and sometimes frustrating extradition processes, which are mostly slower compared to the fast pace of cybercrime [21].

7.2.12 Jurisdictional Challenges

This study finds that the cross-border nature of cybercrime posed jurisdictional challenges during investigations. All the case files investigated in this research were of international dimension, with victims in a different country from the cybercriminal. A look at the amounts involved showed they were all in dollars (Nigeria's currency is the Naira). This is not restricted to the cases investigated in Nigeria, as the cases of *Hushpuppi* and *Invictus* Obi, both involved victims in different countries. This finding aligns with Bello and Griffiths' [5] position that the trans-national nature of cybercrime posed jurisdictional challenges during investigations. This finding is also consistent with Weber's (2003) position that jurisdictional challenges in cybercrime investigation and prosecution could range from the lack of criminal statutes, lack of procedural powers, and lack of enforceable mutual assistance provisions with foreign states. Cassim [8] also noted that the jurisdictional complexities were a significant impediment to prosecuting cybercriminals. These findings support Cohen and Felson's [11] position, as it affects the guardian's capability and motivates the cybercriminal. Therefore, for Nigeria to wage a formidable war against cybercrime, the country will need to broaden and deepen relationship with other nations.

7.2.13 Emerging Technologies

The technological landscape continues to evolve with emerging technologies. This study found that it was challenging to keep pace with emerging technologies. Most participants pointed to the complications and complexities of investigating emerging technologies such as blockchain and cryptocurrency, cloud technology, and others. Mihai et al. [29] supports this position, noting that emerging technologies increased the attack surface and possible vulnerabilities. This finding is consistent with Karie and Venter [25], who identified emerging technologies as technical challenges facing digital forensics. Bello and Griffiths [5] also held that the constantly evolving technological landscape gives cybercriminals the edge over cybercrime investigators. Of particular concern is that this study established a lack of forensic readiness, lack of sustainable funding, and lack of structured training programme; all of which are necessary to stand any chance of putting up a formidable fight against cybercrime in the evolving threat landscape.

7.2.14 Funding Challenges

There was a consensus among all participants that funding was a significant challenge. This position is consistent with the Technology, Organization, and Environment (TOE) Framework, where Leung et al. [27] identified financial readiness as one of the factors for technology adoption from the organizational context. Therefore, this study showed that Nigerian's cybercrime investigation agencies were not financially ready to be forensically ready, and if an organization is not forensically ready, their investigative capacity is greatly weakened. These organizational factors may impede or facilitate innovation and technological adoption at the firm level [3]. The findings of this study are also consistent with Bello and Griffiths' [5] position that funding for cybercrime agencies in Nigeria was inadequate. Chigozie-Okwum et al. [10] and Olayemi [33] also agree with this position, pointing to the poor funding of law enforcement agencies in Nigeria.

7.2.15 The Pace of Cybercrime

Findings from this study show that investigators struggle to cope with the fast pace of cybercrime. The rising caseloads overwhelm the organization's forensic resources. This position is consistent with Li's [28] position that the gap between the blistering pace and the slow wheel of justice gives cybercriminals an edge. Hadlington et al. [20] also pointed out the widening gap between the speed of cybercrime and the speed of investigation. This position is also consistent with the International Telecommunication Union's [21] that the pace of cybercrime is far more than the slow grind of cross-border prosecution. The implication of this finding is that Nigerian cybercrime agencies struggle with the pace of cybercrime, and to overcome this, steps need to be taken to improve their forensic readiness and capability maturity.

Research Subquestion 2: What is the extent of digital forensic tools adoption by Nigerian law enforcement agents?

Adoption refers to an individual's decisions to accept, diffuse and mainstream innovation in an integrated manner (Straub 2009). As organizations continue to invest large sums in new technologies, it is essential to study technology adoption. Such investments may not yield positive results except the right adoption strategies are put in place [3]. This research examined the level of digital forensic technology adoption. One theme emerged from this, summarized in Table 7.3.

Table 7.3 Theme and corresponding literature for research subquestion 2

S/N	Themes	Research findings	Literature
1	Digital forensic adoption	There is a good level of user acceptance of digital forensic technology. However, the lack of access impeded the diffusion of digital forensic technology in both organizations	Bello and Griffiths [5], Ahmed [3], Tonye [41], Leung et al. [27], Olayemi [33], and Oliveira and Martins [34]

7.2.16 Digital Forensic Adoption

The findings of this study show that there was a good level of user acceptance for digital forensic technology. Response by participants showed that law enforcement agents are open and willing to utilize digital forensic technology. However, this willingness is frustrated by the investigators' lack of access to digital forensic tools across different formations. The study found that the lack of funding was a significant reason for both agencies' poor technology diffusion. The study also found that available digital forensic technologies are centralized at the national headquarters, at the expense of the rest of the country. Olayemi [33] corroborated this finding, noting that the Nigeria Police Force did not have a digital forensic laboratory. Tonye [41] also supports this position, noting that the lack of digital forensic tools was a common challenge affecting the efficiency of the investigative process.

Bello and Griffiths [5] also align with this position, stating that the agencies had expired tool licenses due to funding challenges. Beyond the individual's choice to accept technology, the TOE Framework offers a better explanation of technology adoption at the organisational level, consistent with this study's findings. The TOE framework incorporates critical elements of environmental factors [27, 34]. From the Organizational context, Leung et al. [27] condensed the aspects from previous studies in adoption as Financial readiness, technological readiness, and top management support. These organizational factors may impede or facilitate innovation and technological adoption at the firm level [3] and are consistent with this study's findings. The study's findings show that financial crimes investigation agencies in Nigeria are neither technologically ready nor financially ready, which may explain the low adoption and diffusion of digital forensic technology.

Research Subquestion 3: How has the lack of digital forensic resources affected the law enforcement agencies in Nigeria, and by extension, their efficiency in the fight to stop cybercrime?

An analysis of the participants' responses produced one theme, summarized in Table 7.4.

Table 7.4 Themes and corresponding literature for research subquestion 3

S/N	Themes	Research findings	Literature
1	Impact of lack of digital forensic technology	Lack of digital forensic resources seriously impacted financial crimes investigation	Bello and Griffiths [5], Tonye [41], Olayemi [33], Oraegbunam [37], Ehimen and Bola [16], Chigozie-Okwum et al. [10], Mohammed et al. [30]

Note This table summarizes themes and corresponding literature from research subquestion 3

7.2.17 Impact of Lack of Digital Forensic Technology

This research showed a lack of digital forensic resources—competent personnel and digital forensic tools (hardware and software). The findings also show that the lack of digital forensic resources adversely impacted financial crimes investigation in Nigeria. This finding is consistent with Bello and Griffiths [5], who suggested that the law enforcement agencies cannot achieve much with the expired tools licenses and lack of digital forensic resources. Tonye [41] also corroborated this position, noting that the lack of digital forensic tools was a common challenge affecting the efficiency of the investigative process. This result is also consistent with Olayemi [33], who submitted that law enforcement agencies in Nigeria, particularly the Nigerian Police, lack the computer forensic laboratory needed to investigate and analyze cybercrime effectively.

Oraegbunam [37] also echoed this position, noting that there was a need to upscale the digital forensic capabilities of law enforcement agencies across the various formations and not just restricted to an elite law enforcement squad. Ehimen and Bola [16] asserted that the Nigeria Police Force are not technologically savvy and lack the computer forensic skills needed for investigating cybercrimes. This finding is consistent with Chigozie-Okwum et al. [10], who stressed the lack of officers with technological skills as a significant concern and the root cause behind Nigeria's rising status as a haven for cybercriminals. Mohammed et al. [30] also concluded by noting that researchers generally accept Nigerian cybercrime investigators' lack of forensic capacity. This position was also consistent with Olayemi [33], who submitted that the lack of training opportunities meant a shortage of adequately trained personnel, which impacted the prosecution of financial crimes in Nigeria.

Research Subquestion 4: What are the areas of digital forensic skills deficiency needing an upgrade?

One theme emerged from this research question, summarized in Table 7.5.

Table 7.5 Theme and corresponding literature for research subquestion 4

S/N	Themes	Research findings	Literature
1	Digital forensic skills deficiency	The study identified 17 areas of deficiency, needing training	James [23], Hadlington et al. [20], Mohammed et al. [30], Karie and Venter [25], Bello and Griffiths [5]

Note This table summarizes the theme for research subquestion 4

7.2.18 Skills Deficiency

The researchers asked participants to share their perspectives on the areas of skills deficiency they would like to have more training. This study identified a total of seventeen different skill areas where participants needed further training. The training recommended the most by the participants was the broad classification, digital forensic examination training. The following had the joint-third highest nomination from three participants: Computer forensic, network forensics, and cryptocurrency investigation. Mobile forensic training, cloud forensic training, and JTAG/Chip-off/Phone repairs. Figure 2.1 summarizes the various training program suggested by the participants and the participants that nominated them.

Previous studies only identified the need for more training but did not identify the specific areas of deficiency needing training. For instance, James [23] recommended more funding for training to enable law enforcement agents to upskill. Hadlington et al. [20] also supported this by stating a lack of consistent training on cybercrime for law enforcement agencies. Mohammed et al. [30] advocated for sending investigators on specialized training. Karie and Venter [25] said the lack of training programs explains the lack of competent digital forensic experts in law enforcement. Bello and Griffiths [5] also identified the lack of training as a major challenge to cybercrime investigation in Nigeria.

Research Subquestion 5: What is the specific digital forensic training needed by law enforcement agents in Nigeria?

An analysis of Research SubQuestion 4 and Research SubQuestion 5 produced one theme, as shown in Table 7.5. This theme was discussed above and further discussed with the context of research subquestion 5. This study found 17 different areas of skills deficiency that the investigators needed further training. Figure 7.1 summarizes the specific training courses required by financial crimes investigators in Nigeria. Previous studies only showed the need for more training, but none specifically discussed the particular training needs by investigators. For instance, James [23], Hadlington et al. [20], Mohammed et al. [30], Karie and Venter [25], and Bello and Griffiths [5] all concluded that law enforcement agents needed more training in digital forensics. Therefore, the finding of this study is novel and could potentially help in the design of training needs for cybercrime investigators in Nigeria.

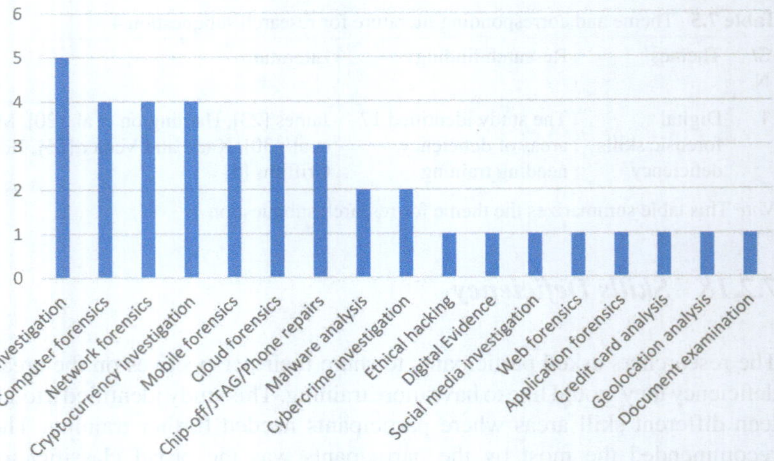

Fig. 7.1 Training courses needed by participants. *Note* This figure shows the top training courses needed by participants

Table 7.6 Theme and corresponding literature for research subquestion 6

S/N	Themes	Research findings	Literature
1	Digital forensic tools needed	The study identified six tools needed by financial crimes investigators in Nigeria	No literature

Note This table summarizes the theme for research subquestion 6

Research Subquestion 6: What specific digital forensic tools are in short supply or with expired licenses needing an upgrade?

This analysis produced one theme, as shown in Table 7.6.

7.2.19 Digital Forensic Tools Needed

The participants were encouraged to suggest tools they would like to have. The responses to this varied between participants, but there were common areas of interest. Also, the areas of specialization of each participant seem to shape their recommendations. This study found financial crime investigators in Nigeria needed the following top six tools: Mobile forensic tools, cryptocurrency investigation tools, trackers/jammers, cloud forensic investigation tools, network forensic investigation tools, and Call Detail Record (CDR) analyzer. The needs is indicative or suggestive of the areas of technological gap. Figure 7.2 summarizes the tools needed.

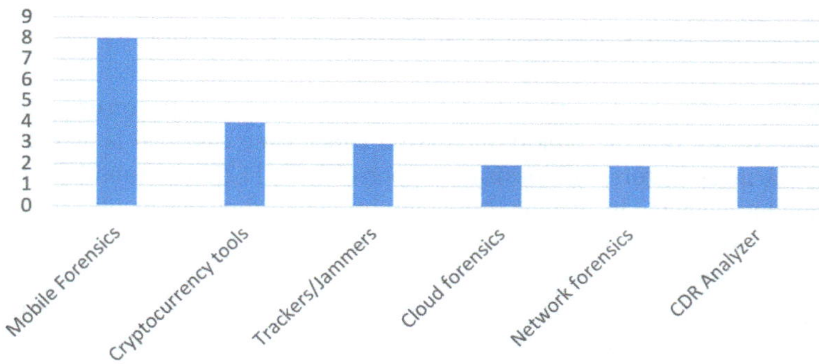

Fig. 7.2 Top 6 tools needed by participants. *Note* This figure shows the top 6 tools needed by financial crimes investigating agencies in Nigeria

Previous studies had shown the need for more investment in tools but did not go into specifics of the tool type or tool category. For instance, Olayemi [33] noted that the lack of a digital forensic laboratory incapacitated the police. Tonye [41] also supports this position, noting that the lack of digital forensic tools was a common challenge affecting the efficiency of the investigative process. Bello and Griffiths [5] corroborated this finding, noting the funding challenge to provide the tools and other logistics needed for effective investigation. This finding also aligns with the RAT framework, with the law enforcement agencies as the capable guardian. It follows that a capable guardian should be one with access to the right tools [5, 11, 18, 26]. This study finds that investing in the recommended tools will improve the forensic capability of law enforcement agencies.

Research Subquestion 7: What are the daily cybercrime caseload and available digital forensics resources?

Two themes emerged from this analysis, summarized in Table 7.7.

Table 7.7 Themes and corresponding literature for research subquestion 7

S/N	Themes	Research findings	Literature
1	Rising caseloads	The rapidly increasing caseload of cybercrime was a challenge to investigators	Eboibi [12], Chigozie-Okwum et al. [10], Cohen and Felson's [11]
2	Top three reasons for rising caseloads	Unemployment, poverty, and peer pressure are the top three reasons behind the rising caseloads.	Chigozie-Okwum et al. [10], Olayemi [33], Adesina [2], Cohen and Felson's [11]

Note This table summarizes themes for research subquestion seven and corresponding literature

7.2.20 The Rising Caseload of Cybercrime

The findings of the study established that there is a surge in cybercrime cases. The study also shows that the rapidly increasing cybercrime caseload is a challenge to cybercrime investigators. This position supports Eboibi [12], who submitted that Law enforcement agencies in Nigeria struggle with cybercrime caseloads. This finding is also consistent with Chigozie-Okwum et al. [10], who stated that the rapidly increasing caseloads of cybercrime put a more significant burden on investigators in Nigeria. The findings of this study also align in part with Cohen and Felson's [11] Routine Activity Theory, that for crime to occur, three conditions must occur. The conditions are a motivated offender, a suitable target, and the absence of a capable guardian. Situating the cybercrime investigators in the mould of the "Capable Guardian", it follows that a low level of forensic readiness is a motivation for the cybercriminal.

7.2.21 Top 3 Reasons for Rising Caseloads

The researchers asked participants to share their perspectives on the rising caseloads. This study identified the top three reasons as primarily economic, social, and cultural. The study findings show that unemployment was the most frequently mentioned reason for the rising caseloads of cybercrime. Poverty and peer pressure were the second and third most mentioned reasons for the increasing caseloads. Greed was the fourth most frequently cited reason. Greed was followed by the relative ease of cybercrime compared to other traditional crimes like robbery, as one reason for the high figures. Poor parenting was also one of the reasons cited by participants. The implication of this finding is that while the lack of forensic resources is a motivation for the cybercriminal, however, the top motivation factors have to do with socioeconomic reasons.

The findings of this study align with Oni et al. [36], who held that unemployment and greed are responsible for the rising cases of cybercrime. These findings also align with Chigozie-Okwum et al. [10], who submitted that unemployment, poverty, and the relatively lower risk of cybercrime serve as an incentive behind the increasing figures. Olayemi [33] also held that cybercrime was increasing due to poverty, greed, and corruption. Adesina [2] also aligns with this position, stating that Nigerian youths turn to cybercrime due to poverty. This finding only aligns in part with Cohen and Felson's [11] Routine Activity Theory, that for crime to occur, three conditions must occur. The conditions are a motivated offender, a suitable target, and the absence of a capable guardian. In this sense, the top three reasons for the rising cybercrime cases did not include a suitable target. The top three factors raised by participants had more to do with the attributes of the criminal than the disposition of the victim. The Economic and Financial Crimes Commission [14] chairman, however, noted in a recent presentation that poverty and unemployment should not be reasons why young people should take to cybercrime.

> **Primary Research Question 2: What is composition and complexity of the cybercrime cases in Nigeria?**
>
> > **Research Subquestion 1: What are the frequent cybercrimes committed in Nigeria?**
> > **Research Subquestion 2: How many persons are convicted of cybercrime in Nigeria?**

To address the primary research question 2, and research subquestions 1 and 2, the researchers relied on official records and statistics from the EFCC, graciously shared by the commission. These statistics and records are useful to better understand the magnitude, dynamics, frequency, and taxonomy of cybercrimes in Nigeria. The following themes emerged from this analysis:

1. Cybercrime Taxonomy and Caseloads
2. Other Cybercrime Dynamics.

7.3 Cybercrime Taxonomy and Caseloads

Understanding the cybercrime typology or taxonomy is important for a lot of reasons. It is indicative of the personal and technological preferences of the cybercriminal. It is also important for planning purposes, from the law enforcement point of view. For instance, knowing the frequently committed cybercrime types can inform your technological choices in attaining forensic readiness and capability maturity. To understand the taxonomy and caseloads, this research relied on the EFCC statistics and official documents. This study found that before 2020, the commission broadly classified cybercrime under 4 taxonomies:

i. Email hacking (BEC)
ii. Internet fraud (Computer related)
iii. Cybercrime (Other forms of Cybercrimes)
iv. Internet Banking Fraud.

However, in 2020, the EFCC conducted an internal review which saw the splitting of some of these and the emergence of new taxonomies. This study showed the following taxonomies by the EFCC, between 2021 and 2022:

i. Email hacking (BEC)
ii. Cybercrime (Other forms of Cybercrimes)
iii. Identity theft
iv. Electronic signature theft
v. Credit card fraud
vi. Theft of electronic device
vii. Fraudulent issuance of e-instruction.

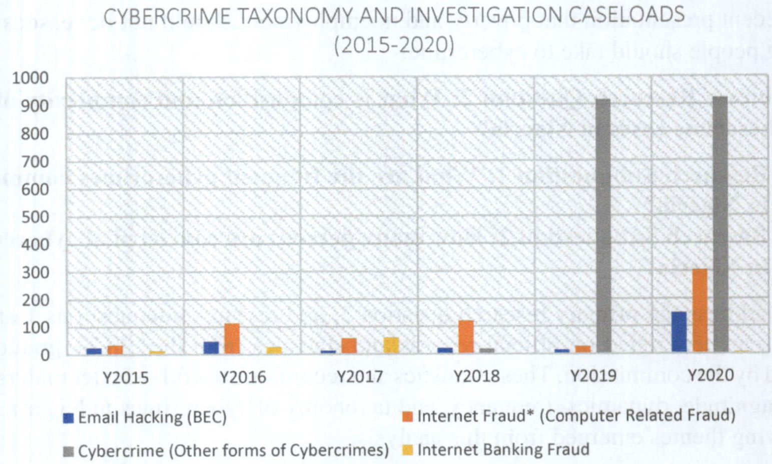

Fig. 7.3 Cybercrime taxonomy and investigative caseloads (prosecution) for 2015–2020. *Note* This figure is a breakdown of the prosecution caseloads, by cybercrime type, from 2015 to 2020

Figure 7.3 shows the breakdown of number of cases investigated for each cybercrime type between 2015 and 2020. As can be seen in the figure, the cybercrime type that had the highest number of investigations between 2015 and 2018 was internet fraud (computer related fraud). Between 2019 and 2020, cyber crime (other forms of cybercrimes) dominated the caseloads.

As stated above, following the redefinition of the cybercrime typology by the EFCC, the dynamics changed in years 2021 and 2022, therefore, the researchers generated a different graph for the two years. This study established that the most investigated cybercrime type for both years was identify theft. The second most investigated cybercrime type was electronic signature theft. This was followed by the cybercrime type, cybercrime (other forms of cybercrime). This was followed by Email Hacking (Business Email Compromise). Figure 7.4 shows the breakdown for 2021–2022.

Figure 7.5 shows the EFCC conviction records for internet fraud from 2015 to 2020, while Fig. 7.6 shows the conviction records for other cybercrime taxonomy in 2022. Figure 7.5 shows that internet fraud spiked between 2019 and 2020. From just 7 convictions for internet fraud in 2019, the number of convictions jumped to 344 in 2019 and 309 in 2020, respectively. However, as noted above, a reclassification of the cybercrime taxonomy by EFCC saw a breakdown to other typologies.

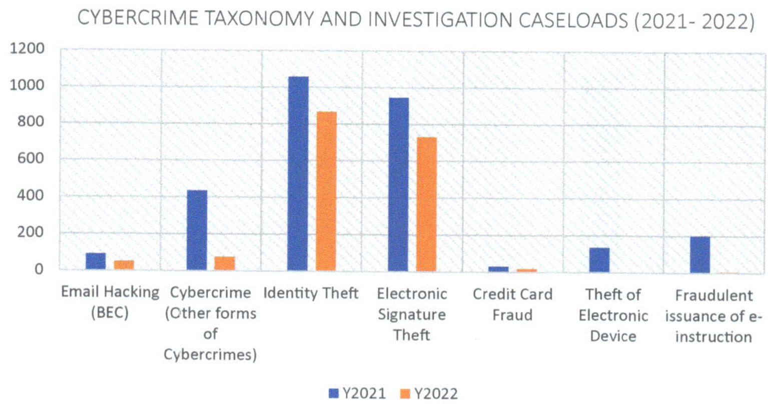

Fig. 7.4 Cybercrime taxonomy and investigative caseloads (prosecution) for 2021–2022. *Note* This figure is a breakdown of the prosecution caseloads, by cybercrime type, from 2021 to 2022

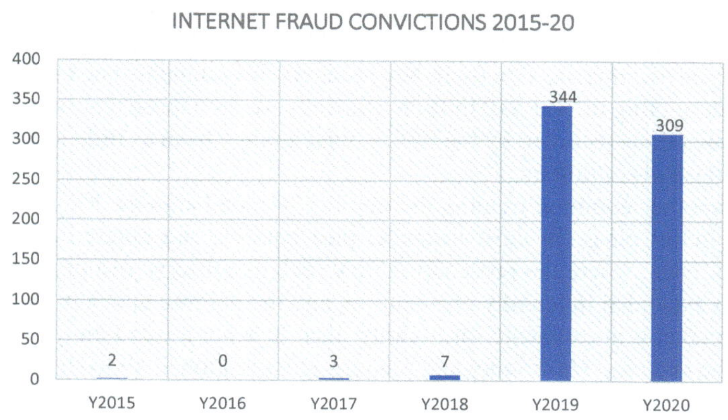

Fig. 7.5 Internet fraud conviction records for 2021–2022. *Note* This figure is a breakdown of the internet fraud conviction record of the EFCC from 2015 to 2020

7.4 Other Cybercrime Dynamics

To understand the dynamics and complexity, this study further drilled into specifics of the casefiles. Table 7.8 summarises the findings from an analysis of the conviction press releases by the EFCC for the month of February 2023. Looking at this, there was a pattern observed in the case type, amount involved, prosecution, and sentencing. First, one quick trend noticed is that all the victims for the cases reviewed (February 2023) are all foreigners and the amounts involved is in foreign currency (mostly dollars).

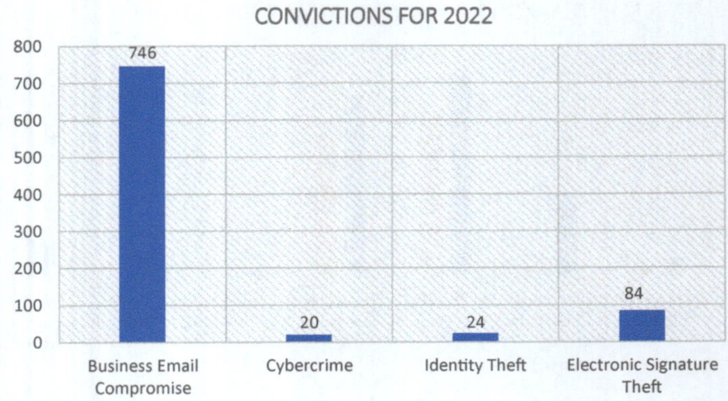

Fig. 7.6 Cybercrime (by type) conviction records for 2021–2022. *Note* This figure is a breakdown of the cybercrime (by type) conviction record of the EFCC from 2015 to 2020

Also, the amounts involved are relatively small, compared to other jurisdictions. For instance, the case of *Ramon Olorunwa Abbas aka "Ray Hushpuppi"* and *Obinwanne Okeke aka Invictus Obi* (both Nigerians) reviewed in this book involved large sums; both running to over \$10 million, respectively. Juxtapose that with the figures for the convictions recorded by the EFCC, which range from as little as \$50 to a few tens of thousands of dollars.

Also, another common trend is the number of plea bargains. Most of the cases ended in guilty pleas. In most instance, plea bargains are entered as a common ground for each, where the prosecution may seek to conserve resources that would have been expended in lengthy prosecution, and the defense appealing for leniency in the sentencing in exchange for a guilty plea. It is not a trend unique to Nigeria, as the reviewed case *Hushpuppi* and *Invictus Obi* mentioned above both ended in a plea bargain.

Despite the similar trend of plea bargains, the sentencing structure is different. In all the reviewed cases in this study, the sentences were mostly 2–3 years, and only a few instances of 5 years. A cursory look at the cases with sensing of 5 years show that the defendants were not charged for violation of the Cybercrime Act 2015, rather they were charged with a state law. Specifically, the cases reviewed with 5 years, the suspects were charged for violation to Section 308 of the Kaduna State Penal Code Law, 2017 and punishable under Section 309 of the Same Law.

However, it is noteworthy that all the convictions reviewed have options of fines, in line with the provisions of the Cybercrime Act 2015. The challenge with this is that the Cybercrime Act 2015 provided for static fines, which did not contemplate inflationary pull, time value for money, and the rapid currency differentials (Naira has lost value by over 100% against the dollar). Here's the challenge with provisions such as this: In 2015 when the Cybercrime was passed into law, N100,000 was about \$560.92 (at N178.28 to \$1 exchange rate). As at November, N100,000 has lost value

Table 7.8 Findings from EFCC press releases for conviction (February 2023)

S/N	Command	Cybercrime taxonomy	Sentence	No. of convictions
1	Port Harcourt, Rivers State command	Internet fraud. Fraudulent impersonation using Telegram, YouTube, etc.	• Pleaded guilty. 2 years in a correctional facility or an option of a fine of N300,000 • Forfeiture of Samsung Galaxy A305	1
2	Kaduna	Internet fraud. Romance scam—fraudulent impersonation via Facebook	• Guilty plea. 5-years imprisonment with an option of N150,000 fine • Forfeiture of one HP Laptop and an Infinity S5	1
3	Kaduna	Internet fraud. 1 count charge of impersonation. Induced victim via Instagram to deliver 27,900 Pakistani rupees	• Guilty plea. Sentenced to 5-years imprisonment or fine of N100,000 payable to Kaduna State Government • Forfeiture of iPhone XR used to commit crime • Ordered to restitute sum of 27,900 Pakistani Rupees to victim	1
4	Abuja	Internet fraud. 1 count of impersonation using various social media • Defendant 1: fraudulently obtained N150,000 from a Chinese • Defendant 2: fraudulently obtained N1,500,000 • Defendant 3: fraudulently obtained $170 from his American victim	• Pleaded guilty • Sentenced to community service • Fines of N50,000, $100 (and refund $70 from stolen funds), and N200,000, respectively • Forfeiture of phones	3
5	Port Harcourt	Internet fraud. Impersonation	• Both pleaded guilty • Defendant 1 sentenced to 1-year imprisonment with fine option of N100,000 • Defendant 2 sentenced to 3 years imprisonment with fine option of N200,000 • Forfeiture of phones	2

(continued)

Table 7.8 (continued)

S/N	Command	Cybercrime taxonomy	Sentence	No. of convictions
6	Port Harcourt	Internet fraud	• Both pleaded guilty • Defendant 1 sentenced to 1-year imprisonment with fine option of N200,000 • Defendant 2 sentenced to 2 years imprisonment with fine option of N300,000 • Forfeiture of 4 phones and 1 laptop	2
7	Kaduna	Cybercrime. Impersonating and dishonestly inducing victim via Instagram to deliver $400	• Sentenced to 5-years imprisonment with fine option of N100,000 • Forfeiture of Infinix phone used to commit crime	1
8	Abuja	Cybercrime. Fraudulent impersonation on Facebook to defraud a Thai citizen and a New Jersey technician	• Pleaded guilty • Sentenced to 1-year imprisonment with fine option of N100,000 • Forfeiture of HP laptop	1
9	Port Harcourt	Romance scam	• Pleaded guilty • Sentenced to 1-year imprisonment with fine option of N50,000 • Forfeiture of Techno phone used to commit the crime	1
10	Makurdi	Internet fraud. Impersonation to defraud victim of $104 worth of bitcoin	• Sentenced to 1-year imprisonment with fine option of N50,000 • Forfeiture of Infinix phone and amount in account	1
12	Port Harcourt	Internet fraud. Fraudulent impersonation using Gmail and Telegram accounts	• Pleaded guilty • Sentenced to 2-years imprisonment with fine option of N100,000 • Forfeiture of mobile devices	1
13	Abuja	Internet fraud. Fraudulent impersonation on social media (Wechat and Instagram), defrauding unsuspecting victims	• Pleaded guilty • Sentenced to 6 months imprisonment without an option of fine • Forfeiture of phone and financial proceeds of crime (N600,000)	1

Note This table summarizes the findings from EFCC Press Releases for Conviction for the month of February 2023 colossally and is now only worth \$110.50 (at the official rate of N905.39 to a dollar) [42].

So, consider a criminal who committed cybercrime in 2015 and asked to pay a fine of N100,000, his fine in dollars would be \$560.92 (Again, remember that this study has established that the proceeds of their crime are mostly dollar-denominated). Today, another cybercriminal who commits same crime and is given the option of a fine in similar amount will be paying the dollar equivalent of only \$110.50. That is, the fine has shrunk by over 80%. The cybercriminal earns in high value dollar, and only pays a paltry fine in a currency weaker in valuation than the proceeds of crime. This appears to be clearly an incentive for the cybercriminal. This section of the Cybercrime Act 2015 needs to be reviewed to accommodate the dynamics of currency differentials, inflationary pull, and other macroeconomic factors.

Also, if you look at this from an inflationary point of view, in October 2006, inflation in Nigeria was at 6.10%, as of October 2023, inflation had risen to 27.33% [9]. Therefore, the penalty has shrunk in value (in dollar terms) and is now an incentive for cybercriminals since the can easily pay this amount. Do not forget that the proceeds of their crime, as established in this study, is largely dollar denominated. Therefore, setting static penalty options in a country with volatile macroeconomic parameters have proved counterproductive and in fact an incentive to the criminals.

7.5 Summary

This chapter analysed the findings presented in Chaps. 5 and 6, and examined the implications for financial crimes in Nigeria. The study made important findings in terms of digital forensic readiness of the cybercrime agencies. Also, other key findings concerning the caseloads, frequency and dynamics of cybercrime were examined.

The study established a lack of digital forensic resources at the financial crimes agencies in Nigeria. Specifically, the study established the lack (insufficient number) of competent forensic professionals in relation to the rising caseloads. The study also established a challenge with tools availability. The study also established a lack of an SOP that is available and mainstreamed. The study also showed that the Cybercrime Act 2015, while a significant improvement, is no longer an efficient legal framework in the wake of emerging realities. Table 7.9 summarized the themes, research findings, and the implications for financial crimes in Nigeria.

Table 7.9 Summary of research findings (from themes) and implications for financial crimes in Nigeria

S/N	Themes	Research findings	Implications and recommendations
1	Personnel adequacy	Agencies lacked personnel	Given the rising caseloads and Nigeria's population, cybercrime agencies are overwhelmed
2	Personnel capability	Personnel of the agencies lacks forensic capabilities	Need for sustained training program
3	Tools availability	Digital forensic tools were in short supply or outdated	Nigerian cybercrime agencies lack the tools to put up an efficient fight against cybercrime. Need to have a sustainable funding structure for law enforcement agencies to build technological readiness
4	Documented processes	No Standard Operating Procedure (SOP) is available and mainstreamed.	The EFCC has an SOP. Need to make it available and mainstreamed. The Nigeria Police needs to develop an SOP to guide their investigation
5	Structured process review	No structured process review	There is the need to have a structured process review mechanism.
6	Policy framework	Cybercrime Act 2015 is the guiding framework	The Cybercrime Act 2015 is not an efficient legal framework. It needs to be amended to reflect emerging realities
7	Tool licensing challenge	The recurrent cost of forensic tools licenses is a significant challenge	The efficiency of the forensic unit is undermined with expired licenses. Need to have a sustainable funding structure for law enforcement agencies to build technological readiness
	Lack of structured training program	The study established the lack of a structured training program	Cybercrime investigators have skills gap and struggle with emerging technologies. Need to have a structured training programme. Need for a sustainable funding structure
	Policy challenges	Lack of an efficient framework for inter-agency collaboration, jurisdictional roadblocks, other legal hurdles, and poor policy implementation mechanism	The lack of an efficient framework for inter-agency collaboration was a challenge. Also need to foster international collaboration to reduce the jurisdictional bottlenecks in the investigation of cybercrime
	Roadmap for digital forensic readiness	No roadmap for digital forensic readiness	The absence of a clear roadmap undermines the agencies abilities to build digital forensic readiness in a structured manner. Having a roadmap for digital forensic readiness is a good first step to building readiness

(continued)

Table 7.9 (continued)

S/N	Themes	Research findings	Implications and recommendations
	Collaboration	The study established the need for more effective collaboration	Need for more collaborations between various stakeholders
	Jurisdictional challenges	The study established that the cross-border nature of cybercrime poses jurisdictional roadblocks	Need to foster international collaboration to reduce the jurisdictional bottlenecks in the investigation of cybercrime
	Emerging technologies	The study concluded that emerging technologies were challenging to cybercrime investigators	Cybercrime investigators have skills gap and struggle with emerging technologies
	Funding	The study established that funding was a significant challenge	Need for sustainable funding structure
	Pace of cybercrime	The fast pace of cybercrime was a challenge to investigators	Need to build forensic readiness. Need for sustainable funding structure. Need for a structured training programme
	Digital forensic adoption	There is a good level of user acceptance of digital forensic technology. However, the lack of access impeded the diffusion of digital forensic technology in both organizations	There is a good level of user acceptance, which is a good encouragement for more investment. More digital forensic laboratories and tools should be set up to promote access
	Impact of lack of digital forensic technology	Lack of digital forensic resources seriously impacted financial crimes investigation	The lack of forensic readiness greatly impacted cybercrime investigation in Nigeria
	Digital forensic skills deficiency	The study identified 17 areas of deficiency, needing training	Need to have a structured training programme to fill the skills gap
	Digital forensic tools needed	The study identified six tools needed by financial crimes investigators in Nigeria	Need to invest more to fill the gaps identified
	Rising caseloads	The rapidly increasing caseload of cybercrime was a challenge to investigators	This is a great concern and overwhelms cybercrime investigators. Need for more resources—personnel, digital forensic resources, intelligence, others
	Top three reasons for rising caseloads	Unemployment, poverty, and peer pressure are the top reasons for the rising caseloads	Until Nigeria solves her socioeconomic challenges, the caseloads will continue to be high

Note This table summarizes findings (from themes) and the implications for financial crimes in Nigeria

References

1. Abu SO, Lateef OM, Echobu J (2018) Determinants of cyber fraud investigation in Nigeria. Acc Taxation Rev 2(2)
2. Adesina OS (2017) Cybercrime and poverty in Nigeria. Can Soc Sci 13(4):19–29
3. Ahmed I (2020) Technology organization environment framework in cloud computing. Telkomnika 18(2):716–725
4. Ajetunmobi RA, Uwadia CO, Oladeji FA (2016) Computer forensic guideline: a requirement for fighting cyber crime in Nigeria now? In: UNILAG research conference 2016, Nigeria. https://ir.unilag.edu.ng/handle/123456789/5833
5. Bello M, Griffiths M (2021) Routine activity theory and cybercrime investigation in Nigeria: how capable are law enforcement agencies? In: Rethinking cybercrime. Palgrave Macmillan, Cham, pp 213–235
6. Carrier B, Spafford E (2004) An event-based digital forensic investigation framework. Digit Invest. https://dfrws.org/wp-content/uploads/2019/06/2004_USA_paper-an_event-based_digital_forensic_investigation_framework.pdf
7. Carrier BD, Spafford EH (2005, August) Automated digital evidence target definition
8. Cassim F (2011) Addressing the growing spectre of cybercrime in Africa: evaluating measures adopted by South Africa and other regional role players. Comp Int Law J South Afr 44(1):123–138
9. Central Bank of Nigeria (2023) Inflation rates (percent). https://www.cbn.gov.ng/rates/inflrates.asp?year=2023
10. Chigozie-Okwum C, Ugboaja S, Micheal D, Osuo-Genseleke M (2017) Proliferation of cyber insecurity in Nigeria: a root cause analysis. AFRREV STECH Int J Sci Technol 6(2):53–60
11. Cohen LE, Felson M (1979) Social change and crime rate trends: a routine activity approach. Am Sociol Rev 588–608
12. Eboibi FE (2017) A review of the legal and regulatory frameworks of Nigerian Cybercrimes Act 2015. Comput Law Secur Rev 33(5):700–717
13. Eboibi FE (2021) Cybercriminals and coronavirus cybercrimes in Nigeria, the United States of America and the United Kingdom: cyber hygiene and preventive enforcement measures. Commonw Law Bull 47(1):113–142
14. Economic and Financial Crimes Commission (2023) Poverty, unemployment no excuses for cybercrimes-Bawa. https://www.efcc.gov.ng/efcc/news-and-information/news-release/9246-poverty-unemployment-no-excuses-for-cybercrimes-bawa
15. Economic and Financial Crimes Commission (2022) Unveiling of manuals: Buhari commends Bawa, urges other agencies to emulate EFCC. https://www.efcc.gov.ng/efcc/news-and-information/news-release/7858-unveiling-of-manuals-buhari-commends-bawa-urges-other-agencies-to-emulate-efcc
16. Ehimen OR, Bola A (2010) Cybercrime in Nigeria. Bus Intell J 3(1):93–98
17. Elyas M, Maynard SB, Ahmad A, Lonie A (2014) Towards a systemic framework for digital forensic readiness. J Comput Inform Syst 54(3):97–105
18. Grabosky PN (2001) Virtual criminality: old wine in new bottles? Soc Leg Stud 10(2):243–249
19. Grobler CP, Louwrens CP (2007, May) Digital forensic readiness as a component of information security best practice. In: IFIP International information security conference. Springer, Boston, MA, pp 13–24
20. Hadlington L, Lumsden K, Black A, Ferra F (2021) A qualitative exploration of police officers' experiences, challenges, and perceptions of cybercrime. Policing J Policy Pract 15(1):34–43
21. International Telecommunication Union (2012) Understanding cybercrime: phenomena, challenges and legal response. http://www.itu.int/ITU-D/cyb/cybersecurity/docs/Cybercrime%20legislation%20EV6.pdf
22. Interpol (2017) Global cybercrime strategy. https://www.interpol.int/en/Crimes/Cybercrime
23. James JI (2017) How businesses can speed up international cybercrime investigation. IEEE Secur Priv 15(2):102–106

24. James JI, Gladyshev P (2013) Challenges with automation in digital forensic investigations. arXiv preprint arXiv:1303.4498
25. Karie NM, Venter HS (2015) Taxonomy of challenges for digital forensics. J Forensic Sci 60(4):885–893
26. Leukfeldt ER, Yar M (2016) Applying routine activity theory to cybercrime: a theoretical and empirical analysis. Deviant Behav 37(3):263–280
27. Leung D, Lo A, Fong LHN, Law R (2015) Applying the Technology-Organization-Environment framework to explore ICT initial and continued adoption: an exploratory study of an independent hotel in Hong Kong. Tour Recreat Res 40(3):391–406
28. Li JX (2017) Cybercrime and legal countermeasures: a historical analysis. Int J Crim Justice Sci 12(2):196–207
29. Mihai IC, Pruna Ş, Petrica G (2017) A comprehensive analysis on cyber-threats against elearning systems. ELearning Softw Educ 3:344–351. https://doi.org/10.12753/2066-026X-17-225
30. Mohammed KH, Mohammed YD, Solanke AA (2019) Cybercrime and digital forensics: bridging the gap in legislation, investigation, and prosecution of cybercrime in Nigeria. Int J Cybersecur Intell Cybercrime 2(1):56–53
31. Nwankwo W, Ukaoha KC (2019) Socio-technical perspectives on cybersecurity: Nigeria's cybercrime legislation in review. Int J Sci Technol Res 8(9):47–58
32. Office of the National Security Adviser (2021) National cybersecurity policy and strategy. https://cert.gov.ng/ngcert/resources/NATIONAL_CYBERSECURITY_POLICY_AND_STRATEGY_2021.pdf
33. Olayemi OJ (2014) A socio-technological analysis of cybercrime and cyber security in Nigeria. Int J Sociol Anthropol 6(3):116–125
34. Oliveira T, Martins MF (2011) Literature review of information technology adoption models at firm level. Electron J Inform Syst Eval 14(1):110–121
35. Omodunbi BA, Odiase PO, Olaniyan OM, Esan AO (2016) Cybercrimes in Nigeria: analysis, detection, and prevention. J Eng Technol 1(1):37–42
36. Oni S, Berepubo KA, Oni AA, Joshua S (2019, April) E-government and the challenge of cybercrime in Nigeria. In: 2019 Sixth international conference on eDemocracy & eGovernment (ICEDEG). IEEE, pp 137–142
37. Oraegbunam IK (2015) The Nigerian police and problems of cybercrime investigation: need for adequate training. Niger Law J 18(1):1–28
38. Pooe A, Labuschagne L (2012, August) A conceptual model for digital forensic readiness. In: 2012 Information security for South Africa. IEEE, pp 1–8
39. Straub ET (2009) Understanding technology adoption: theory and future directions for informal learning. Review of educational research 79(2):625–649
40. Tan J (2001) Forensic readiness. @ Stake, Cambridge, MA, pp 1–23
41. Tonye WS (2018) Cyber forensic and data collection challenges in Nigeria. Glob J Comput Sci Technol 18(3)
42. Trading Economics (2023) Nigerian naira. https://tradingeconomics.com/nigeria/currency
43. Tseloni A, Wittebrood K, Farrell G, Pease K (2004) Burglary victimization in England and Wales, the United States and the Netherlands: a cross-national comparative test of routine activities and lifestyle theories. Br J Criminol 44(1):66–91
44. Weber AM (2003) The council of Europe's convention on cybercrime. Berkeley Technol Law J 18(1):425–446
45. Yar M (2005) The novelty of 'cybercrime': an assessment in light of routine activity theory. Eur J Criminol 2(4):407–427

Chapter 8
Conclusion and Recommendations for Digital Forensic Readiness of Nigerian Financial Crimes Agencies

Abstract This chapter presents a summary of the key findings of this study and the implications for financial crimes in Nigeria. The chapter started by presenting a summary of the methodology of the study. The study was structured as a qualitative case study, relying on interviews and review of official documents and records of the Economic and Financial Crimes Commission (EFCC) and the Nigeria Police Force. The chapter presented a summary of research contributions to knowledge—theory, policy, and practice. This chapter ended by presenting a set of practical recommendations for the digital forensic readiness of both the EFCC and the Nigerian Police Force.

Keywords Cybercrime · Financial crimes · Economic and Financial Crimes Commission · Nigeria Police · Digital forensic readiness

8.1 Introduction

The Nigerian law enforcement agencies have been struggling to cope with the pace, scale, and magnitude of financial crimes, particularly cybercrime and internet fraud. Studies have identified gaps in digital forensics resources amongst financial crime agencies in Nigeria as one of the significant factors preventing effective prosecution [4, 28–31]. For instance, the Economic and Financial Crime Commission's (EFCC) digital forensics unit at the agency's head office has just an 8-man team. With caseloads averaging about two per day—each with a possibility of multiple devices—it is difficult for an 8-man team to cope [29]. While these studies suggested the lack of forensic resources and capabilities by both the Nigerian financial crimes agencies and the justice system, no available studies have drilled deeper into it. Specifically, no studies examined the specific skills gap and resources needed in Nigeria's financial crimes agencies. With such growing concern for the lack of digital forensic capabilities for financial crime agencies, this study identified resource deficiencies and how

R. T. Sibe and C. Kaunert, *Cybercrime, Digital Forensic Readiness, and Financial Crime Investigation in Nigeria*, Advanced Sciences and Technologies for Security Applications, https://doi.org/10.1007/978-3-031-54089-9_8

this affects caseloads and prosecution. The outcome of this study could be a good starting point for developing a roadmap for digital forensic readiness and capability maturity for the law enforcement agencies in Nigeria.

This chapter summarized the findings of this research. The results established an apparent lack of digital forensic resources by Nigeria's two major financial crime investigation agencies—The Nigerian Police Force and the Economic and Financial Crimes Commission (EFCC). The study also identified the key challenges responsible for the low adoption of digital forensic technology. The significant challenges from the results are tools licensing, poor funding, lack of structured training program, policy challenges, lack of a clear roadmap for digital forensic readiness, poor collaboration, jurisdictional roadblocks, emerging technologies, and the fast pace of cybercrime. The study made unique contributions to theory, knowledge, practice, and policy. In this chapter, specific recommendations were made addressing the identified challenges affecting the fight against cybercrime in Nigeria. The chapter ended with an important contribution of a Roadmap for Digital Forensic Readiness for the agencies.

8.2 Methodology

This study was structured to investigate the digital forensic readiness of cybercrime institutions in Nigeria. This study also investigated the specifics of what constitutes the cybercrime caseloads in Nigeria—the actual figures, the number of convictions, the cybercrime taxonomy, and any other trend or dynamics behind the surge. The study also investigated the lack of forensic resources amongst financial crimes agencies in Nigeria. This study was structured as a qualitative case study, utilizing semi-structured interviews to understand the subject. In Nigeria, following the enactment of the EFCC Act 2004, the Economic and Financial Crimes Commission (EFCC) was set up with the sole purpose of investigating and prosecuting financial crimes [27, 46]. Also, the Nigerian Police Force has a Fraud Investigating Unit dedicated to investigating fraud and financial crimes. They also have a dedicated cybercrime unit with a mandate to crack down on cybercrime [25, 48].

Therefore, the research population consisted of the Nigerian Police Force and the Economic and Financial Crimes Commission (EFCC). Eighteen participants were carefully selected from related departments to ensure a deep understanding of the subject. The sample consisted of five persons from the Cybercrime department of the Nigeria Police Force and thirteen officers of the EFCC, drawn from four different related (forensic or forensic-dependent) departments within the organization—Digital Forensic department, Cybercrime Department, Advance Fee Fraud Department, and Legal (Cybercrime Prosecution) Department. This diversity was necessary to ensure different perspectives.

Following informed consent from the participants (after prior authorization from the two organisations), the researchers used Sony digital audio recorder for recording participant interviews. The digital recordings were transcribed, and the researchers used the qualitative software NVivo to analyze the transcription of recorded interviews. This tool codified themes from the interview transcripts. This study used theoretical thematic analysis for the categorization of interview data. A thematic analysis could come in three forms: inductive analysis, theoretical analysis, and that which comes with constant comparison [33]. This research adopted the theoretical analysis method. This method allowed some pre-determined themes were generated from existing literature and research questions while also being flexible to creating new ones inductively from patterns observed in the interview transcripts. Data collected was analyzed to look out for repeating patterns and themes. The study was structured to follow the analytic procedure recommended by Marshall and Rossman [19]. This study produced themes and emergent themes that are valuable contributions to the body of knowledge—theory, policy, and practice.

8.3 Summary of Research Contributions

This research made several contributions that could potentially shape policy formulation in both organizations. It established the lack of digital forensic resources and made specific findings in this regard. The study made a unique contribution to digital forensic adoption studies of law enforcement agencies. The research made novel contributions by producing a list of tools and training needed by Nigeria's financial crimes investigating agencies. It established the absence of an effective collaboration mechanism among agencies. The study also added to the literature on the jurisdictional roadblocks and impact on cybercrime, big data challenge, and other challenges faced by the agencies in Nigeria. This study also established the specifics of Nigeria's cybercrime caseload, and a breakdown of the taxonomy and other dynamics.

Six themes and twenty-five subthemes emerged from the analysis of the interviews. The main themes are personnel, digital forensic technology, digital forensic training, processes, policy, and challenges. The personnel theme had subthemes for personnel adequacy and personnel capability. The digital forensic technology theme had the following subthemes: tool availability, tool licensing challenge, tools needed, digital forensic adoption, and the impact of lack of digital forensic technology. The digital forensic training theme had the following subthemes: structured training and training need. The process theme had the following subthemes: defined processes, structured process reviews, and process challenges.

The policy theme had four subthemes: policy framework, policy challenges, and the roadmap for digital forensic readiness. The challenges theme had the following subthemes: collaboration, jurisdictional, emerging technologies, funding, the pace of Cybercrime, rising caseloads, top 3 reasons, information governance, big data challenge, and the roadmap for digital forensic readiness. Challenges identified include lack of an efficient framework for collaboration, jurisdictional challenges, emerging technologies, poor funding, the fast pace of cybercrime, big data challenge, and the lack of a roadmap for digital forensic readiness. The themes reveal the perspectives shared by participants drawn from the two agencies. The researchers analyzed the research questions within the context of these themes.

This study made significant findings and unique contributions to theory and knowledge. It could positively and potentially impact the policy and practice of cybercrime investigation in Nigeria. This research outcome could help strengthen the financial crimes investigation capability of both the Nigerian Police Force and the Economic and Financial Crimes Commission in Nigeria. This chapter presents these contributions within the context of theory contribution, knowledge contribution, and Policy and Practice Contribution.

8.3.1 Theory Contribution

Two theoretical frameworks guided this study: Routine Activity Theory (RAT) and the Technology-Organization-Environment (TOE). RAT is a famous theory in criminology developed by Cohen and Felson [8]. Essential aspects of the theory—such as the concept of the capable guardianship—shaped this study. The TOE framework is a technology adoption framework that is suitable for studying adoption at the firm level. This study made significant contributions to both theories.

Routine Activity Theory. Routine Activity Theory is a renowned situational theory of crime developed by Cohen and Felson [8]. The theory states that for crime to occur, three conditions must occur. The conditions are a motivated offender, a suitable target, and the absence of a capable guardian. This study is rooted in the third element: the absence of a capable guardian. There have been debates as to the suitability of this theory in other areas beyond the terrestrial world. Specifically, there are varying perspectives and arguments regarding RAT's suitability to analyze the causation of cybercrime and Internet fraud. For instance, Yar [49] thinks given the Spatio-temporal nature of cyberspace and the ecological nature of the RAT, it cannot explain the causation of Internet crime reliably. Grabosky [11] submitted a contrary position, suggesting that the three conditions applicable in the terrestrial world also apply in the cyberworld. Leukfeldt and Yar [17] also posited given the similarities of the terrestrial world and cyberspace, RAT is suitable in both worlds.

Other research has supported Grabosky's [11] position. For instance, Pratt et al. [35] used RAT to explain Internet Fraud. Hutchings and Hayes [12] used RAT to study and explain phishing victimization. Kigerl [15] went beyond the individual level to use RAT to explain cybercrime determinants at the national level. Reyns [37] used RAT to explain online victimization. Samonas [38] narrowed in by using used RAT to analyze and explain insider threats. Bello and Griffiths [4] also used RAT to study Nigerian cybercrime investigative agencies as capable guardians. This theory pointed out all three factors that must be present for a crime to happen, but the findings of this study only align with two—the capable guardian and a motivated offender.

Tseloni et al. [45] define guardianship as the capability of the persons and objects to prevent the crime. The concept of capable guardianship applies widely. Yar [49] expanded the scope of this definition, suggesting this concept could be the property owner, custodian, law enforcement, Computer Emergency Response Teams, Banks, or any other, whose presence may discourage the occurrence of the crime in question. Bello and Griffiths [4] posited that the awareness of the presence of a capable guardian is a demotivating factor to the criminal. This study contributed to this theory by expanding the scope of factors affecting the capability of financial crime agencies (the guardian). The research introduced other factors such as the number of personnel, available technology (in this case, digital forensics), skillset, need for constant training, need for a robust policy framework, and need to provide better funding. This study also reinforced that the absence of a capable guardian is a motivating factor for crime to occur.

However, this study also showed that while the lack of a capable guardian is a motivation for crime to occur, it is not the major motivation for cybercriminals in Nigeria. This study specially showed that the top reasons why the cybercriminals take to crime in Nigeria have more to do with the socioeconomic factors, than the lack of a capable guardian. Furthermore, the study showed an exponential increase in the conviction numbers, which is also an indication of the improved capability and diligent prosecution by the law enforcement agencies. This increased prosecution success rate (and by inference a more capable guardian) does not seem to be a deterrent to the cybercriminals as the caseloads continue to increase. Specifically, this study found that the top three reasons motivating people to take to cybercrime in Nigeria are Unemployment, poverty, and peer pressure. In conclusion, this study showed that to holistically tackle cybercrime in Nigeria, it is important to improve the forensic readiness and capability maturity of the financial crime agencies as well as take adequate steps to also tackle the socioeconomic issues such as poverty, unemployment, and others.

Technology-Organization-Environment Framework (TOE). Adoption refers to an individual's decisions to accept, diffuse and mainstream innovation in an integrated manner [39]. As organizations continue to invest large sums in new technologies, it is crucial to study technology adoption. Such investments may not yield positive results except the right adoption strategies are put in place [2]. This situation is more apparent given the need to study the innovation adoption of emerging technologies and the rapidly evolving landscape. There are several adoption theories, but Technology-Organization-Environment (TOE) framework offers a better explanation of technology adoption at the firm or organisational level. Leung et al. [18] noted that an essential feature of the TOE framework is incorporating environmental factors, helpful in explaining technology adoption.

Technological context includes all relevant technologies in the firm. This context comprises existing related tools as well as emerging technologies [2]. Tornatzky et al. [44] describe technological context as internal and external technologies relevant to the firm. While internal technologies have to do with practices and technologies already adopted by the firm, external technologies refer to available technologies in the market. Following this, Leung et al. [18] hold that technological context primarily focuses on technological characteristics in the technology adoption process. Leung et al. [18] summarized the factors in the technical contexts condensed from previous technological adoption studies as perceived direct benefits, indirect benefits, and cross-technology compatibility [6, 13, 36]. This study contributes to this theory by reinforcing the technological context as a significant adoption consideration. The study established the lack of digital forensic technology as a fundamental reason for Nigeria's poor adoption among law enforcement agents. The study also showed a general willingness by law enforcement agencies to use digital forensic technology; however, the lack of availability of these tools made diffusion impossible.

From the Organizational context, Leung et al. [18] condensed the factors from previous studies in adoption as financial readiness, technological readiness, and top management support. These organizational factors may either impede or facilitate innovation and technological adoption at the firm level [2]. The components summarized by Leung et al. [18] could apply to this study, which was structured to investigate the lack of forensic resources and digital forensic readiness of financial crime agencies in Nigeria. For instance, financial readiness and technological readiness can explain the lack of technology adoption in a firm. Introducing and mainstreaming an emerging technology such as digital forensics technology will be affected or enhanced by organizational factors, which this study was also structured to investigate. This study reinforced this by establishing that the lack of financial readiness, technological readiness, and sustained top management support affect the adoption of digital forensic technologies in Nigeria's financial crimes investigation agencies.

Environment context focuses on the space the firm or organization conducts its business [2]. This space extends to external factors presenting either opportunities or constraints for technological innovation. The environmental context also encompasses the firm's industry, competitors, and governmental interface and policies [44]. These factors affect the adoption of innovation and technology at the firm level. For instance, Al-Hujran et al. [3] established that the regulatory framework was one of the main environmental factors that affected adoption. The findings of this study further reinforce the environmental context as a factor in adoption studies. For instance, following Tornatzky et al. [44] extension of the scope of the environment to include externalities, such as other agencies and stakeholders, this study reinforces this by highlighting the lack of an efficient inter-agency collaboration framework as a reason behind the poor success rate of cybercrime investigation, and by extension the use of digital forensic resources. The study also established jurisdictional complexities and the lack of efficient and timely handshake mechanisms with other nations as one of the key challenges faced in the efficient prosecution of cybercrime.

8.3.2 Contribution to Knowledge

This study made several contributions to the body of knowledge. The study made useful findings to extend and deepen the knowledge and practice of policing, hi-tech crime investigation, and financial crimes investigation in Nigeria. Six themes and 25 sub-themes emerged from this study, all of which resulted in significant contributions to the body of knowledge. Previous studies only pointed to the lack of forensic resources as a significant setback to cybercrime investigation [4, 30, 31]. This study made a significant contribution by investigating deeper to unravel and establish the extent of this lack. The following section summarizes specific contributions.

Skills Gap and Training Need. Previous studies pointed to the need for continuous training for cybercrime investigators and digital forensics experts in Nigeria's financial crimes agencies, but none investigated the specifics of the training needs [1, 7, 9, 30, 31]. This study made a unique contribution to the body of knowledge by investigating this and making recommendations for training needs. This study found seventeen different areas of skills deficiency that the investigators needed further training.

The top three nominations for training found by this study are as follows. Digital forensic investigation training had the highest nomination. This broad skill set reflects that the majority of the participants felt deficient in a general sense and would instead generalize their training needs. Three specialist areas had the joint second highest nominations for training need. They are computer forensics, network forensics, and cryptocurrency investigation training. Three specialist areas got the joint third-highest nominations. They are mobile forensics, cloud forensics, and chip-off/JTAG/Phone repairs training. This finding is a unique contribution to internet fraud and cybercrime investigation in Nigeria, as no previous studies had reported such. It could be beneficial for developing a training program for cybercrime investigators in Nigeria, and by extension other developing economies. Training (to attain capability maturity and stay up-to-date) is also an essential component of a roadmap for readiness. The outcome of this study could be potentially helpful in developing a functional roadmap for digital forensic readiness.

Digital Forensic Technology Gap/Needs. Previous studies alluded to a lack of digital forensic technology as a significant challenge in cybercrime investigation. Bello and Griffiths [4], Mohammed et al. [21], Tonye [43], Chigozie-Okwum et al. [7], Oraegbunam [31], Olayemi [30], and Ehimen and Bola [10] all submitted that the lack of digital forensic tools was a significant setback to cybercrime investigation in Nigeria. These studies, however, did not give specifics of the actual technological gap. The outcome of this study addressed this gap by making specific findings on the extent of the lack of these digital forensic tools and recommendations. These gaps were derived from qualitative interviews of the cybercrime investigators, who are in a good position to know their technological gaps.

This study found the following top six tools recommended by participants (starting with the topmost): Mobile forensic tools, cryptocurrency investigation tools, trackers/jammers, cloud forensic investigation tools, network forensic investigation tools, and Call Detail Records (CDR) analyzer. The researchers de-emphasised the actual product name so as not to promote particular product names over the other. This finding is a unique contribution to internet fraud and cybercrime investigation in Nigeria. Technology is an essential aspect of the TOE framework and an integral component of a roadmap to digital forensic readiness. For an efficient adoption, the organization needs to be technologically ready. Therefore, the outcome of this study could be particularly useful in developing a functional roadmap for digital forensic readiness of Nigerian financial crimes investigation agencies in Nigeria (and, by extension, all law enforcement agencies in Nigeria as well as other developing economies). This study is the first scholarly work to boldly examine the specific forensic technology needs of cybercrime investigating agencies in Nigeria, and even elsewhere.

Lack of Digital Forensic Resources. Previous studies had pointed to the lack of digital forensic resources and indeed attempted studying the impact [4, 7, 21, 43]. Out of these, only Bello and Griffiths [4] looked at it from a broad law enforcement point of view, which included wider stakeholders involved in the cybercrime war in Nigeria. This study limited perspectives strictly to key practitioners—law enforcement agents directly involved in financial crimes prosecution that either uses digital forensic tools themselves or is directly affected by the lack of these tools. This study made contributions to knowledge by reinforcing the earlier findings (that the lack of digital forensic resources had a significant impact on the cybercrime investigation) but from a unique insider perspective. The law enforcement agencies are a major stakeholder in the fight against cybercrime, therefore, their opinions carry significant weightings.

This study made unique findings not previously reported with such clarity and from a law enforcement perspective. This research established a lack of digital forensic resources—competent personnel and digital forensic tools (hardware and software). The outcome of this study also suggested that of the two organizations, the Nigerian Police Force lacked more digital forensic resources. The study established that the Economic and Financial Crimes have a well-equipped digital forensic laboratory at the head office and some minor technological presence at the zonal offices. This study's findings showed that the centralized concentration of digital forensic resources at the headquarters leaves the states and regional offices grossly underserved. This study also showed that the rising caseload was overwhelming, and there was a need to invest more in digital forensic resources. This research also reinforced the fact that the lack of digital forensic resources adversely impacted financial crimes investigation in Nigeria. These findings are unique and a valuable contribution of this study to cybercrime policing in Nigeria.

Digital Forensic Adoption. The findings of this study show that there is a good level of user acceptance for digital forensic technology. Response by participants shows that law enforcement agents are open and willing to utilize digital forensic technology. However, this willingness is frustrated by the investigators' lack of access to digital forensic tools across different formations. This fact is a novel contribution since there are no previous studies on the adoption of digital forensic technology by Nigeria's law enforcement agencies. This contribution is an important outcome that could form the basis for further research applying different technology adoption models and expanding the scope to other law enforcement formations in Nigeria.

Challenges Posed by Emerging Technologies. The technological landscape continues to evolve with emerging technologies, and cybercriminals leverage this evolving landscape to perpetrate crimes. Previous studies have pointed to this challenge [4, 14, 20], but none drilled down on how emerging technologies specifically affected financial crimes investigating agencies in Nigeria. This study found that it was challenging to keep pace with emerging technologies. Most participants pointed to the complications and complexities of investigating emerging technologies such as blockchain and cryptocurrency, cloud technology, and others. This finding is important from a law enforcement point of view and a notable contribution to the body of knowledge in cybercrime investigation in Nigeria.

Challenges Preventing Nigeria's Law Enforcement Agencies from Having Adequate Forensic Capabilities and Being Forensically Ready. Previous studies pointed out the lack of digital forensic resources as a significant challenge facing cybercrime investigative agencies in Nigeria [4, 9, 30, 31]. There are no available studies that comprehensively examine the factors preventing law enforcement agencies in Nigeria from being forensically ready. This study made an essential contribution to the body of knowledge by comprehensively unearthing these challenges facing the agencies from a law enforcement perspective. Documenting these challenges is a crucial achievement of this study and a unique contribution to the body of knowledge.

The challenges found by this study in this regard include the recurrent challenge of the cost of tool licensing. The lack of structured training programs in the organizations was also a significant reason preventing the agencies from being forensically ready. The study also identified funding as a significant challenge. This result provided more profound insight into the funding gap from a practitioner's view. The study also identified the lack of a clear roadmap for forensic readiness for law enforcement agencies in Nigeria. The absence of such roadmap means there is no clear pathway for forensic readiness of law enforcement agencies in Nigeria. The study also identified the lack of an efficient collaboration mechanism, jurisdictional bottlenecks, and the dynamic landscape of emerging technology as some of the reasons. The study also identified the blistering pace of cybercrime as a major challenge faced by investigators. The findings, examined individually from a law enforcement perspective, are unique contributions to the body of knowledge of internet fraud policing and cybercrime investigation in Nigeria.

Roadmap for Forensic Readiness of Law Enforcement Agencies in Nigeria. The findings from this study show that there was no well-articulated roadmap for digital forensic readiness that was ready, available, and mainstreamed in both organizations. There are no previous research findings that support or refute the presence of a digital forensic readiness roadmap in Nigeria's financial crime investigative agencies. Available literature only points out elements of the readiness framework, like the lack of technology, the need for training, and others. Therefore, the findings from this study uniquely contribute to the growing body of knowledge. This study made a unique contribution by developing a roadmap for forensic readiness for cybercrime investigative agencies in Nigeria. Figure 8.1 shows the proposed roadmap for digital forensic readiness of the EFCC. Figures 8.2 and 8.3 shows the proposed locations for establishing digital forensic laboratories for the EFCC and the Nigeria Police Force, respectively.

The Big Data Challenge. With the massive data available, it becomes increasingly difficult to carry out digital investigations. The findings from this study showed that the big data challenge affected cybercrime investigation in terms of analysis, processing capability, and the storage dilemma. The study found this challenge to be more prominent at the Nigerian Police. The study found out that the EFCC was taking steps to address this by ensuring focused investigation. Also, with support from the British government, the commission recently invested in a large data center to alleviate the storage dilemma.

Cybercrime Taxonomy and Caseloads. To answer Primary Research Question 2, this research further Triangulated Supporting Information for Cybercrime Caseloads, Taxonomy, Dynamics, Complexity, and frequency of cybercrime incidents and conviction in Nigeria. This research further analysed data from four sources (1) Official conviction record of the EFCC (2) Analysis of official press release of the EFCC from their website (3) detailed conviction records of last 3 years, and (4) court judgments and charge sheets for cybercrime prosecution. The findings of this research established the specifics of the caseloads and the cybercrime types. Understanding the cybercrime typology or taxonomy is important for a lot of reasons. It is indicative of the personal and technological preferences of the cybercriminal. It is also important for planning purposes, from the law enforcement point of view. Therefore, this is an important finding and contribution to the body of knowledge.

Other Cybercrime Dynamics. This research also made significant findings in terms of other cybercrime dynamics. For instance, this research established common trends and patterns in cybercrime prosecution and conviction in Nigeria. The study established a common sentencing pattern of terms ranging from 1–2 years imprisonment, but with an option of fine ranging from ₦100,000 to ₦200,000. The study showed almost all the cases ended in plea bargain, with the suspects opting to pay fine options instead of serving prison terms. The study also showed that most sentencing made pronouncements for restitution, where amount recovered from suspect is channeled back to the victim. This study could not confirm instances where amount restituted actually got to the victim, However, the court documents show this pronouncement. This study also compared this findings on cybercrime prosecution in Nigeria to the investigation and prosecution of two celebrated cybercrime cases involving Nigerians, but prosecuted in the United States of America. Specifically, the study reviewed the cases of *Ramon Olorunwa Abbas aka "Ray Hushpuppi"* and *Obinwanne Okeke aka Invictus Obi* (both Nigerians), respectively, and established trends and patterns of both in comparison with Nigeria. The study established that in comparison, the amount involved in the prosecuted cybercrime cases in Nigeria are relatively small (typically less than $10,000) when compared to the reviewed cases in the United States of America, running to over $10 million, respectively. However, like the cybercrime cases prosecuted in Nigeria, these two celebrated cases also ended in plea bargain.

8.3.3 Contribution to Policy

This study made several findings that could be directly applicable to both organizations and shape policy formulation. This study established the absence of an effective collaboration mechanism among the agencies. Cybercrime investigation often involves roles that cut across different agencies, and the efficiency of the investigative process depends on the level of collaboration between these agencies. This study also added to the growing literature on the jurisdictional roadblocks and the impact on cybercrime investigation. The study findings showed the need to amend the Cybercrime Act 2015, following the emerging technology landscape and the evolving challenges of cybercrime investigation. The study made a unique contribution by identifying the absence of Standard Operating Process (SOP) documents that guide the operations of cybercrime investigation and digital forensic investigation for the Nigeria Police Force. However, this study found that the EFCC has launched an SOP but could not verify if same has been properly mainstreamed.

The study also showed that cybercrime investigations were affected by the increasing information governance demands. For instance, with the issuance of the Data Protection Regulation (NDPR) in 2019, by the National Information Technology Development Agency (NITDA), and the passage of the Nigeria Data Protection Act [26] by the National Assembly, organisations that processes large datasets with Personally Identifiable Information (PII) are expected to take steps to protect data. Digital forensic investigation is an exploratory discipline that involves analysing devices and hard drives containing PII's, therefore this will have implications for cybercrime investigation. The study identified the lack of funding (or inappropriate) for the various forensic departments of law enforcement agencies in Nigeria. This result could potentially shape the funding policy of both organizations.

This research shows the absence of a structured training program at Nigeria's financial crime investigating agencies. This finding could potentially shape both organizations' (EFCC and the Nigeria Police Force) policies on the training program. This study also contributed to the growing literature on the top reasons why more Nigerians are turning to cybercrime. This study uniquely contributed to this topic from a practitioner's point of view. The previous studies did not explore this perspective sufficiently. The study found that the top reasons for the rising cases of cybercrime are primarily socioeconomic. Specifically, the study found the top three reasons as unemployment, poverty, and peer pressure. Other reasons found by this study include the relative ease of cybercrime compared to other traditional crimes like robbery, as one reason for the high figures and poor parenting. This finding is a significant contribution that could potentially help shape broader economic policies in Nigeria's quest to tackle the cybercrime challenge in Nigeria.

Participants of this study made other policy suggestions that could strengthen the capacity of cybercrime agencies in Nigeria. Participants recommended that big-tech companies set up branches in Nigeria (to help smoothen out some of the jurisdictional roadblocks during investigations involving their platforms). Participants from the legal department recommended the need to fuse lawyers in the forensic department to ensure synergy of investigation and prosecution. Participants also recommended the need for cybercrime orientation to enlighten the public on the ills of cybercrime. Participants recommended more investment in research and development (to encourage indigenous innovations in digital forensics). Participants recommended creating an autonomous funding structure for the digital forensic unit to address the funding challenges currently faced. Finally, participants recommended the review of existing cybercrime laws (to ensure stiffer punishment) and the need for the protection of the mental health of digital forensic practitioners given the exposures in the course of work. Table 8.1 summarises the unique contributions of this study.

Table 8.1 Summary of unique contributions of research

S/N	Contribution	Summary of contribution
1	Theory contribution	Routine Activity Theory (RAT) • This study contributed to the application of RAT in cybercrime investigation in Nigeria • This study expanded the scope of factors affecting the capability of financial crime investigators to include the number of personnel, digital forensic technology, skillset, training, funding, and a robust policy framework Technology-Organization-Environment (TOE) • This novel study applied TOE to study digital forensic technology adoption in Nigeria's law enforcement agencies • This study established that financial readiness, technological readiness, and sustained management support affect the adoption of digital forensic technology in Nigeria's financial crimes agencies • Established that the financial crimes agencies in Nigeria were not technologically ready, and therefore not forensically ready • This study established that Nigeria's financial crime agencies were not financially ready to be forensically ready • This study reinforced environment context as a factor in technology adoption
2	Contribution to knowledge	The study made the following contributions to the body of knowledge: • Themes and emergent themes • The study established areas of the digital forensic skills gap and specific training needs • The study identified digital forensic tools needed by financial crimes investigators in Nigeria • The study established the extent and impact of the lack of digital forensic technology in financial crime investigating agencies in Nigeria • This study is a novel contribution to digital forensic technology adoption by Nigerian law enforcement agencies • The study identified challenges preventing Nigeria's law enforcement agencies from being forensically ready • The study made significant findings that could potentially aid the development of a digital forensic readiness roadmap for Nigeria's financial crimes agencies

(continued)

Table 8.1 (continued)

S/N	Contribution	Summary of contribution
3	Policy contributions	The following findings could be helpful in policy formulation: • Need for an efficient inter-agency collaboration framework • Need for process optimization to boost the efficiency of investigative processes • Need for more international collaboration to smoothen out jurisdictional complexities and challenges • Need for more funding • Need for independent and sustainable funding • The need to review the Cybercrime Act 2015 • Need for documented Standard Operating Procedure mainstreamed in the agencies • Need to have a decentralization policy that encourages the establishment of forensic laboratories in regional and states formation, beyond just the headquarters • The study identified the need to have a structured training program • The study identified the top three reasons for rising caseloads of cybercrime

Note This table summarizes the key contributions of this study

8.4 Recommendations/Roadmap for Digital Forensic Readiness

The five critical components of the Digital Forensic Readiness model identified by Pooe and Labuschagne [34] shaped the following recommendations. These five components are People, Process, Policy, Technology, and Data. The researchers grouped the recommendations (for the themes and emergent themes) under the five components to keep things focused and organized.

People

The specific themes from the study that falls under the people classification are: personnel adequacy, personnel capability, and Digital Forensic Skills deficiency.

8.4.1 Personnel Adequacy

The World Bank (2022) estimates the population of Nigeria to be about 218 million. The staff strength of the Economic and Financial Crimes Commission (EFCC) is put at about 2220, across different departments, out of which about 850 are police officers seconded to the commission [16]. This puts it at one officer of the commission for every 98,441 citizens. This leaves us with an overwhelming gap, as there is no way a ratio of 1:98,441 can produce efficient results.

As bad as the result above is, it is even worse when you factor in the fact that only a handful of the personnel above are digital forensic examiners. While there was no specific figure put out, the researchers estimate the personnel with advanced digital forensic capabilities at between 10 and 30 in the entire commission (please note that this is not an official figure; it was derived from interviews and physical observations). If you nomalise the upper limit (of 30 personnel) over the population of the country, that leaves us with a terribly low ratio of 1:7,284,707. That means there is only one competent officer with digital forensic capabilities for every 7,284,707 citizens. For context, compare this with the 14,300 full time employees at the 409 publicly funded laboratories in the US [47].

Another way to look at this is to view it against the conviction statistics. In 2022, the EFCC recorded a total of 3785 convictions. Assuming all investigations required digital forensic examination, that will leave us with a ratio of 1:126. That is, a caseload of about 126 per annum for every digital forensic examiner. This is going to be overwhelming for the forensic examiner to follow through with the painstaking process of documentation, evidence acquisition and preservation, examination, analysis, report writing, and possibly appearing in court as expert witness. This is an overwhelming caseload, and the current digital forensic examiners must be putting in extra shift to cope with this.

To address this challenge, this study recommends that digital forensic laboratories should be set up at all 15 commands of the EFCC spread across the nation. Currently, only the Head Office (and perhaps, Lagos Office) have a good forensic laboratory. Our recommendation is that over the next 5 years, this should be replicated across the nation. Fifteen digital forensic examiners and technicians should be employed for each command office. That will mean the recruitment of at least 225 additional digital forensic examiners. The recruited digital forensic examiners should be of mixed skillset and experience levels. The recommended specialization/designation and numbers are:

1. Laboratory Manager—1
2. Digital Forensic Examiner (Computer)—3
3. Digital Forensic Examiner (Mobile)—5
4. Digital Forensic Technicians—5
5. QA/QC Officer—1.

For the Nigeria Police Force, the staff need is even more. The Police have presence in all 36 states of the federation, and the Federal Capital Territory. In addition to this, the Police have 17 zonal Police Commands. The Nigeria Police Force Laboratory also do more than just investigating financial crimes. The caseloads requiring digital forensic examinations involve different criminal cases, beyond financial crimes. The researchers make the following recommendations, for consideration over the next 5 years:

1. At least one mini digital forensic laboratory in all 36 states (7 digital Forensic Examiners and Technicians). This should be scalable to grow to a full forensic laboratory status within 10 years.

2. One Digital Forensic Laboratory in all 17 zonal commands (15 Digital Forensic Examiners and Technicians in each proposed laboratory).

8.4.2 Personnel Capability, and Digital Forensic Skills Deficiency

Digital forensics is a high-tech discipline requiring sophisticated forensic skills. This study established an obvious digital forensic skills gap. Specifically, this is the first study that law enforcement agents that are digital forensic examiners freely discussed specific areas they need training. The study also established the lack of a structured and sustainable training programme. The study showed that cybercrime investigators struggle with the pace of cybercrime as well as with the complexity of emerging technologies. This study makes the following recommendations, to address this:

1. The financial crimes agencies (EFCC and Nigeria Police Force) need to have a structured training programme. The training should reflect the skills gap established by this study.
2. Funding is a major issue in training, as digital forensic courses are generally expensive. Given the budgetary constraints of Nigeria's public procurement cycle, the researchers recommend a sustainable funding model, that is free from bureaucratic bottlenecks. For instance, the Nigeria Police Trust Fund could provide dedicated and sustainable funding for training digital forensic examiners and cybercrime investigators.
3. There are more available cybersecurity and digital forensic expertise in the private sector than in the public sector. The Financial Crime Agencies can leverage this resource strategically and economically. The agencies can recognize and accredit competent privately owned laboratories and personnel, that can be assigned digital forensic investigations, particularly when the caseloads are too high to cope with internally. In 2022, Nigeria signed into law, the Chartered Institute of Fraud and Certified Forensic Investigators (CIFCFIN). This institute can be equipped to standardize the practice of digital forensics, accredit digital forensic laboratories, and digital forensic examiners. This can be done with support from the financial crime agencies.
4. Cybercrime is a cross-border crime. As we have seen in this study, majority of the victims of Nigerian cybercriminals are not in Nigeria. Therefore, the Nigerian Cybercrime challenge is not just a national challenge; it has an international dimension given the international spread of the victims. Therefore, there should be structured training exchanges, where developed economies can support the Nigeria cybercrime investigators with sustained training programme. This will go a long way to build capacity and well as deepen collaboration.

Technology

This study established that to be forensically ready, an organization needs to be technologically ready. The study established that the lack of forensic readiness by the financial crimes agencies in Nigeria, greatly impacted their output. The specific themes from the study that falls under the technology classification are: Tools Availability, Roadmap for Digital Forensic Readiness. Tools availability and Tool licensing challenge are discussed below, while roadmap for digital forensic readiness will be discussed at the end of this chapter.

8.4.3 Tools Availability/Tool Licensing Challenge

The financial crimes agencies in Nigeria have their digital forensic resources centralized at the headquarters. Currently, only the Head Office (and perhaps, Lagos Office) of the EFCC have a well-equipped forensic laboratory. There are a handful of digital forensic tools at the command offices, but not enough to call it a well-equipped digital forensic laboratory. The Nigeria Police Force only have a poorly equipped digital forensic laboratory. It is unacceptable that Nigeria, with a population of about 218 million [41], will have less than five standard publicly funded digital forensic laboratory. Compare this with the United States of America, with a population of 333 million [42], and with at least 11,000 digital forensic laboratories [22]. Out of this, there are about 409 publicly funded crime laboratories (performing extraction and analysis of digital evidence, among other forensic activities) in the United States, spread among federal, state, county, and municipal authorities [47]. If you nomalise over the approximate figures, you will see that in the United States, there is at least one publicly funded laboratory mapped to 814,181 citizens. Compare this with Nigeria with the shocking statistics of about 43.6 million citizens mapped to a laboratory. Nigeria will have to address this gap to make significant progress in the fight against cybercrime.

Another major challenge established by this study is the recurrent cost of renewal of licenses for digital forensic tools. Most digital forensic tools have tenured license. That is, it is not enough to just buy the tool; the agency will have to contend with the high cost of annual renewal of licenses. As presently constituted, the paltry sum set aside for maintaining forensic laboratories in Nigeria is grossly insufficient. For context, compare with the 409 publicly funded laboratories in United States with annual operating expenditure in 2014 put at $1.68 billion [47]. This amount, when converted to Naira is almost the entire budget of ₦299.6 billion appropriated for the Nigeria Police Force in 2014 [32].

To overcome this challenge, this research makes the following recommendations:

1. **Roadmap for Forensic Readiness**—Technological readiness must be achieved to be forensically ready. Therefore, the financial crimes agency will need to come up with a workable roadmap for forensic readiness. This should be drafted factoring in funding availability, personnel, and other variables. This study made

a unique contribution by proposing the roadmap for forensic readiness for the EFCC, as showed in Fig. 3.1.

2. **Digital Forensic Laboratories**—This study recommends that digital forensic laboratory should be set up at all 15 commands of the EFCC spread across the nation. For the Nigeria Police Force, this study recommends at least one mini digital forensic laboratory in all 36 states (with 7 digital Forensic Examiners and Technicians in each mini-laboratory). This should be scalable so it will be expanded to a complete digital forensic laboratory over the next 10 years. In addition to this, the study recommends that the Nigeria Police Force will need to set up one well-equipped Digital Forensic Laboratory in all 17 zonal commands. Each digital forensic laboratory (for both the EFCC and the Nigeria Police) will have at least 15 personnel, consisting of a Laboratory Manager, Digital Forensic Examiners (Mobile and Computer forensics), Forensic Technicians, and QA/QC Officer. Each forensic laboratory should follow established standards for the setting up of digital forensic laboratory and should have modern tools to perform computer forensics, mobile forensics, network forensics, cloud forensics, JTAG/Chip-off forensics, video forensics, audio forensics, data recovery, Open Source Intelligence (OSINT), Blockchain analytics, forensic workstations, forensic laptops, forensic duplicators, write blockers, hard drives, enterprise data storage solutions, accessories, among others.
3. **Multi-year Tool Licensing Procurement**—One of the findings of this study was the challenge of recurrent renewals of digital forensic tools, given the complicated budgetary challenges in Nigeria. This study is recommending one-time 5-year tool license for all tools, so this does not become an annual challenge. By the third year, the agencies can commence another procurement process to ensure availability of funds for the licenses for another 5-year licensing cycle when it expires at the 5th year. This will eliminate the licensing gaps established by this study.
4. **Work Out a Sustainable Funding Structure**—The Nigerian budgetary cycle and funding dynamics makes it impossible or very difficult to make timely availability of funds for the running of critical services such as laboratories. To overcome this challenge, the agencies need to set up an independent and sustainable funding structure that is insulated from the bureaucratic bottlenecks of the Nigerian budgetary cycle. For instance, the police can leverage the Police Trust Fund to bridge their technological deficit.
5. **Outsource to Private Laboratories**—Given the rising caseloads, the technological and skills gaps, and the poor funding, the financial crimes agencies will continue to face the challenge of coping with the surge in numbers. This study is recommending outsourcing to privately owned laboratories, with proven expertise and a track record of excellence and professionalism. There are a few privately owned digital forensic laboratories in Nigeria. The financial crimes agencies can work with organisations such as the Chartered Institute of Fraud and Certified Forensic Investigators (CIFCFIN) to accredit the private laboratories and forensic

personnel. Upon accreditation, the agencies can outsource digital forensic jobs to the laboratories. To achieve standard results, the financial crimes agencies will have to develop an SOP to guide the private laboratories to ensure consistency in processes, analysis, and reporting.

6. **Encourage Research and Development**—As at the time of concluding this research, one of the leading global mobile forensic companies stopped selling their tools to all African nations, citing export control restrictions. This has frustrated on-going prosecution of cybercrime as most financial crimes agencies in the continent have been relying on this tool for years. Challenges such as this shows that funding is not the only obstacle. To address this, Nigeria must take proactive steps to develop their own homegrown solutions so they are not forced into unfriendly technological hold such as this. Very little effort is put in research and development in both organisations, and public institutions in Nigeria generally. Nigeria is a "consuming" nation, and currently there is not a single digital forensic tool that was designed and developed in the country. This study is recommending that the agencies work with other relevant agencies such as the National Information Technology Development Agency (NITDA) to partner with private sector software development, digital forensic companies, and the academia to come up with locally made digital forensic solutions. A 10-year roadmap can be developed for this.
7. **Open-Source Tools**—There are some open source tools that have been standardized and accepted in the scientific communities and in courtrooms, globally. Given the obvious funding challenge, the agencies can leverage these alongside the commercial tools to save cost. The NIST [23] forensic tool catalog shows a list of digital forensic tools with good acceptability and ratings.

8.4.4 Policy

This research established that the lack of an efficient framework for inter-agency collaboration was a challenge. The study also established the need to foster international collaboration to reduce the jurisdictional bottlenecks in the investigation of cybercrime. The following specific recommendations are made:

1. Different agencies of government currently play different roles in fighting cybercrime in Nigeria. While there are handshakes between them, the findings of this study show the need for an efficient collaboration for more efficiency. The last edition of the National Cybersecurity Strategy and Policy which was released by the Office of the National Security Adviser [28] made provision for the National Cybersecurity Coordination Centre (NCCC). Also to be domiciled under the NCCC is the National Digital Forensic Laboratory (NDFL), to provide the requisite tools and facilities for investigation and intelligence gathering of cyber related issues. The National Cybersecurity Strategy and Policy also made provision for the Cybersecurity Advisory Council (CAC) [28]. These bodies can be optimized and refocused to serve as an efficient vehicle for better collaboration between agencies and stakeholders.

2. Better collaboration with other nations to facilitate cross-boarder investigation of cybercrime.
3. The findings of this study show that Cybercrime Act 2015 needs to be amended to reflect emerging realities. In recognizing the need for the amendment, the National Cybersecurity Strategy and Policy recommended that the Cybersecurity Advisory Council (CAC) should coordinate the amendment [28]. This research is endorsing this recommendation, and urges the CAC to make wider consultations with stakeholders to achieve a better cybercrime legislation.
4. One of the challenges faced by the Nigerian cybercrime agencies is the jurisdictional gap both with other offshore agencies, as well as with the Big Tech companies who mostly reside in the United States. In 2022, the National Information Technology Development Agency [24] announced a policy compelling social media companies like Twitter, Facebook, and TikTok to appoint contact persons in-country. Steps like this can attempt to bridge the gap, and this research recommends that this be properly refined and expanded to capture strategic interests that will facilitate cybercrime investigation.

8.4.5 Processes

This study established that the EFCC have a Standard Operating System (SOP). However, the paper could not ascertain if this has been mainstreamed in the organization. This study also established that the EFCC Digital Forensic Laboratory has the following ISO certifications: ISO 9001—Quality Management System and ISO 17025—The international standard for testing and calibration laboratories. The study did not find any trace of the availability of an SOP that is mainstreamed in the Nigeria Police Force. Also, there is nothing suggesting that the Nigeria Police Force have a standard laboratory that has gone through certifications, like that of the EFCC. This study makes the following recommendations:

1. It is encouraging to note that the EFCC has an SOP document. This study recommends that the SOP is fully mainstreamed and made available to all staff. As at the time the interviews of this study was conducted, there was no SOP in place, therefore, this study could not ascertain if the SOP was mainstreamed and made available to all staff.
2. Carry out periodic reviews of the SOP.
3. The Nigeria Police Force needs to develop a Standard Operating Procedure that is mainstreamed in the organization.
4. The Nigeria Police Force should get their forensic laboratories ISO Certified (recommended: ISO 9001 and ISO 17025).
5. One of the findings of this study is the gap in processes. For instance, there is the gap between the investigation, legal (prosecution), and the forensic team. This study recommends the harmonization of the processes to ensure a seamless handshake. The study also recommends that the representation of the legal team,

the cybercrime team, and the Advance Fee Fraud team should be fused in the forensic team for easy coordination and harmonization.

8.4.6 Data

Digital forensic investigation is a data-centric exercise. Like many other countries around the world, Nigeria has witnessed increasing awareness for the responsible use of data (data protection). For instance, with the issuance of the Nigeria Data Protection Regulation (NDPR) in 2019, by the National Information Technology Development Agency (NITDA), and the recent passage of the Nigeria Data Protection Act [26] by the National Assembly, organisations that processes large datasets with personally identifiable information are expected to take steps to protect data. This study showed that cybercrime investigations were affected by the increasing information governance demands. Specific recommendations include:

1. Need for more awareness for cybercrime investigators on the newly passed Nigeria Data Protection Act [26].
2. Due to the cross-border nature of digital forensic investigation, examiners should also be trained on data protection laws and regulations in other climes, such as General Data Protection Regulation (GDPR) for the EU region.
3. Need to Appoint a dedicated Data Protection Officer in each organisation as recommended by the NDPR and the Nigeria Data Protection Act [26].
4. Need to invest in cybersecurity tools and controls to ensure the protection of personally identifiable information during investigation.
5. This study also found that one of the challenges faced is the challenge of big data and the storage dilemma due to growing size of data. This study recommends investment in enterprise data storage systems such as direct-attached storage (DAS), network-attached storage (NAS), and storage area networks (SANs).

8.4.7 Others

The following recommendations are also made:

1. **International Support**—This study established the lack of forensic resources by Nigeria's financial crimes agency. The study also established the rising caseloads, and the fact that most of the victims are not resident in Nigeria. Therefore, the cybercrime scourge in Nigeria is not localized in Nigeria. This study recommends improved cooperation and strategic assistance (both technical, legal, and logistical) to be given to the Nigerian cybercrime agencies. Developed economies such as the United States of America, United Kingdom, Germany, France, South Korea, should be encouraged to support Nigeria better with intelligence sharing, legal assistance, donation of digital forensic tools and accessories (hardware and software), training support, and research and development.

2. **Cybercrime Act**—The findings of this study show the need to review the cybercrime Act 2015 to reflect emerging dynamics and realities. This needs to be expedited.
3. **Cybercrime Awareness**—The findings of this study show the disturbing rising caseloads of cybercrime. A review of the case file show that most of the cybercriminals are young people—undergraduates, young graduates, etc. There is the need for sustained cybercrime awareness campaign across all segments of the society.
4. **Harmonised ID System**—Nigeria have a lot of Identity systems—international passport, driving license, National Identity card, Voters Card, Bank Verification Number (BVN), and others—all having unique numbers, respectively. This makes it difficult for investigators to correlate identity information of suspects. This study recommends the need for the harmonization of the disparate ID systems and databases.
5. **Research and Development**—The cybercrime agencies need to invest more in research and development.
6. **Socioeconomic Concerns**—This study showed the top three reasons behind the surge in numbers of cybercrime in Nigeria are Socioeconomic in nature. This study recommends that the socioeconomic factors identified by this study should be comprehensively addressed from a national scale. To effectively tackle the cybercrime scourge in Nigeria, Nigeria must tackle the underlying causes of poverty, unemployment, and other socioeconomic issues that is attracting young people to cybercrime.
7. **Collaboration with Private Sector**—There is a lot of technical expertise in the private sector. The financial crime agencies can leverage this expertise through effective partnerships and collaborations.

8.5 Roadmap for Digital Forensic Readiness for the EFCC

This study showed that the financial crime agencies in Nigeria are not forensically ready. The study also showed that both agencies studied—the Economic and Financial Crimes Commission and the Nigeria Police Force—do not have an articulated roadmap for digital forensic readiness. This study adopted the five critical components of the Digital Forensic Readiness model identified by Pooe and Labuschagne [34]—People, Process, Policy, Technology, and Data.

To develop a sustainable roadmap for digital forensics requires a lot of both technical and non-technical details, which are were not all available to the researchers at the time of this study. Some of these factors includes annual budget, specific number of staff available, inventory of digital forensic tools available, and others. However, based on the findings of this study, after interviewing 18 personnel of the financial crime agencies from relevant units, and after reviewing official documents and statistics made available, this study made a unique contribution by developing a roadmap for digital forensic readiness as one of the key contributions of this study.

The roadmap for the EFCC is showed in Fig. 8.1. Also presented below are maps generated as part of this study, showing proposed distribution of new digital forensic laboratories for EFCC (Fig. 8.2) and for the Nigeria Police Force (Fig. 8.3).

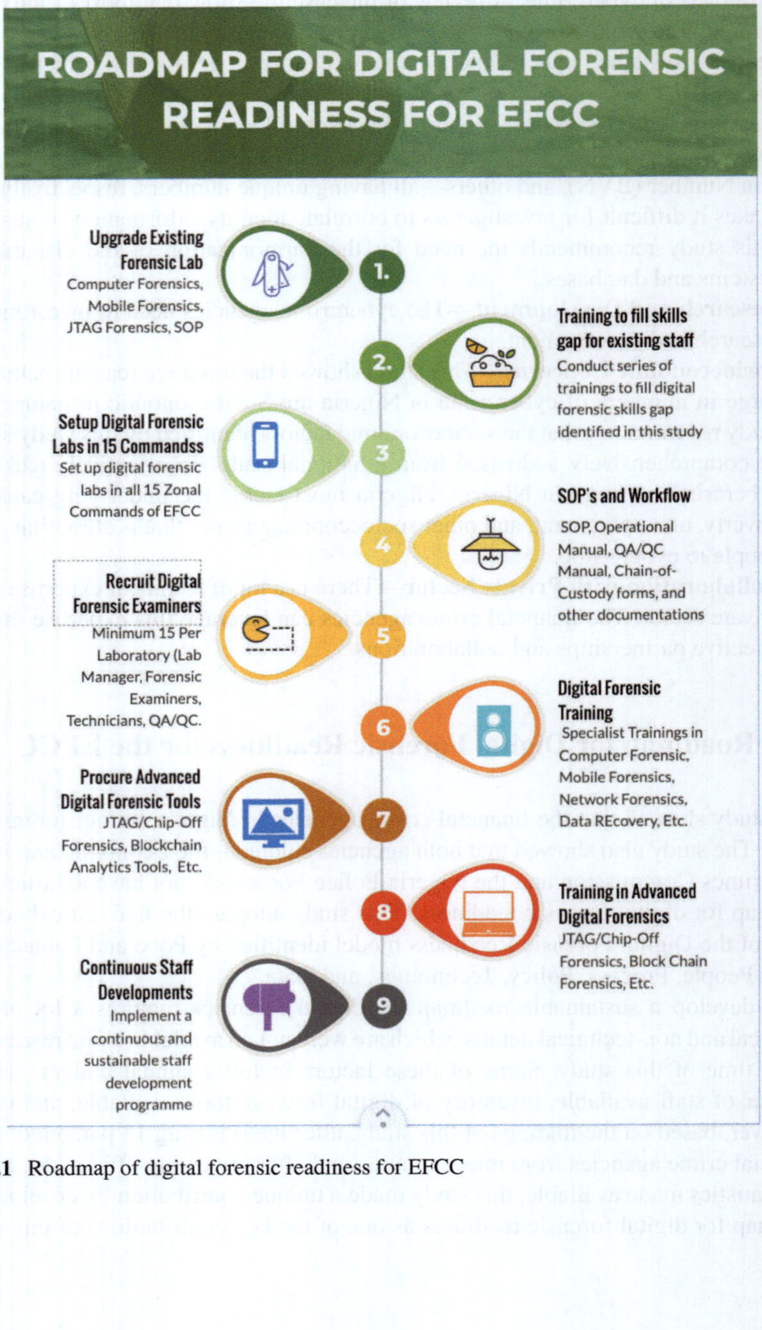

Fig. 8.1 Roadmap of digital forensic readiness for EFCC

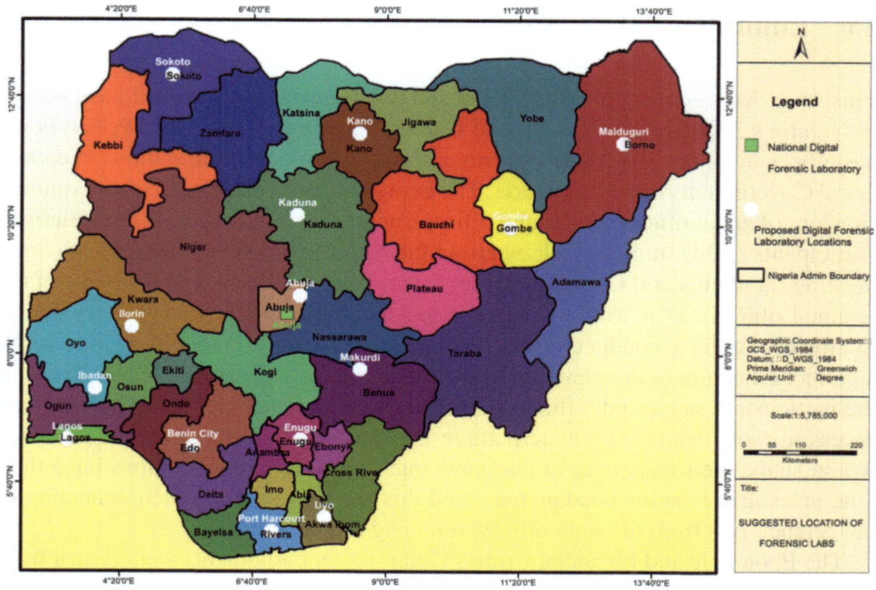

Fig. 8.2 Recommended location for setting up digital forensic laboratories in zonal commands of EFCC

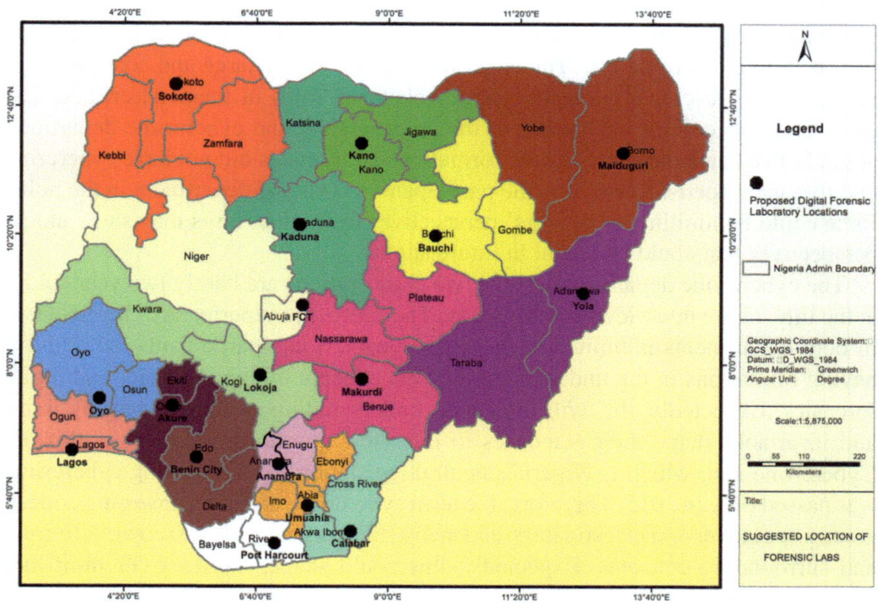

Fig. 8.3 Recommended location for setting up digital forensic laboratories in zonal commands of the Nigeria Police Force

8.6 Limitations of the Study

This study has certain limitations. First, the two organizations studied have offices in Nigeria's 36 states and the Federal Capital Territory. The Nigeria Police Force has offices in all the 774 Local Government Areas (with multiple stations in certain Local Government Areas) of Nigeria. The Economic and Financial Crimes Commission has 14 zonal offices (command offices), apart from the corporate headquarters. Participants of this study were drawn from the respective Headquarters of both organizations at the Federal Capital Territory (apart from a solitary case from one of the regional offices), as it would have been logistically draining to visit every Police Station in Nigeria to conduct interviews. The chosen sample in this study may not be a perfect reflection of the views of all the officers in both organizations. As some of the participants suggested, officers in the headquarters often get better training and access to tools than their counterparts in the states and other remote areas, which would shape their responses to interview questions. Both organizations have their elite investigators at the headquarters, and this may not be a complete reflection of the perspectives from the state offices, rural and remote offices.

The Economic and Financial Crimes Commission participants were drawn from all the related departments: the digital forensic department, the advance fee fraud department, the cybercrime department, and the legal department. Participants' responses might have been influenced by their respective backgrounds, given the unique complexities of each unit. The participants from the police were drawn from just the cryptography and cybercrime department (now restructured, as at the time of concluding this research). The Nigeria Police Force is a large and complex organization with several investigative or prosecutorial roles in financial crimes. This study chose to delimit the sample to the cryptography and cybercrime department at the Police headquarters since the formations at the states did not have cybercrime and forensic experts. Restricting the participants to just one department in the police force could be limiting, as officers' perspectives from other units may show unique perspectives that could be useful in future studies.

The cybercrime departments of the two organizations are barely two years old as at the time of the interviews for this study. Therefore, the experience of investigators in both departments is limited to those two years. Some participants did admit to having limitations in the understanding of the concept of cybersecurity and digital forensics. Expectedly, this will limit their understanding of some emerging issues and invariably shape their responses to interview questions. Apart from this, the Cybercrime Act, which is Nigeria's central legislation for combatting cybercrime, was passed only in 2015. Therefore, the term cybercrime is still an emerging concept among operatives and investigators, and many still struggle with the scope, definition, and surrounding concepts. Expectedly, this could shape, influence, or limit their responses to their limited or fledgling understanding. Experience (or inexperience) could be a limitation in research such as this.

This study was limited to the Technology-Organization-Environment (TOE) framework in studying the adoption of digital forensic technology. There are other adoption theories which if applied to this study, could offer new perspectives and findings. For example, there are other technology adoption theories, such as the Theory of Reasoned Action (TRA), the theory of Planned Behaviors, the Technology Acceptance Model (TAM), and the Unified Theory of Acceptance and Use of Technology (UTAUT), highlighted in Chap. 2. These theoretical frameworks could have possibly offered new perspectives to this study.

8.7 Implications for Future Study

Sample Size, Composition and the Need for More Diversity

This study, like other studies, had limitations. Therefore, there are implications for future studies. First, there is an opportunity to broaden the scope of investigation for the Nigerian Police Force. This study only involved interviews of five Police officers from the Cryptography and Cybercrime department. There are two reasons why this happened. First, the unit is a relatively new unit set up in 2019 with only about ten personnel. Therefore, our sample constituted about 50% of the departmental workforce. Furthermore, by the 5th interview, the interview had hit saturation, with no new issues coming up.

However, in practice, the Nigerian Police Force has other departments investigating and prosecuting fraud and financial crimes, both at the federal and state levels. Broadening the scope of research to these different departments could reveal new findings. For instance, a future study could include interviewing personnel from the fraud investigation unit from the other states in Nigeria. This study suggests the total absence of a well-equipped digital forensic laboratory or resources at the state level. Therefore, it would be interesting to hear their (at the state level) perspectives from this deeper level of lack. Apart from the Police, the Economic and Financial Crimes Commission has 14 zonal offices. This study sample only included one participant from the regional offices. A future study could be structured to drill further into the perspectives of investigators and operatives from the zonal offices with lesser access to digital forensic resources.

Funding Gap

The findings of this research also show a severe funding challenge across both organizations. This research, although semi-structured, constrained itself to get perspectives on funding adequacy and not specific figures needed. The theoretical framework, Technology, Organization, and Environment (TOE), shaped this study. One of the factors influencing technological adoption and impeding or facilitating innovation diffusion in an organization is financial readiness. Therefore, funding is vital in understanding the lack of digital forensic resources in Nigeria's financial crimes investigation agencies. There is a research opportunity from the findings of this study, as a future study could be structured to investigate the scope and extent of this funding lack. Such research could be a quantitative or mixed study to get numerical specifics and perspectives.

Bureaucratic Bottlenecks and Collaboration Opportunities

Participants in this study repeatedly noted a lack of cooperation as a challenge. There are several agencies and stakeholders of interest in the fight against internet fraud and cybercrime. This study showed the lack of an effective collaboration framework among these agencies in Nigeria and their counterparts in other countries. This situation presents a good research opportunity for future studies to drill into the existing collaboration mechanics and make recommendations for an efficient handshake.

Beyond the challenges of inter-agency collaboration, this study also found out that there are intra-agency bottlenecks during an investigation. Some of the participants did allude to this and made certain suggestions to smoothen the investigative process. There is an opportunity for a study to drill down in each organization and adequately examine the processes. Such studies can provide better insight into the bottlenecks and recommend process optimization and dismantling of identified roadblocks that impede investigative efficiency.

Technology Adoption

One of the research questions of this study was to look at the digital forensic technology adoption in the two organizations sampled. This study was limited to the Technology-Organization-Environment (TOE) framework in studying the adoption of digital forensic technology. There are other adoption theories which if applied to this study, could offer new perspectives and findings. For example, there are other technology adoption theories, such as the Theory of Reasoned Action (TRA), the theory of Planned Behaviors, the Technology Acceptance Model (TAM), and the Unified Theory of Acceptance and Use of Technology (UTAUT) highlighted in Chap. 2. These theoretical frameworks could have offered new perspectives to this study. Therefore, there is a research opportunity to design a study specifically to study the adoption of digital forensics, using any of the combinations above or other models to gain more insight.

Roadmap for Digital Forensic Readiness

To be adequately empowered to investigate Nigeria's growing Internet fraud cases, the country's financial crime agencies will need to attain a considerable level of forensic readiness. Digital forensic readiness has two primary objectives: to maximize the usefulness of evidence collected; and minimize the cost of investigations [40]. The findings of this study show the lack of an articulated roadmap for forensic readiness of the financial crimes investigative agencies in Nigeria. The study showed technological gap, personnel gap, skills gap, funding gap, and others. This study developed a roadmap for digital forensic readiness for the EFCC. However, a more accurate roadmap will need to incorporate some other variables such as annual budgets and funding dynamics, specifics of existing forensic technology available, and others. This roadmap could potentially help achieve both operational and infrastructural readiness [5]. Therefore, the outcome of such a study could be very useful in Nigeria's fight against internet fraud and cybercrimes.

References

1. Abu SO, Lateef OM, Echobu J (2018) Determinants of cyber fraud investigation in Nigeria. Acc Taxation Rev 2(2)
2. Ahmed I (2020) Technology organization environment framework in cloud computing. Telkomnika 18(2):716–725
3. Al-Hujran O, Al-Lozi EM, Al-Debei MM, Maqableh M (2018) Challenges of cloud computing adoption from the TOE framework perspective. Int J E-Bus Res (IJEBR) 14(3):77–94
4. Bello M, Griffiths M (2021) Routine activity theory and cybercrime investigation in Nigeria: how capable are law enforcement agencies? In: Rethinking cybercrime. Palgrave Macmillan, Cham, pp 213–235
5. Carrier B, Spafford E (2004) An event-based digital forensic investigation framework. Digital Investigation. https://dfrws.org/wp-content/uploads/2019/06/2004_USA_paper-an_event-based_ digital_forensic_investigation_framework.pdf
6. Chau PY, Tam KY (1997) Factors affecting the adoption of open systems: an exploratory study. MIS Q 21(1)
7. Chigozie-Okwum C, Ugboaja S, Micheal D, Osuo-Genseleke M (2017) Proliferation of cyber insecurity in Nigeria: a root cause analysis. AFRREV STECH Int J Sci Technol 6(2):53–60
8. Cohen LE, Felson M (1979) Social change and crime rate trends: a routine activity approach. Am Sociol Rev 588–608
9. Eboibi FE (2021) Cybercriminals and coronavirus cybercrimes in Nigeria, the United States of America and the United Kingdom: cyber hygiene and preventive enforcement measures. Commonw Law Bull 47(1):113–142
10. Ehimen OR, Bola A (2010) Cybercrime in Nigeria. Bus Intell J 3(1):93–98
11. Grabosky PN (2001) Virtual criminality: old wine in new bottles? Soc Leg Stud 10(2):243–249
12. Hutchings A, Hayes H (2009) Routine activity theory and phishing victimisation: who gets caught in the 'net'? Curr Issues Crim Just 20(3):433–452
13. Iacovou CL, Benbasat I, Dexter AS (1995) Electronic data interchange and small organizations: adoption and impact of technology. MIS Q 465–485
14. Karie NM, Venter HS (2015) Taxonomy of challenges for digital forensics. J Forensic Sci 60(4):885–893
15. Kigerl A (2012) Routine activity theory and the determinants of high cybercrime countries. Soc Sci Comput Rev 30(4):470–486
16. Kingsley N, Enumah A (2021) Shake-up imminent in EFCC as 850 Police. https://www.thisdaylive.com/index.php/2021/02/22/shake-up-imminent-in-efcc-as-850-police
17. Leukfeldt ER, Yar M (2016) Applying routine activity theory to cybercrime: a theoretical and empirical analysis. Deviant Behav 37(3):263–280
18. Leung D, Lo A, Fong LHN, Law R (2015) Applying the Technology-Organization-Environment framework to explore ICT initial and continued adoption: an exploratory study of an independent hotel in Hong Kong. Tour Recreat Res 40(3):391–406
19. Marshall C, Rossman GB (2014) Designing qualitative research. Sage Publications
20. Mihai IC, Pruna Ş, Petrica G (2017) A comprehensive analysis on cyber-threats against elearning systems. ELearning Softw Educ 3:344–351. https://doi.org/10.12753/2066-026X-17-225
21. Mohammed KH, Mohammed YD, Solanke AA (2019) Cybercrime and digital forensics: bridging the gap in legislation, investigation, and prosecution of cybercrime in Nigeria. Int J Cybersecur Intell Cybercrime 2(1):56–53

22. NIST (2022) Digital investigation techniques: a nist scientific foundation review. https://nvlpubs.nist.gov/nistpubs/ir/2022/NIST.IR.8354.pdf
23. NIST (2023) Computer forensics tools & techniques catalog. https://toolcatalog.nist.gov/index.php
24. National Information Technology Development Agency (2022) Nigeria to require social media platforms to open local offices. https://www.reuters.com/world/africa/nigeria-require-social-media-platforms-open-local-offices-2022-06-14/
25. News Agency of Nigeria (2016) Police to create special unit to tackle cybercrime. Guardian Newspaper. https://guardian.ng/news/police-to-create-special-unit-to-tackle-cybercrime/
26. Nigeria Data Protection Act (2023). https://ndpc.gov.ng/Files/Nigeria_Data_Protection_Act_2023.pdf
27. Obuah E (2010) Combatting corruption in Nigeria: the Nigerian economic and financial crimes (EFCC). Afr Stud Q 12(1)
28. Office of the National Security Adviser (2021) National cybersecurity policy and strategy. https://cert.gov.ng/ngcert/resources/NATIONAL_CYBERSECURITY_POLICY_AND_STRATEGY_2021.pdf
29. Okolorie GR (2020, December 22) Uncovering patterns in complex investigations is no match for Nigeria's Economic and Financial Crimes Commission (EFCC) [Interview]. Cellebrite. https://www.cellebrite.com/en/uncovering-patterns-in-complex-investigations-is-no-match-for-nigerias-economic-and-financial-crimes-commission-efcc/
30. Olayemi OJ (2014) A socio-technological analysis of cybercrime and cyber security in Nigeria. Int J Sociol Anthropol 6(3):116–125
31. Oraegbunam IK (2015) The Nigerian police and problems of cybercrime investigation: need for adequate training. Niger Law J 18(1):1–28
32. Oyedele T (2014) Nigeria: Nigeria's 2014 budget—tax and economic analyses. https://www.mondaq.com/nigeria/tax-authorities/288146/nigerias-2014-budget---tax-and-economic-analyses
33. Percy WH, Kostere K, Kostere S (2015) Generic qualitative research in psychology. Qualitative Rep 20(2):76–85
34. Pooe A, Labuschagne L (2012, August) A conceptual model for digital forensic readiness. In: 2012 Information security for South Africa. IEEE, pp 1–8
35. Pratt TC, Holtfreter K, Reisig MD (2010) Routine online activity and Internet fraud targeting: extending the generality of routine activity theory. J Res Crime Delinq 47(3):267–296
36. Ramdani B, Chevers D, Williams DA (2013) SMEs' adoption of enterprise applications: a technology-organisation-environment model. J Small Bus Enterprise Dev
37. Reyns BW (2015) A routine activity perspective on online victimisation. J Finan Crime
38. Samonas S (2013) Insider fraud and routine activity theory. LSE Research Online. http://eprints.lse.ac.uk/50344/1/Samonas_Insider_fraud_routine_2013.pdf
39. Straub ET (2009) Understanding technology adoption: theory and future directions for informal learning. Rev Educ Res 79(2):625–649
40. Tan J (2001) Forensic readiness. Cambridge, MA:@ Stake, 1–23
41. The World Bank (2022a) Population, total—Nigeria. https://data.worldbank.org/indicator/SP.POP.TOTL?locations=NG
42. The World Bank (2022b) United States. https://data.worldbank.org/country/united-states?view=chart
43. Tonye WS (2018) Cyber forensic and data collection challenges in Nigeria. Glob J Comput Sci Technol 18(3)
44. Tornatzky LG, Fleischer M, Chakrabarti AK (1990) Processes of technological innovation. Lexington Books
45. Tseloni A, Wittebrood K, Farrell G, Pease K (2004) Burglary victimization in England and Wales, the United States and the Netherlands: a cross-national comparative test of routine activities and lifestyle theories. Br J Criminol 44(1):66–91
46. Umar I, Samsudin RS, Mohamed M (2016) Understanding the successes and challenges of Anti-Corruption Agency (ACA) in Nigeria: a case of Economic and Financial Crimes Commission (EFCC). Asian J Multidisc Stud 4(5):27–33

47. United States Department of Justice (2016) Publicly funded forensic crime laboratories: resources and services, 2014. https://bjs.ojp.gov/content/pub/pdf/pffclrs14.pdf
48. Vanguard Newspaper (2020) Nigeria police, interpol arrest three suspects over cybercrime. Vanguard Newspaper. https://www.vanguardngr.com/2020/07/nigeria-police-interpol-arrest-3-suspects-over-cybercrime/
49. Yar M (2005) The novelty of 'cybercrime': an assessment in light of routine activity theory. Eur J Criminol 2(4):407–427

47. United States Department of Justice (2016) Publicly funded forensic crime laboratories: resources and services, 2014. https://bjs.ojp.gov/content/pub/pdf/pffclrs14.pdf
48. Vanguard Newspaper (2020) Nigeria police, interpol arrest three suspects over cybercrime. Vanguard Newspaper. https://www.vanguardngr.com/2020/07/nigeria-police-interpol-arrest-3-suspects-over-cybercrime/
49. Yar M (2005) The novelty of 'cybercrime': an assessment in light of routine activity theory. Eur J Criminol 2(4):407–427

Appendix
Selected Interview Quotes

Theme 1.1 Personnel Adequacy

P08 stated that "I don't think we have enough staff; the cases are overwhelming. Yeah, they are overwhelming based on the number of cases that we receive on a daily basis or weekly basis. It's quite overwhelming". This position was consistent across all the departments of both organizations represented and was reflected in their submissions. P04, a cybercrime investigator from Organization A, stated that "we are not enough. We need more numbers, more equipment to go further. Because they are not slowing down in committing that crime. The rate is increasing; it is not decreasing".

P14 from Organization B, and with a legal background, stated:

> What I'll tell you for a fact is we need a lot of manpower; not just "Organisation B" but almost all the law enforcement agencies need manpower. Not just manpower, but manpower that can be utilized, that can be effective, reliable, and dependable...We're getting it right, but for now, manpower is a big challenge. Manpower, but not just the manpower; you'll have to have this manpower and train them.

P15, a Cybercrime investigator from organization B, stated:

> Yes, obviously, there is a shortage of manpower to curtail this trending menace; cybercrime and advanced fee frauds. Because we have a lot of youths who are engaging in it and the manpower is not adequate as to curtail it as expected, but however, we are still trying our best with the available resources, we are trying to nip it in the bud.

P16, an Advance Fee Fraud investigator from organization B, stated:

> Unfortunately, I will say the answer is still no because with the load of cases we have, apart from the cybercrime and AFF cases we are handling, they normally assign other cases to us. Like which day we just realized that we have so many AFF cases that we've not even attended to because I think each team should have at least eight to ten considering the work that we do, but you will see that we have like four men with the team leader, four to five

R. T. Sibe and C. Kaunert, *Cybercrime, Digital Forensic Readiness, and Financial Crime Investigation in Nigeria*, Advanced Sciences and Technologies for Security Applications, https://doi.org/10.1007/978-3-031-54089-9

men with the team leader, which maybe I can think they're not adequate to tackle what we are doing. It is just that sometimes we have to go out of our way; we stay late just to see that we finish this work, and normally, I think up until now in Nigeria, we are not really exposed to this digital forensics up till now.

P06, a digital forensic investigator, stated:

It's not enough, we don't have enough, because if not now we are still pioneers, most people run away when they hear anything technical, they say no it's a hard job, and apart from that, it's a new field, a virgin area. Most people are not keen into it because they feel its a mental work and no no no, sometimes you'd be surprised to know that…sometimes when you are trying to do a job, and you really want to get headway, you'll be here till like 9 pm when your mates are leaving here 5 pm, sometimes you come Saturday. It is tasking, but for the fact that it's giving you results, it's ok. But we are understaffed.

Theme 1.2: Personnel Capability

P01 stated:

We still have digital forensic officers who are still able to dig investigations in those areas. Like my boss is very vast, he's very good. He was opportune to go for courses like financial crime courses, money laundering, and all of that outside the country and that has made him eeeh….we've been, working under him, we are actually learning a lot with the kind of knowledge and the way he goes about it.

P02 submitted that:

I have already said that some investigations need to be done at the highest level. They cannot be done at the divisional level. So that is to tell you that there is a need to have the equipment and the training for other staff at the divisional level and other formations so that they can be able to handle that.

P06 suggested staff had certifications. The participant (P06) said "with the coming of this present administration, I am proud to beat my chest and tell you all our licenses are active, and we are working towards getting retrained because we've already had the certifications".

Theme 2.1: Tools Availability

P01 said, "as per availability, we have limited technology, and that has actually made investigation here hectic…the outcome of investigation take longer than it should be".

P011 said:

Well, there's still room for improvement, and there is a lot that still needs to be done. We still have other agencies coming to the commission to forward other cases they are handling, and there is a need for forensic analysis. This goes to say that those agencies are not funded in that aspect, and in our end, what we have is not also sufficient to cater for our needs too. So there is still lots to be done in funding and getting and getting equipment.

P03 said:

> We really need a lot of equipment, that is the truth. I think presently we have access to phone extraction, but it's not adequate. We need more. You know the subscription alone is something. It runs into millions. For example, our department, if we in the department can have like one or two extractions, which most of the time, if we arrest this suspects their phones are locked, some things are deleted which we'll need to pass through forensic examination to discover a lot of things that are deleted which would help in your investigation. So, if we, for now, if we can have extractor, it's very important, the one we have is not enough because that's what the whole department is using. So, I think more extractors would assist us in carrying out our investigation work.

P04 said:

> In Nigeria, to go for the crime the way the cybercrime is going, I don't think we are up to it. Because you see sometimes, you'll have a case, and they'll be asking you how do you do this, you'll be asking them how far did you do this definitely that means they don't have. So, to me in Nigeria, we are still on 20% in this technology, if not less. We are still on 20% because I can remember when we travelled to Israel, on tracking ourselves, I see the way they do it.

Participants P13, P03, and P06 indicated varied satisfaction with the available digital forensic tools. P13 said:

> I'm not exaggerating EFCC is one of the highest law enforcement agencies that I think possess almost all the digital forensics tools that the CIA is using, FBI is using, the Korean Police is using…What we just need is actually more staff and training and retraining because as I said crimes are done daily in different ways, likewise if you are to like convert that you also have to find a way of coming up with the technique to combat those that are threats.

P10 did not quite know whether the other law enforcement agencies lacked the digital forensic tools needed or not. P10 stated as follows:

> I'm sure you've gone to our digital lab, and I'm sure you are impressed. Well, I think we are not doing badly as a commission, but I do know that some other commissions do come to EFCC to get their stuff done. So that's the much I know, so I cannot say what they have, whether they are inadequate or adequate, but for EFCC, I think we're good.

Theme 4.1: Defined and Documented Processes

P09 stated that:

> We have documents, but again, there are still work in progress every now and then. Especially for us here, we are moving towards getting our lab accredited in line with the ISO 17025. This process is still ongoing, and we are working vehemently to meet that requirement, and that requirement will require having documented processes. With work in process, we have some documents deficiencies we have identified. We are working vehemently to make sure that we meet that standard, so there are documents, and there are still some we have identified and working towards having them developed.

Theme 4.2: Structured Process Review Mechanism

P02 stated that:

> One of the problems we have in this country is the policy review. Not only on this, if you consider other parts other things in the country, you'll see that something has been there for over 20 years 10 years without reviewing it, while the crimes the way the crimes are committed, they are being upgraded, people every day they are upgrading themselves. Criminals are upgrading, but the policy is not upgrading, and other things. So actually, there are so many policies that they are outdated that if you say you will even look at those policies, you can't achieve anything, so you just have to like make sure that you do what is needed.

Theme 5.1: Policy Framework

P03 said, "yeah, I think in Nigeria, we have a cybercrime act… I think that's what guides our operation: the cybercrime Act".

Theme 2.2: Tool Licensing Challenge

P01 said:

> That's true, yes…you know, that's a challenge on its own too. When it's expired, like I said, funding is an issue. And even not in Nigeria alone, even in developed countries, they're underfunded. Funding has been an issue. So, you come to realize that when your Cellebrite or some of your devices expires, renewing it, the license becomes an issue, and for those times, you go blank. That's when you'll be having complaints that we can't do this now, we cant do that now. So it's a challenge on its own, and we wish such things can be subsidized or the cost can be controlled to half…just to make sure we work.

P08 said:

> Secondly, license expiring and being able to explain and convince for the renewal of licenses, but I think that issue has been settled since we have the new Chairman, that one has really, really been settled.

P05 said:

> You know, we know a lot of forensic tool kits, and we are using them. But the problem is most of them we don't have their license, so maybe we must have used them for trial period, some better versions and that's the end. So, if we will be able to have the licensed tools, it's going to go a long way.

Participants P13 and P09 submitted that licensing is not such a challenge. P09 submitted that:

> Like I said, we have some relationship with international organizations which we partner. Some of them are law enforcement agencies within and outside the country. They support us. We tell them through the appropriate channel of communication of things that we think if we have will help enhance our work, and they make contribution. Yearly budget also, we make budget to the management, management designates some amount of money to build up our capability and renewal of license.

Theme 3.1: Lack of Structured Training

P06 said:

> When it comes to training, that is one thing you'll give Organization B; they don't give half measures. I told you I was in general investigation before they moved me to forensics. I was sent to London for a training by the Guidance Software, that's where they trained me… I spent three weeks there and came back. I was sent to Dubai for Forensics ToolKits; that's FTK. Some of the software we use for computer data recovery. They later sent me to Sweden. Apart from that, we've had a series of people coming into the country; the last was the Korean national police. Apart from that, I think I can list like four, five other agencies that came in to make sure we are abreast with the happenings. So if it comes to knowledge, we are not lacking. We are trained, and they keep retraining us. As I'm talking to you now, I'm certified. I have like four certifications with different software that I could use from proficient level to the highest level.

Theme 5.2: Policy Challenges

P01 said:

> Well, in as much as we are aware that we have Cybercrime Act, that prohibits and pointed out sanctions for whoever that violates, that commits offence regarding the internet, we also know that there are some policies that have been on ground but seriously to me are really, really not working and, like I said, like the one I told you in terms of information sharing between institution and organizations now. When you look at the NFIU now or the NIBBS, when you want to get information from them, it takes you time.

Theme 5.3: Roadmap for Digital Forensic Readiness

P18 said:

> Yes, for the forensic readiness roadmap and probably cybercrime investigation roadmap, I must tell you everything is in the pipeline. Sincerely, the committees have been set up to look into some of these crucial things because lately, because of change of government in the commission, so things are taking shape, things that are not in place we've started working on them, so at least we'll be among the elite institutions that we'll be able to reckon with when it comes to cybercrime investigations, digital forensics in the world.

P04 said, "honestly, no".

Theme 6.1: Collaborations

P07 said:

> With the help of the UK government, we were able to get a centralized server where we store our data because the volume was increasing, and it became an issue for us to store this…in fact, there was a point we needed to delete some of the things on our hard drive till they came for our rescue, so we had a centralized server where we store our data.

Theme 6.2: Jurisdictional Challenges

P18 submitted that:

> I can say I'm in the know of what is going on in Europe as Europe has a data protection law and even restrict some of the things we normally get from the open-source, for instance, getting the data about a domain, the IP address, who is, who owns it? Who does it belong to? They are holding up your investigation; you now discover that you have to go through the pain of mutual legal assistance to central authority and what we normally deal with in cybercrime world oftentimes, they are volatile data that can be altered, that can disappear within the twinkle of an eye…and again you discover that the subject would have been able to move the funds around before you get the response if it belongs to this, it belongs to that, you know it has been quite tedious. So, I think the organization they are looking into that, to report to the right entities and some times for the ones that concern the US, we get in touch with the legal in the US Embassy, working with the FBI, in the UK the NCCU, they do help, they do assist us as well and Canada the RCMP - Royal Canadian Mounted Police, so informally they normally assist us, informally the German police as well they do to get some of those signals without following all these unnecessary bureaucratic procedures.

Theme 6.3: Emerging Technologies

P09 said:

> Well, generally worldwide, you know all the organizations to the best of my knowledge are lagging behind because again the criminals, they invest all their resources in getting the tools, especially now that we have the dark web, the tools are on the shelf you can actually acquire them. What we do is that, when we find an incident that now becomes a trend, we begin to develop our capabilities, and we have got some international partners, some agencies that partner with the commission.

Theme 6.4: Funding Challenges

P11 submitted that:

> Investigation takes a lot of funding. There are some cases that take you ten, fifteen years to really clamp down on. So, there's no time limit to really estimate how you can close down cases. A lot needs to be done relating to funding. We need to move ahead of these guys. And it's being modest when you say you don't need funding. Technology takes funding. So many things that you need to attain with funding, and so when funds are available, you move, and your efforts are majorly, majorly preventive, not reactionary, but when you wait till some of these vices occur, then you are reactive, then the deed is done already so you really need to move ahead to stay on the time.

P12 said:

> Yes, I would say we don't have enough funds to do that, and then why it affects us is because most of the victims involved in cybercrime are foreign nationals. So, we'll need a lot of funding. The investigator will need to, if possible, go to the country where the victims are to be able to conduct their investigation. If not, they will have to be able to either contact the embassy or police or whatever the agency is saddled with such responsibility in such country. So we'll need enough funding to do that which is not really there. So it actually tampers or rather slows our investigation or rather adequate investigation at the end of the day.

P05 stated that:

> You know the thing is, generally, the police is being underfunded. You know, if you look at the budget throughout the years, you will see that Police hardly get up to 40% of their annual budget disbursement. And if you compare what other security agencies are being given, whose responsibilities are less than that of the police, you will find out that there is a very wide disparity… I know if you put the budget of the military put together, military, Army and Airforce, it is like, it is at least five times the budget of the police, but they get about 90% disbursement or 100% sometimes. But the police has little as it is we hardly get up to 40%.

P08 submitted that: "funding, lack of tools is still part of it, and lack of manpower but funding is number one, lack of training".

Theme 6.5: Speed of Cybercrime

P15 said:

> Training as a whole for law enforcement is poor, and in the cybercrime department, it's really poor because these boys move at the speed of light, and we are moving at a slow pace. For every ten yards they make, we just make one step forward. So most of us sometimes resort to personal training using self-help. We have to train ourselves to better the work, just because of the love we have for the job, but if it's to comment on training in the cybercrimes unit, it is very, very poor.

P18 stated that:

> Yes, the data is enormous, the crime rate is high, the need for proficiency is high, and what have you? Now I'm very sure there are some peculiar challenges before now with our organization. We discovered that you send the devices to the forensic department, they'll not be able to respond at a reasonable time. We have even concluded the whole investigation, forwarded the case to legal if possible, convicted the suspect without digital evidence. So, we just rely on the other evidence that we have because of the inability to meet the timing, because of probably expired license, inability to have the right software.

Theme 6.8: Information Governance

P10 submitted that:

> Well, let me just tell you that we don't have any data protection law now. What we have is a policy under the NITDA, and I don't know you see policies have no bite. It's just a guiding principle, but somewhere along the line, there's this consciousness of data protection. It has sipped through all the consciousness of Nigeria in the light of cybercrime. So, in the light of that, there are awareness to that effect the need to protect data and certain organizations are putting up those data protection principles. Putting them in place within their own organization to protect against cybercrime. However, there is a provision in the cybercrime Act that empowers law enforcement to go to court right, and get an order, an interim order, ex parte order to search vessels. There is a requirement under the Cybercrime Act for Internet Service Provider, mobile service providers to retain…. well, the law says traffic data, but they don't keep data. What they keep is mostly login details. So, they maintain those login details, and they are available for law enforcement. So the law gives law enforcement some sort of immunity within a certain level of control to investigate and to breach privacy, where necessary, for security purposes.

Theme 6.9: Big Data Challenge

P08 said:

Yeah, that has really been solved in my organization because we have currently at the data center, we have a server. I can't remember the capacity here now that whatever we are doing, the imaging we pull it there, but it was a very big challenge for us that time it was a very big challenge because we use to, we have hard disk - an external hard disk within our SOC that we just plugged-in. It got to a point that the capacity of those destination drives, most of them were… the highest was 2 terabytes and when you have a computer that the source drive is 2 terabyte capacity and you need to connect to a drive - a destination drive that is higher than that of the source drive, it became, it was a very big issue to us. So, what we are doing now is that, if we are using FTK to make the image, what I do is that after making the image, we pull it into the server, yeah we pull it into the server and then you clean up the drive waiting for another one to come or if we are using … to image directly, we just image directly to the server.

Theme 2.4: Digital Forensic Adoption

P12 said:

I'll say it is something that we have accepted, and then for even the end result, that's the court. It's something that is quite new, but you could see the willingness from the part of the court to accept it, to learn from it to be able to understand and appreciate what it is.

P14 said:

The truth is you cannot bring in anything new when you don't train people to understand the concept of what you're bringing to them. Just as I told you earlier, our law enforcement works the analog way, and if you want to bring technology, of course, they'll rebel against it. Some are not rebelling against it not because they want to rebel, but it's because they do not know how to do the application of that new technology, so you have to train them. You have to prepare them for that technology.

Theme 2.5: Impact of Lack of Digital Forensic Technology

P03 said:

The truth is it has really affected law enforcement in Nigeria. It has really affected crime-fighting in Nigeria. That is the truth because the unavailability of these forensic apparatus has really dealt a big blow because at the end of the day, you go to court, and your cases are thrown out because you can not prove most of these cases because we don't have forensic apparatus to really go a long way to convince the judge that yes, yes this is what this person has done. So really, it has really affected prosecution of criminals and crime-fighting in Nigeria. That is the reality as it stands.

P02 said:

Actually, in some states, or let me say in some formations, they cannot even look at cases that has to do with Forensic Investigation. They cannot even handle it except that case has to be transferred, which I think that each and every State Police…. but unfortunately, majority of the cases you see….once a case has to do with forensic investigations…it has to be transferred to the highest level.

Theme 3.2: Skills Deficiency

P18 said:

> I think we need more training under cryptocurrency investigation, starting with metadata that are related to cryptocurrencies; try to harmonize wallet address; do blockchain analysis on them; and see who is the owners of the pointers or signatures that will lead you to the main owner or the real owner of the wallet address. Training on cryptocurrency investigation and the ever-evolving cybercrime trend, I think it's just for us to be updated and know what's going on.

Theme 2.3: Digital Forensic Tools Needed

P01 submitted that "mobile SIM card analysis, one could actually check on a sim card and get all the ...call logs and some other things. These are some of the devices I wish we can have it". P18 said that "we need that, for instance...Chainalysis, we need that as well. At least, that will assist in cryptocurrency investigations; will go a long way as we do our investigations".

P02 said:

> We have to be equipped with tracking network crimes; crimes that are being committed on the network... like the way this new world is into cryptocurrency, forex and other things we have to have facilities, equipment that can handle that. So, I think if we can have a good funding on that because that is what is.

P01 said:

> As investigators, you always want to go after a criminal; you need to track the person down. We have been tracking, but to me, with what we have, like you said earlier on, that the increase in the technology they use, how do we deal with....Now I am now telling you, there is need for us...in tracking them...we need a very sophisticated one that will give an exact result.

Participant P10, however, questioned the premise for the claims of a high caseload. P10 said:

> Number one, your premise is wrong. I do not agree with you. So, from that point, I'm talking on an international level. They keep saying Nigeria, Nigeria, Nigeria. When you go abroad, you'll find that the Nigerian passport is easy to get. Most of those people are not Nigerians, or some of them are not Nigerians; they just claim Nigeria, and when they are caught, they bring out their green passport, and they are not Nigerians. I do not say that Nigerians don't commit cybercrime now but if you're to have a fair judgment of Nigerians and Nigerians in the area of crime, now look at the population of Nigeria and now look at the percentage of those that committed the crime then weigh it vis a vis smaller country. Then you'll see that the percentage of Nigerians per head is less. It's just because we are many, so if a million Nigerian commit cybercrime, how many percent? It's not even up to one percent. But if a million persons in a small country it's like ooh, it's a huge chunk, but for us, it's just a drop in a lot.

Theme 6.7: Top 3 Reasons for Rising Caseloads

P15 said:

> I cannot really attribute it to poverty because if somebody can raise money to buy iPhone of 700000, the person is not poor. But the greed that I want to be rich, quick rich, I want to get rich as soon as possible, is one of the factors. And secondly, they feel that the risk is very minimal; you don't sweat, just press a button on a system and make your money… either romance scam, extort money from people, Business Email Compromise. It's basically to get money they did not work for from other people.

Supplementary Findings

Policy suggestions. P11 said:

> I feel in the forensic department, there should also be the legal aspect to forensic department. I don't think there are lawyers there; lawyers need to be trained on document and how to prove cases relating to signatures, forgery, and all that. You need lawyers trained in that aspect, and I feel there's a gap there. Where you need to have lawyers trained to give testimonies in court, experts in that line.

P01 said:

> Well, in as much as we are aware that we have Cybercrime Act that prohibits and pointed out sanctions for whoever that violates, that commits offense regarding the internet, we also know that there are some policies that have been on ground, but seriously to me are really, really not working and, like I said, like the one I told you in terms of information sharing between institution and organizations now. When you look at the NFIU now or the NIBSS, when you want to get information from them, it takes you time. Okay, When you are into cybercrime investigation; when you are into Internet investigation, I feel policies that will give you access to database where you can get informations. People's database, National database, access, direct access that could help you to get timely investigation.

P14 said:

> I think it's just for the crime lab to expand to all other zones. Yes, to all other zones of the office so that the reliance in the headquarters would reduce in other to allow them function effectively and deliver results in time.

MIX
Papier aus verantwortungsvollen Quellen
Paper from responsible sources
FSC® C105338

If you have any concerns about our products,
you can contact us on
ProductSafety@springernature.com

In case Publisher is established outside the EU,
the EU authorized representative is:
Springer Nature Customer Service Center GmbH
Europaplatz 3, 69115 Heidelberg, Germany

Printed by Libri Plureos GmbH
in Hamburg, Germany